'Chris Anastasi has written an invaluable practical guide to strategic stakeholder engagement. It combines a comprehensive explanation of the decision-making landscape in the public sector with a wealth of insights, born of long (and sometimes challenging) experience, into how to establish, organise and manage the resources within businesses to interact effectively with a broad range of counterparties in the public sector. There's no magic formula to engagement with government; it's a long, hard road that requires and repays the establishment and maintenance of trusted relationships with a broad range of interlocutors. Absorbing and acting on Chris' practical guidance would be a great start for any business intending to create or enhance a public affairs function.'

Sir Adrian Montague CBE, Chairman of Aviva plc

'Many CEOs and Finance Directors struggle to appreciate the real value of stakeholder engagement. They should read this book to understand how crucial a focused campaign can be to commercial success. The case studies are illuminating on what works and what not to do. They depend on building trust and relationships based on strong ethical standards. Most importantly, there's an understanding of the hands-on role of a Company's leaders in the stakeholder dialogue and building credibility. This is a team effort.

The other key audience for this book is Government Affairs professionals. Those running, or setting up, these departments will find the step-by-step guide to a targeted programme invaluable. Chris Anastasi describes audiences to target, the many tiers of influencers that shape policy, the importance of galvanising wider support, and above all a focused approach to securing opportunities and managing risks. The case studies show how tangible value can be measured and delivered. Government relations professionals can use this unique book as a benchmarking resource or a template for success. It plugs a gap in the field of stakeholder relations.'

Robert Armour OBE, Former Deputy Chair of NuGeneration

'Society today has given voice to many diverse views. People and institutions expect to have a voice in issues that affect their government, their society and their lives. Successful institutions, both public and private, need to find ways to speak to these diverse and (sometimes) competing views such that all stakeholders feel their positions and opinions have been fairly and fully considered. This book gives excellent guidance based examples of successful stakeholder engagement programs and the experience of leaders who have been successful in effective stakeholder engagement.'

Bill Coley CBE, Former President of Duke Power
and CEO of British Energy

Strategic Stakeholder Engagement

New Government policy and regulation affect the environments in which organisations operate, bringing both risks that need to be mitigated and potential opportunities to exploit. A key question is whether organisations are engaging with decision-makers and other key actors as effectively as they could. Are they managing to influence the policy and regulatory regime that shapes the markets in which they operate? Even more fundamentally, do they know who they should be interacting with or understand the formal and informal processes whereby they can present their concerns, views and ideas?

Strategic Stakeholder Engagement addresses these important questions. The content of this book is wide-ranging, presenting much useful information, ideas and approaches, and provides concrete examples to demonstrate important aspects of strategic stakeholder engagement. The approach needed to deliver an effective programme and the role of internal stakeholders are discussed in detail. Many of the ideas and approaches presented in this book are drawn from experience in the energy sector, but their consideration leads to generic lessons that can be applied more widely across different sectors and stakeholders, and in different countries.

This book is a standard reference book for the area, one that will challenge existing practices and stimulate new innovative activity. It is essential reading for public affairs practitioners.

Chris Anastasi is one of the UK's leading corporate experts on Stakeholder Engagement and Government Affairs. He has also been an academic and an advisor to national and international institutions, and held a number of executive and non-executive roles for various organisations.

Strategic Stakeholder Engagement

Chris Anastasi

LONDON AND NEW YORK

First published 2018 by Routledge

2 Park Square, Milton Park, Abingdon, Oxfordshire OX14 4RN

52 Vanderbilt Avenue, New York, NY 10017

Routledge is an imprint of the Taylor & Francis Group, an informa business

First issued in paperback 2020

British Library Cataloguing-in-Publication Data
A catalogue record for this book is available from the British Library

Library of Congress Cataloging-in-Publication Data
A catalog record for this book has been requested

ISBN: 978-1-138-10664-2 (hbk)
ISBN: 978-0-367-60591-9 (pbk)

Typeset in Times New Roman
by Apex CoVantage, LLC

To my mother and father

Contents

List of illustrations   xiii
List of case studies   xv
Foreword   xvi
Preface   xviii
Acknowledgements   xxi
Selected acronyms   xxiii

1   Setting the scene for strategic stakeholder engagement   1

    1.1 An influential case study 1
        1.1.1 Poor decision-making in a changing market 2
        1.1.2 Missed opportunities by British Energy and the
              Government 3
        1.1.3 Causes of failure and what might have been 8
    1.2 The importance of strategic stakeholder engagement 9
        1.2.1 Expert Panel views 11
    1.3 Key questions for an organisation 16

2   Decision-makers   20

    2.1 Stakeholder spectrum 20
    2.2 Political institutions 22
        2.2.1 Westminster Parliament in the UK 23
        2.2.2 Devolved Administrations 28
    2.3 Parliamentary Committees 33
        2.3.1 Westminster 33
        2.3.2 Devolved Administrations 34
    2.4 Local Government 36
    2.5 European Union political institutions 38
        2.5.1 UK decision to leave the EU (Brexit) 41

3   Key influencers   47

   3.1 Key influencers on Government and Parliament 47
      3.1.1 Civil Service in the UK 49
      3.1.2 Civil Service support for the Devolved
         Administrations 50
   3.2 Influential independent Non-Departmental Public Bodies 52
   3.3 European Institutions supporting the political process 54
   3.4 Influential third parties 57

4   Stakeholder engagement processes   66

   4.1 Understanding engagement processes 66
   4.2 Formal processes 67
      4.2.1 Consultations and Inquiries 67
      4.2.2 Legislation 71
      4.2.3 Using Parliamentary Questions and the Freedom of
         Information Act 72
      4.2.4 Recourse to the Judicial Review and law courts 75
      4.2.5 Royal Commissions for ad hoc Inquiries 76
      4.2.6 Task forces and Missions 76
      4.2.7 Exiting the European Union 77
   4.3 Informal processes 79
      4.3.1 Informal engagement opportunities 79
      4.3.2 Trade Association activities 80
      4.3.3 Specialist forums 82

5   Organising for stakeholder engagement   91

   5.1 Context for an organisation's stakeholder engagement 91
      5.1.1 Defining the activity space for an organisation 91
      5.1.2 Licence to operate 93
      5.1.3 Ethical considerations associated with lobbying 95
   5.2 Developing an engagement programme 97
      5.2.1 Getting organised internally 97
      5.2.2 The importance of leadership 99
      5.2.3 A professional Government Affairs, Policy and
         Regulation team 100
      5.2.4 Drawing on all the organisation's capabilities 101
      5.2.5 The role of internal experts 105
   5.3 Developing the internal infrastructure 105
      5.3.1 Resources fit for purpose 105

5.3.2 *Developing and applying a stakeholder management 'tool' 108*

5.3.3 *Carrying out a political risk analysis 112*

5.3.4 *The importance of a Risk Register 114*

5.3.5 *A Briefings Booklet for executives 117*

5.3.6 *Regular highlights and briefings for the CEO and the executive team 118*

5.4 *Developing a 'story' and engagement strategy 118*

5.5 *Building alliances and getting independent advice 121*

5.5.1 *The importance of independent advice 124*

6 Delivering the stakeholder engagement strategy 148

6.1 *The importance of formal and informal processes 148*

6.2 *Submissions to Consultations, Inquiries and Reviews 150*

6.3 *Briefing key audiences 153*

6.3.1 *Political decision-makers 153*

6.3.2 *Engaging with officials in the Civil Service 156*

6.3.3 *Engaging with Non-Departmental Public Bodies 158*

6.3.4 *Participation in sector working groups, roundtables and other forums 159*

6.4 *Responding to Brexit 161*

6.5 *Raising the organisation's profile 163*

6.5.1 *Reporting performance 163*

6.5.2 *Speeches, presentations and discussion forums 163*

6.5.3 *Supporting Government initiatives 165*

6.5.4 *Sponsorship of selected events 167*

6.5.5 *Gaining recognition for individuals in an organisation 168*

6.5.6 *Using all forms of media 170*

6.6 *Reviewing progress 171*

6.6.1 *The importance of an annual review 171*

6.6.2 *Measuring success 173*

7 Reflection 196

7.1 *Policy arena is rich with opportunities for stakeholder engagement 196*

7.1.1 *Stakeholder engagement by officials 198*

7.2 *Strategic stakeholder engagement in different countries 198*

7.3 *The importance of reflection 202*

7.3.1 On the context for stakeholder engagement 202

7.3.2 On key stakeholders 204

7.3.3 On stakeholder processes 205

7.3.4 On organisational issues 206

7.3.5 On stakeholder engagement 207

Index   209

Illustrations

1.1	The rise and fall of British Energy	4
1.2	British Energy response to Climate Change Levy policy initiative	7
1.3	Importance of external affairs across the world	10
1.4	Some fundamental questions for an organisation	17
2.1	Stakeholder spectrum	21
2.2	UK Parliamentary system	24
2.3	UK Government Cabinet in 2017	26
2.4	Devolved Administrations in the UK	30
2.5	Devolved Administration Executives	32
2.6	Organisation of Local Government in the UK	35
2.7	Local Government responsibilities	37
2.8	European Parliament composition	40
3.1	Influencing UK political institutions	48
3.2	Generic organisational structure within Whitehall Civil Service in the UK	51
3.3	Executive agencies and public bodies	55
3.4	Informing UK political decisions	58
3.5	Influential third parties	60
4.1	Formal processes for engagement	69
4.2	Legislation process through Parliament in the UK	73
4.3	Policy assessment across the economy following Brexit	78
4.4	Engagement through informal processes	81
5.1	Desired activity space	92
5.2	Social licence to operate	94
5.3	Elements of an effective lobbying programme	98
5.4	Drawing on organisational capabilities	102
5.5	Governance process for external engagement	104
5.6	Matching resources to ambition	107
5.7	Stakeholder mapping options	109
5.8	Stakeholder mapping	111
5.9	Dealing with political risk	113
5.10	Quantifying risks	116
5.11	Developing the organisation 'story'	119

5.12 A wealth of knowledge and experience to draw on   123
5.13 Advisory Boards across the economy   126
5.14 Assessing options for external advice   128
5.15 Expert analysis and comment can influence policy   130
5.16 Mitigating specific risks   140
6.1   Elements of an effective engagement programme   149
6.2   Engaging with political decision-makers   155
6.3   Engaging with policy and regulation key influencers   157
6.4   Participating in national and international forums   160
6.5   Potential energy sector implications of Brexit   162
6.6   Building credibility and trust by reporting performance   164
6.7   Engagement through informal processes   169
6.8   Workshop activity reviewing performance   172
7.1   Example policy areas across the economy   197
7.2   Engagement with political institutions   199
7.3   Decision-makers in representative countries   201
7.4   Workshop activity to aid organisation positioning   203

Case studies

2.1	Government policy can be transformational	42
2.2	Devolution increasingly important in policy development	43
2.3	Europe an important influence on national policy	45
3.1	The importance of expert reviews	62
3.2	Non-departmental public bodies can be highly influential	63
3.3	A role for strong independent voices	64
4.1	Participating in Select Committee inquiries	84
4.2	Recourse to the law	85
4.3	Using assets to deliver strong messages	86
4.4	Building relationships with Devolved Administrations	88
4.5	Raising credibility of the organisation with key stakeholders	89
5.1	On the rewards of ambition	132
5.2	Stakeholder mapping is an essential activity	133
5.3	Getting organised to meet specific challenges	136
5.4	Focusing on risks to the business	137
5.5	The importance of governance protocols	141
5.6	Briefings Booklet for executives and managers	142
5.7	Building alliances	144
5.8	Importance of independent advice	145
5.9	Strategic stakeholder engagement programme review	146
6.1	Positioning the organisation for external stakeholders	176
6.2	Dealing with risk through active stakeholder engagement	177
6.3	Escalating issues in decision-making institutions	178
6.4	On the vagaries of Government policy	180
6.5	When politics trumps argument	181
6.6	Dealing with Government policy uncertainty	183
6.7	Working with local Members of Parliament	184
6.8	Dealing with Brexit	185
6.9	Challenging erroneous messages	188
6.10	Raising an organisation's credibility with officials	189
6.11	Public speeches a powerful engagement vehicle	191
6.12	Novel approaches to delivering messages	192
6.13	Gaining recognition for employees	194

Foreword

Energy policy has never been far from the front pages since Margaret Thatcher's Government embarked on the privatisation of the electricity supply industry in England and Wales in the late 1980s. Energy, perhaps above all other sectors, necessitates a close interaction between, on the one hand, Government and other public authorities and, on the other, the participants in the chain of activities required to bring power to consumers: generation, transmission, distribution and supply. That's because, as in other sectors, Government sets the rules of energy policy and defines the regulatory framework that creates the parameters within which the companies provide power to millions of consumers, both business and household, around the country. But energy, more than any other sector, involves a flow of particularly sensitive political issues as bills are a considerable cost in the household economies of many families, and the fitness of purpose of regulation to balance the need for continued investment with the delivery of power to consumers at reasonable prices is of keen interest to politicians.

Government is also looking to industry as its vehicle to meet the challenges of climate change, and stimulating investment in renewable energy has necessitated changes to the structure of the industry to provide incentives for the development of the young technologies that are expected to deliver the transition to a carbon-free economy. The resulting 'trilemma', how to balance the competing and sometimes conflicting demands of the security of supply, climate change and the supply of affordable energy to consumers, is a continual preoccupation of Government, and so all participants in the energy sector find it extremely valuable to engage closely with Government and a broad range of influential stakeholders to monitor emerging thinking in this important area.

If close engagement with Government is a clear priority for the energy sector, it is nonetheless also at the heart of managing business in many other sectors where the government has an important role to play: the automotive sector, the other utilities and financial services, to name just three. And changes in the perception of business have made stakeholder engagement all the more relevant for business. In the old laissez-faire days before the global financial crisis, businesses were able to maintain more of an arm's-length relationship with Government. No longer, as continued pressure on living standards and the erosion of public confidence in business have incited governments everywhere to scrutinise business more closely and prompted an increasing level of intervention. Never before has it been so vital for business to ensure that its side of the story is properly told and understood.

Against this background, Chris Anastasi has written an invaluable practical guide to strategic stakeholder engagement. It combines a comprehensive explanation of the decision-making landscape in the public sector with a wealth of insights, born of long (and sometimes challenging) experience, into how to establish, organise and manage the resources within businesses to interact effectively with a broad range of counterparties in the public sector. There's no magic formula to engagement with Government; it's a long, hard road that requires and repays the establishment and maintenance of trusted relationships with a broad range of interlocutors, but it's a worthwhile process because, as a distinguished Permanent Secretary once remarked to me, 'there are no closed minds in Whitehall'. Absorbing and acting on Chris's practical guidance would be a great start for any business intending to create or enhance a public affairs function.

Sir Adrian Montague CBE,
Chairman of Aviva plc

Preface

Markets of all kinds are changing rapidly, driven by the pace of technological change and new consumer needs. Organisations usually have the capability and tools to be able to respond to these drivers to survive in an increasingly competitive world. They can measure their success or otherwise by, for example, the profit and shareholder value they generate, their ability to invest in the future, the continued well-being of their employees, and the respect of the communities they serve.

What is less obvious is the influence of Government policy. The prime purpose of this book is to help those in public relations across the stakeholder spectrum as they engage with decision-makers in Government, Parliament and beyond to the Civil Service, regulators and other independent public bodies.

The idea for *Strategic Stakeholder Engagement* came about because there is remarkable ignorance in organisations about how best to engage with decision-makers and key influencers in the policy and regulatory arena. This is partly because lobbying by commercial organisations is still frowned upon, although this is changing as governments increasingly consult stakeholders and organisations are encouraged to express their views and ideas. This book, then, is timely and highly relevant.

New government policy and regulation affect the markets in which organisations operate, bringing both risks that need to be mitigated and potential opportunities to exploit. There are many developments that also have an impact; for example, the way in which policy is implemented is increasingly devolved to the regional and even local community level, while Brexit will largely remove policy and regulatory development at the European level from the UK. It is important, then, that organisations understand that they can influence policy outcomes, and that they need to engage at all levels of decision-making if they are to protect their interests.

A key question is whether organisations are engaging with decision-makers and other key actors as effectively as they could. Are they managing to influence the policy and regulatory regime that shapes the markets in which they operate? Even more fundamentally, do they know who they should be interacting with or understand the formal and informal processes whereby they are able to present their concerns, views and ideas? This book provides basic information and potential approaches that will help public affairs practitioners address these important questions.

A holistic engagement programme will involve decision-makers in Government and its executive, and a large and varied group of stakeholders that influence policy development. Getting organised internally is an essential requirement. It needs a strong in-house capability, one that draws on all the talents and expertise in the organisation, working in a coordinated and concerted manner. It must also draw on the considerable advice and support available in the external domain if it is to make the most of its position in the market. The approach needed to deliver an effective programme, and the role of the internal stakeholders, are discussed in detail.

This book draws on almost 20 years of experience in the energy sector and the detailed practices of four major companies at a time of considerable change for the industry, much of which had been brought about by major Government interventions at the national and EU level. Some companies in the sector prospered while others did not, and the critical observation is that those in the former group engaged more effectively with decision-makers than those in the latter. The generic lessons learned and the approaches highlighted are applicable to organisations across the economy, commercial and otherwise, small and large; the issues that concern them and their objectives may differ but the decision-makers in the form of Ministers, officials, regulators and so on, and the formal and informal engagement processes involved, are broadly the same for all.

The content of this book is wide-ranging, presenting much useful information and many ideas and approaches, and provides concrete examples to demonstrate important aspects of strategic stakeholder engagement; the focus is on decision-makers and those who influence them. The many institutions that serve society, and the formal and informal processes they are engaged in, are described in sufficient detail to help provide the bedrock on which a stakeholder engagement programme can be effective. But it is also essential that practitioners in the policy arena become as well-informed about their stakeholders as they can be and to develop relationships with them; and practitioners must also be innovative in their thinking in this important area.

Chapter 1 explains why strategic stakeholder engagement is increasingly important around the world. It uses an influential case study and the views of experts to establish what needs to be covered by practitioners in this area. Chapters 2, 3 and 4 explain what is meant by stakeholders and focus on decision-makers and key influencers and their institutions, at the national, Devolved Administration and local levels; the formal and informal processes available to organisations to engage with these key stakeholders are also discussed in detail.

Chapters 5 and 6 explain how companies should organise themselves, and how the nature and scope of the engagement programme is defined by the internal resources available; several tools to aid the programme are discussed, as are the metrics for success. The elements of a successful strategic stakeholder engagement programme are highlighted and each of these elements is discussed.

Chapter 7 highlights the fact that the policy arena is rich in new initiatives across economies and that there are opportunities to engage with strategic stakeholders in many countries around the world. Finally, the need for reflection on all aspects of the engagement programme by key internal stakeholders is discussed and a process presented to help with this activity.

Although many of the ideas and approaches highlighted in this book are drawn from experience in the energy sector, their consideration leads to generic lessons that can be applied more widely across different sectors and stakeholders, and in different countries. The book has many illustrations and case studies that are free-standing and complement the material in the main text.

The book will be helpful to those who are already active in the general field of public relations and to those responsible for government affairs, policy and regulation in their organisations. For these practitioners, it is possible that some of the ideas and approaches are already familiar but it is also likely that some have not been adopted, or that seen afresh and in a different context may stimulate new activity that would be helpful to their programmes. For those organisations with limited resources and capability, this book is an essential aid, providing basic information on key stakeholder groups, some ideas and approaches to help develop an effective programme of activities, and helpful insights on how to use resources effectively. This is equally true for companies that have been attracted into new markets and who are on a steep learning curve on how best to engage with decision-makers.

This book will also be essential reading for those in political and public administration circles, helping to inform them on how organisations, commercial and otherwise, go about the business of engaging with them. It will also help them develop their own stakeholder engagement programmes and encourage them to consider new ideas and approaches as they go about developing their own capability in this important area.

Acknowledgements

There are many people who have helped make this writing project a reality. I would like to thank Kristina Abbots who saw potential in the subject matter and moved the project quickly and successfully though the Routledge process; Kristina was always there to answer my questions and support my efforts to publish this book. Likewise, my heartfelt thanks to Jeannie Cohen who acted as my reader, and who encouraged and challenged me in equal measure to deliver a book that can reach as many stakeholders as possible; the book is richer for her observations, comments and advice. I am very grateful to Charlie Charman for helping me to create illustrations that I hope engage and inform, and are effective in both colour and greyscale, which is no easy task. Special thanks also to Tony Marinaro, a friend and former colleague, for ensuring that my office was set up with all the IT equipment needed for me to work efficiently, and for always delivering a solution when the inevitable glitches in the system arose.

I have been very fortunate to work with some wonderful colleagues over the years without whom it would not have been possible to deliver successful stakeholder engagement programmes. I am very grateful to Chris Bronsdon, David Butler, Stuart Woodings, Mark Johnson, Angela McClowry, Niall Riddell, Peter Haslam, Peter Inglis, Craig Stevenson, Wilma Wilkie and Yvonne Del Corno from the British Energy/EDF Energy years; and to James Flanagan, Laura Bartle, Phil Broom, Libby Glazebrook, Neil Smith, Harriet Guano, Andy Rimmer and Yasemin Arduini in the International Power/GDF SUEZ years. Their work is the bedrock on which this book is written.

I have been privileged to work with and learn from Bill Coley, Steve Riley and Robert Armour, excellent leaders in our organisations. They encouraged, supported and participated in the external engagement programmes, and I am very grateful to them for providing the right environment for us to make a genuine contribution in this important area.

I am also very grateful to the members of the Expert Panel who very willingly provided their views and helped frame the content of this book; their contributions have enriched the text with their wise words. My thanks also to Sir Adrian Montague for writing the Foreword to the book and by doing so contributing his experience and keen insights on strategic stakeholder engagement.

Writing this book was a very enjoyable adventure, made more so by the wonderful encouragement and support by all members of my family. They really are special, and made the discipline, commitment and hard work needed to deliver a fair manuscript to the publishers so much easier.

Selected acronyms

AM	Assembly Member
BEIS	[Department for] Business, Energy and Industrial Strategy
BIS	[Department for] Business Innovation and Science
CBE	Commander of the Order of the British Empire
CBI	Confederation of Business and Industry
CCC	Committee on Climate Change
CCL	Climate Change Levy
CEO	Chief Executive Officer
CHP	Combined Heat and Power
CJEU	Court of Justice of the European Union
CMA	Competition and Markets Authority
CPS	Carbon Price Support
CR	Corporate Responsibility
CSR	Corporate Social Responsibility
DCLG	Department for Communities and Local Government
DECC	Department of Energy and Climate Change
DEFRA	Department for Environment, Food and Rural Affairs
DExEU	Department for Exiting the European Union
DH	Department of Health
DIT	Department for International Trade
DTI	Department of Trade and Industry
EA	Environment Agency
EC	European Commission
ECB	European Central Bank
ECC	Energy and Climate Change Committee
ECO	Energy Companies Obligation
EEAS	European External Action Service
EESC	European Economic and Social Committee
EIB	European Investment Bank
EMR	Electricity Market Reform
EU	European Union
EU ETS	European Union Emissions Trading Scheme
FOI	Freedom of Information
FTSE	Financial Times Stock Exchange

GHG	greenhouse gases
GW	Giga-Watt
ICC	International Chamber of Commerce
IED	Industrial Emissions Directive
IG	Independent Generator
IGG	Independent Generators Group
IoT	Internet of Things
JR	Judicial Review
JV	Joint Venture
LCF	Levy Control Framework
LEC	Levy Exemption Certificate
MBE	Member of the Order of the British Empire
MEP	Member of the European Parliament
MP	Member of Parliament
MSP	Member of the Scottish Parliament
MW	Mega-Watt
MWh	Mega-Watt-hour
NAO	National Audit Office
NDPB	Non-Departmental Public Body
NED	Non-Executive Director
NETA	New Electricity Trading Arrangements
NGO	Non-Governmental Organisation
NHS	National Health Service
NIC	National Infrastructure Commission
NNB	Nuclear New Build
NRW	Natural Resources Wales
OBE	Officer of the Order of the British Empire
OECD	Organisation for Economic Co-operation and Development
Ofcom	Office of Communications
Ofgem	Office of Gas and Electricity Markets
Ofwat	[Office of] Water Service Regulation Authority
PECO	Philadelphia Electric Company
PGES	Parliamentary Group on Energy Studies
POST	Parliamentary Office of Science and Technology
PPP	Purchasing Power Parity
PQ	Parliamentary Question
PWR	Pressurised Water Reactor
RO	Renewable Obligation
SEPA	Scottish Environmental Protection Agency
SMEs	small and medium-sized enterprises
SSE	Scottish and Southern Energy
UK	United Kingdom
USA	United States of America
VAT	Value Added Tax
WBCSD	World Business Council for Sustainable Development

1   Setting the scene for strategic stakeholder engagement

Summary

This chapter provides a context for the book and begins by relating developments that led to the demise of British Energy, the UK's largest electricity generation company in 2002. What is clear with hindsight is that a lack of an effective stakeholder engagement programme was a major contributing factor in its spectacular failure in the market. The lessons learned from the financial collapse of the company and its subsequent rehabilitation show what can be achieved with the right approach to stakeholder engagement. This chapter also contains the views of experts in this area, their comments helping to inform what needs to be addressed for a successful engagement programme; their views confirm that this book is essential reading for practitioners in this area, in organisations across the economy, in the UK and in many other countries around the world.

1.1 An influential case study

In 2002, the Board of British Energy Group went to the Government seeking financial support to carry on operating. This was an unusual request from a private company but this was no ordinary company; it was the operator of the UK's eight most modern nuclear power stations, producing around 25% of the UK's electricity supplies and deemed essential for the economic well-being of the country. The Government provided an emergency loan facility to allow the company to continue operating. In the following weeks and months, the Government was confirmed as the single biggest shareholder of the company, and a long rehabilitation process began under a new Board and management.

Fast-forward to 2009 and British Energy was sold to EDF Energy for £12.5 billion. In the intervening period, the company's charismatic CEO Bill Coley and a small expert Executive Team, supported by an excellent Chairman in Sir Adrian Montague and his Board, led the company back into financial health and managed to improve operational performance, solving some major engineering problems in the process. The Government received a total of £6.7 billion through two sales of shares, with the money going to the Nuclear Liabilities Fund to help meet the long-term liabilities associated with the decommissioning of the plants and treatment of the waste streams.

Fast-forward again to 2016, and the Government confirmed the contracts awarded to EDF Energy and its financial partner China General Nuclear (CGN) under new market arrangements that would facilitate the building of nuclear reactors at Hinkley Point C and Sizewell C.

This outcome has significant implications for the UK's nuclear industry. A country that gave the world its first civil nuclear power station at Calder Hall in 1956, and then built, operated and life-extended 15GW of Magnox, AGR and PWR technologies over the next 60 years would now rely heavily on foreign investment and technology to fund and build the next generation of nuclear power stations.

1.1.1 Poor decision-making in a changing market

The UK has been very successful in encouraging significant inward investment into the electricity sector, as it has in other parts of the economy. But it is also fair to say that there may also have been a missed opportunity for the UK to remain a leader in the nuclear power sector with all the wider long-term benefits that would bring, for example, to the industrial base of the country.

There was, then, an alternative world out there for British Energy, one in which it was a national champion in the UK's nuclear renaissance, using its bedrock of expertise, sites and relationships with the regulator and supply chain. But a number of important developments in the years following its privatisation in 1996 were ultimately not helpful to the company:

- A highly competitive market brought about by the Government's New Electricity Trading Arrangements (NETA), which served to drive wholesale prices below the cost of generating a kilowatt-hour of electricity in nuclear power stations.
- The forays by British Energy into the US and Canada, which were undoubtedly successful ventures when viewed from the monies raised once they were sold under fire-sale conditions, but which may have diverted resources, both monetary and human, away from the core business in the UK operations.
- The failure by British Energy to compete with EDF Energy to buy London Electricity, a company that had more than two million customers in the London area and a gas distribution business. This would have been a strategic acquisition that would have allowed British Energy to realise value from the domestic retail sector as prices declined in the wholesale market.
- A significant overpayment for Eggborough coal-fired power station by the company, which allowed greater trading flexibility, but was subsequently written down in value. The plant did prove its worth in later years because its flexible power generation complemented the relatively inflexible generation from the nuclear stations.
- The dividend policy that gave significant benefit to shareholders at a time when the money could have been used to maintain the company through difficult market conditions.

- The original, inflexible, arrangements under which British Energy was privatised, and the costs associated with the fuel contracts with British Nuclear Fuels Ltd (BNFL) and other liabilities, which did not reflect changing market conditions.
- The failure of negotiations with BNFL, a publicly owned company, on a new cost structure for the fuel contracts, one that linked price of fuel to the electricity price in the wholesale market. Had the negotiations been successful, this would have provided financial relief for the company at a time when it was under considerable cost pressure in a difficult market.
- The Board's overreliance on a single study by consultants that wrongly projected that wholesale prices would remain low for a considerable period. This undoubtedly influenced the Board's decision to seek support from the Government when it had a major loan facility to draw on to maintain operations until the market improved.

It is not possible to say that one of these had an overriding effect on the demise of British Energy, although the low wholesale prices brought about by the introduction of NETA certainly put enormous financial pressure on the company; rather, it was likely to have been a combination of these factors. But whatever the truth, hindsight suggests the problems were exacerbated because of the company's inadequate engagement and lack of influence with decision-makers in the policy development arena during the period between privatisation in 1996 and the call on support from Government in 2002.

1.1.2 Missed opportunities by British Energy and the Government

The New Electricity Trading Arrangements (NETA) were introduced in early 2001, raising competition to new levels and leading to lower electricity prices to the benefit of domestic and industrial consumers, at least in the short to medium term. The potential impact of NETA on nuclear must have been understood, particularly by those who had constructed the market framework: the officials and the regulator. That there was no concern about the pressure on 25% of the UK's electricity supplies is surprising, but perhaps they were complacent because of British Energy's spectacular share price, which climbed from an opening price of 203 pence on privatisation in May 1996 to 733 pence three years later, at about the time the new trading arrangements were being developed.

It is interesting to note that the Government would later say that it could not intervene in the market for the benefit of a single company because of the need to ensure fair competition in the electricity market, even though imposing NETA on an existing market naturally favoured some technologies over others and some companies over others.

NETA, then, had some severe ramifications for British Energy. An active engagement programme with key decision-makers in Government, at an early stage, in which the longer-term implications of the new market arrangements for the company were highlighted, might have brought a more sympathetic hearing

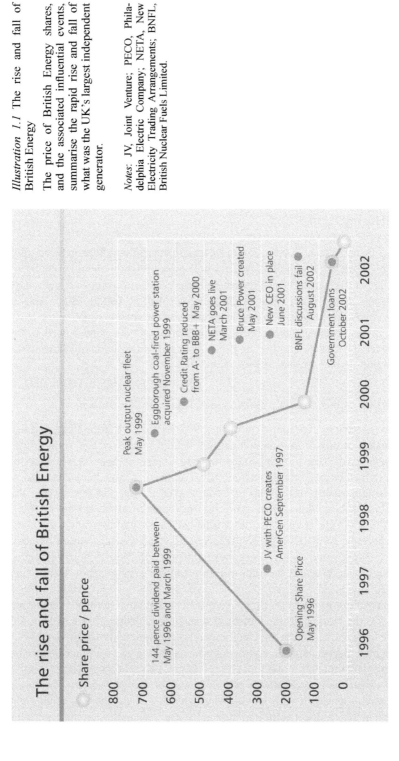

The rise and fall of British Energy

Share price / pence

800
700 — 144 pence dividend paid between May 1996 and March 1999
600
500
400
300
200 — Opening Share Price May 1996
100
0

1996 1997 1998 1999 2000 2001 2002

Peak output nuclear fleet May 1999

Eggborough coal-fired power station acquired November 1999

Credit Rating reduced from A- to BBB+ May 2000

NETA goes live March 2001

Bruce Power created May 2001

New CEO in place June 2001

BNFL discussions fail August 2002

Government loans October 2002

JV with PECO creates AmerGen September 1997

Illustration 1.1 The rise and fall of British Energy

The price of British Energy shares, and the associated influential events, summarise the rapid rise and fall of what was the UK's largest independent generator.

Notes: JV, Joint Venture; PECO, Philadelphia Electric Company; NETA, New Electricity Trading Arrangements; BNFL, British Nuclear Fuels Limited.

when the next policy developments were being considered: the Climate Change Levy (CCL) and the Renewable Obligation (RO). There were opportunities to influence these policy developments, to improve the competitiveness of nuclear generation in the market through the CCL and to limit the cost to the business of the RO; success in one or the other, or both, initiatives would have had a beneficial impact on the finances of the company.

Climate Change Levy

The Marshall Report in 1996 suggested that some form of carbon taxation was an appropriate response to the challenge of climate change, with the options being carbon taxation or a market-based carbon trading scheme. This led to the creation of the CCL to encourage energy efficiency, and through this a reduction in carbon emissions within UK business.

The CCL was a tax on the business use of energy. It was the first policy initiative to address carbon emissions and came into force on 1 April 2001 following extensive consultation. It was designed to be broadly revenue-neutral with some of the revenue used to cut employer national insurance contribution (although these were subsequently increased again a short time later), and to promote the development and deployment of low-carbon technologies.

Following an active lobbying campaign by several stakeholders, most notably non-governmental organisations (NGOs), electricity from renewables and Combined Heat and Power (CHP) was made exempt from the CCL and awarded Levy Exemption Certificates (LECs) for each MWh generated; LECs could then be sold to suppliers who used them to prove that they had supplied non-domestic customers with renewable electricity. However, beyond these exemptions no distinction was made between carbon (i.e., fossil) and low-carbon (i.e., nuclear and hydro) sources of electricity, with both being subject to the CCL.

British Energy operations made, arguably, the largest contribution to carbon reduction in the UK, with almost 50 million tonnes avoided each year at that time, when compared to the prevailing fossil fuel mix. The UK Government in its various climate change consultation documents acknowledged the contribution that nuclear power made, and would continue to make, in mitigating carbon emissions. The company believed there should be financial recognition for this low-carbon nuclear electricity. It felt the Government could do this by:

- Total exemption of nuclear generation from the CCL, which would make it more competitive in the wholesale market.
- Partial exemption of nuclear from the levy (i.e., the levy could be less than the original cost of 0.43 pence/kWh).
- Exemption for electricity generated from projects beyond business-as-usual, for example, those improving the output of the stations or those leading to life extension of the stations both of which would benefit the UK's climate change efforts and maintain security of supply in the longer term.

A full or partial exemption of British Energy's output in 2000 could have allowed the company to keep operating through the wholesale price nadir until the market recovered to more sustainable levels, as it subsequently did; it would also have recognised the important contribution nuclear generation was making to the UK's decarbonisation agenda.

> British Energy's nuclear generators are responsible for 20 per cent of total electricity generation and it plays a part in contributing to the reduction of CO_2 emissions.
>
> *Patricia Hewitt MP, former Secretary of State for*
> *Trade and Industry, Hansards, House of Commons debate,*
> *28 November 2002*

> The Government claim that the Climate Change Levy forms part of their strategy to meet our climate change commitments. As nuclear power is the main energy source that does not produce carbon dioxide emissions, the Government's policy is an absurd contradiction.
>
> *Tim Yeo MP, former Shadow Secretary of State for*
> *Trade and Industry, Hansards, House of Commons debate,*
> *28 November 2002*

In its submissions to Government, British Energy supported carbon taxation but favoured a market-based emissions trading scheme to deliver a cost for carbon on fossil generation responsible for carbon emissions. In the event, Government came forward with both the CCL and a very limited voluntary UK Emissions Trading Scheme, neither of which helped low-carbon nuclear generation. The organisation's engagement programme was limited, focusing almost entirely on a few officials in Whitehall and on briefing the odd supporter of nuclear in the House of Lords. The issue was raised with officials several times by different company executives, but the Government was reluctant to offer more exemptions so early in the lifetime of the CCL, and particularly to an unpopular nuclear sector.

As a result, the engagement initiative failed. Even when the financial pressures on British Energy were threatening the very survival of the company, the response from officials in Whitehall was muted at best, and no CCL exemption for nuclear generation was forthcoming. The real damage was caused because of poor engagement much earlier in the process, at the time of the formulation of the CCL. Renewables and the CHP sector were given exemption from the CCL, and this was achieved by having a good narrative, strong support, and a highly effective lobbying strategy; in contrast, the nuclear operators, despite having strong arguments, failed.

In an interesting postscript, exemption of nuclear (and large-scale hydro) would essentially have converted the CCL to a carbon tax. Ten years later, and in the wake of a very low market price for carbon in the EU Emission Trading Scheme, the CCL was modified to accommodate a Carbon Price Floor; the latter was

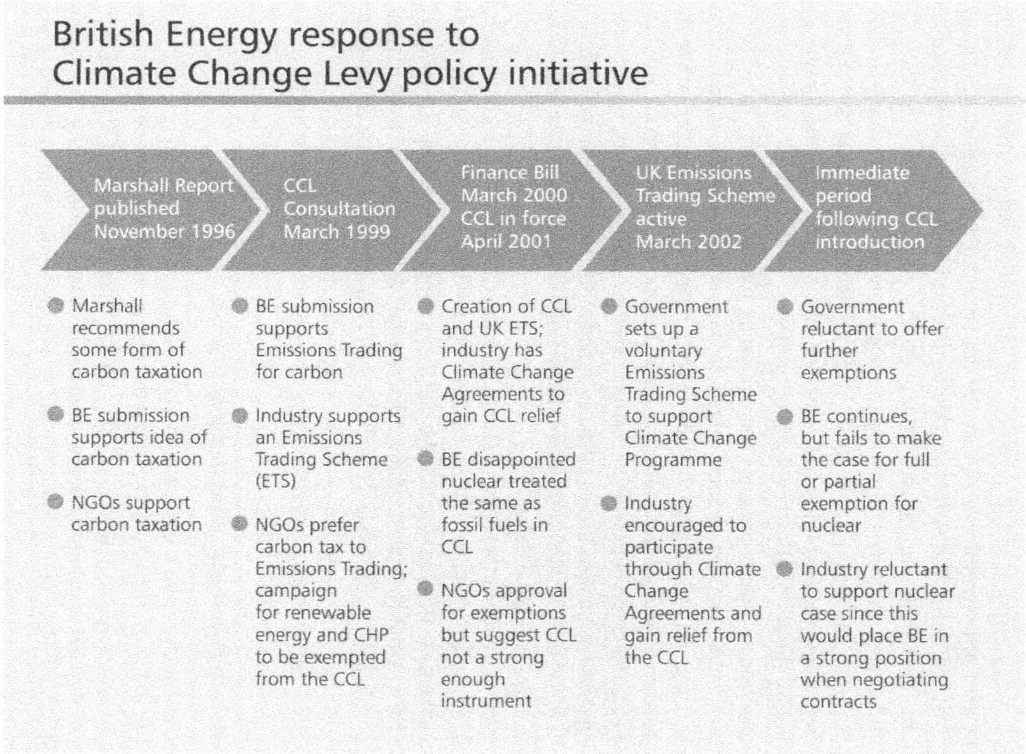

British Energy response to Climate Change Levy policy initiative

Marshall Report published November 1996	CCL Consultation March 1999	Finance Bill March 2000 CCL in force April 2001	UK Emissions Trading Scheme active March 2002	Immediate period following CCL introduction
• Marshall recommends some form of carbon taxation	• BE submission supports Emissions Trading for carbon	• Creation of CCL and UK ETS; industry has Climate Change Agreements to gain CCL relief	• Government sets up a voluntary Emissions Trading Scheme to support Climate Change Programme	• Government reluctant to offer further exemptions
• BE submission supports idea of carbon taxation	• Industry supports an Emissions Trading Scheme (ETS)	• BE disappointed nuclear treated the same as fossil fuels in CCL	• Industry encouraged to participate through Climate Change Agreements and gain relief from the CCL	• BE continues, but fails to make the case for full or partial exemption for nuclear
• NGOs support carbon taxation	• NGOs prefer carbon tax to Emissions Trading; campaign for renewable energy and CHP to be exempted from the CCL	• NGOs approval for exemptions but suggest CCL not a strong enough instrument		• Industry reluctant to support nuclear case since this would place BE in a strong position when negotiating contracts

Illustration 1.2 British Energy response to Climate Change Levy policy initiative

Carbon pricing should have been a significant financial benefit to carbon-free nuclear generation in the UK; in the event, the Climate Change Levy treated nuclear and fossil generation the same.

Notes: BE, British Energy; NGOs, non-governmental organisations; CHP, Combined Heat and Power; CCL, Climate Change Levy; ETS, Emissions Trading Scheme.

introduced to raise the cost of carbon and increase the wholesale price of electricity to help investment in low-carbon technologies, including new nuclear build. As a result of this initiative, low-carbon generation from the existing nuclear (and hydro) stations is now being well-rewarded.

Renewables Obligation

There was ample opportunity for organisations to engage with the policy development process for the UK Government's Renewables Obligation (RO). The RO placed an obligation on all licensed suppliers to source a specified proportion of their electricity to their customers from renewables or, if they failed to do so, to pay a penalty; both the level of obligation and the penalty price would rise over time.

British Energy supported the principle of integrating renewable generation into the market and agreed that the key to the Government's approach should be the use of market-based solutions combined with some flexibility to allow suppliers to meet their obligations. However, the company felt that Government should ensure that the Obligation did not promote some climate-friendly technologies (i.e., new renewables and emerging technologies) at the expense of other beneficial technologies (i.e., nuclear and hydro), nor encourage one form of energy diversity at the expense of another.

The Government's stated key aims for supporting renewables were 'to assist the UK to meet national and international targets for the reduction of emissions including greenhouse gases'. Electricity supplied from British Energy's nuclear power stations was essentially carbon-free, yet under the RO proposals, the company would be treated the same as companies with carbon-intensive generation. The company was a licensed supplier with a direct sales business aimed at the industrial and commercial sector, and this meant it would incur significant additional costs in meeting its RO obligations, costs it could ill-afford.

The company believed there was a strong case for excluding low-carbon nuclear generation from the Obligation. It would have been administratively simple in the new arrangements to demonstrate that the electricity supplied was from a low-carbon source; and there would be little financial impact on the overall renewables programme. Despite considerable correspondence with the then Department of Trade and Industry (DTI) on this issue, these arguments did not meet with success. Once again, the company was burdened with unwarranted additional costs, making it less competitive.

1.1.3 *Causes of failure and what might have been*

In one sense policy-makers contributed to the failure of British Energy. They put measures in place that would drive down the electricity price to benefit consumers (NETA) and help the UK achieve its climate change targets (CCL and RO), but these initiatives were also clearly detrimental to the profitability of the only large-scale low-carbon technology in nuclear generation. And politicians and officials were subsequently reluctant to modify their policies when they had the chance.

The impact of the exemptions from the CCL and RO being sought by British Energy were relatively small in relation to the overall policy initiatives. Had the Government allowed the exemptions, the company could have continued trading, giving it an opportunity to return to profitability as the wholesale price rose and its overseas investments provided a valuable new income stream. In that world, British Energy could have been at the forefront of the nuclear renaissance, bringing with it enormous benefit to UK business.

There are several reasons why the company failed so spectacularly in its engagement with key decision-makers in Government and officials in White-hall. For example, the company had not made the changes needed to act like other private companies in a highly competitive market; in this world, organi-sations engaged in strategic stakeholder engagement to protect their inter-ests. It had only recently come out of public ownership where it had always had access to decision-makers; indeed, many in the company still considered themselves part of the 'establishment'. It did not help that nuclear remained an unpopular technology with its messages often ignored, particularly in the early years of a sceptical New Labour administration when the company was in financial trouble.

Nonetheless, the company should and could have done much better with the cards it was dealt. In contrast, the rehabilitation of British Energy, and nuclear energy in the UK, in the period from late 2002 to early 2009 when the company was sold to EDF Energy, was a period of considerable stakeholder engagement. It was a successful programme because it utilised all the talents that resided in the company and the wider industry, and involved an array of innovative approaches.

It is also fair to say that since 2009 EDF Energy has been excellent in its engage-ment with decision-makers and beyond, which has culminated in the Government signing contracts with the company to build several new nuclear power stations at two of its sites. This is not by chance but through good leadership, a clear strategy, and a highly effective stakeholder engagement programme.

1.2 The importance of strategic stakeholder engagement

The highly reputable consultancy firm McKinsey carries out surveys of executive views on the importance or otherwise of external affairs to their businesses. The last survey in 2015 involved a sample of 1,334 executives drawn from organisa-tions active in many different markets and across the world – they published their findings in an article titled: 'How to reinvent the external-affairs function', pub-lished in July 2016. This excellent survey came to several important conclusions:

- External affairs as an activity now ranks as a top or top-three priority for more than half of CEOs who participated in the survey.

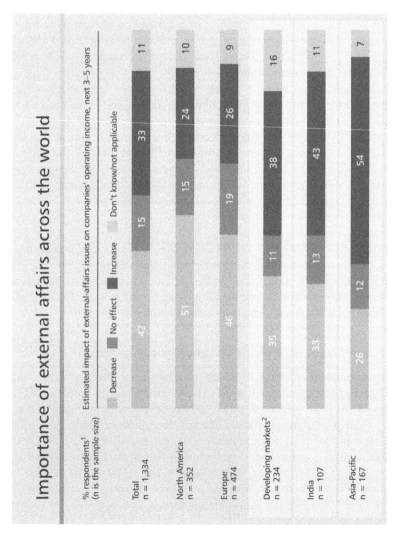

Importance of external affairs across the world

% respondents[1]
(n is the sample size)

Estimated impact of external-affairs issues on companies' operating income, next 3–5 years

Decrease ■ No effect ■ Increase Don't know/not applicable

Region	Decrease	No effect	Increase	Don't know/not applicable
Total n = 1,334	42	15	33	11
North America n = 352	51	15	24	10
Europe n = 474	46	19	26	9
Developing markets[2] n = 234	35	11	38	16
India n = 107	33	13	43	11
Asia-Pacific n = 167	26	12	54	7

Illustration 1.3 Importance of external affairs across the world

There is strong evidence that policy and regulatory issues are a priority for executives all over the world, irrespective of political and market context.

Source: Exhibit from 'How to reinvent the external-affairs function', July 2016, McKinsey & Company, www.mckinsey.com. Copyright © 2017 McKinsey & Company. All rights reserved. Reprinted by permission.

Notes: 1 Illustrations may not sum to 100% because of rounding; 2 Includes China and Latin America.

- Executives believe Government departments and regulators will have the greatest effect on their companies' value (along with their customers), and most believe this influence will increase further in the future.
- A significant number of executives, particularly in mature economies such as those in North America, believe that the risks associated with Government and regulator intervention in their markets outweigh the opportunities and that this will be detrimental to their business. However, some executives, notably in developed countries in the Asia-Pacific region, believe that opportunities will outweigh risks in this arena and that an effective external affairs programme could benefit their business.
- Organisations that have strong external affairs capability tend to be more successful than those in their sector that do not. Nonetheless, even those with relatively strong capability could enhance their performance through better organisation of the external affairs function, by engaging directly and more effectively with stakeholders, and by setting the external agenda through active engagement.
- Successful companies tend to have active CEO participation in their external affairs programmes.

It is very encouraging to see that there are many executives who believe there are opportunities as well as risks associated with issues emerging in the public affairs arena. However, despite a growing awareness that active stakeholder engagement is very important for all kinds of businesses in markets across the world, it is also apparent that there is considerable room for improvement in their performance, even in those organisations that have been relatively successful with their programmes.

1.2.1 Expert Panel views

It is also highly instructive to hear the views of experts drawn from across civil society. Eleven such experts were asked to answer a number of questions that touch on different aspects of engagement with decision-makers and key influencers as part of the research for this book; their views are summarised to help provide valuable context to the material presented in the chapters. All panel members have had long successful careers and held high office; with the odd exception, the panel members have experience of more than one stakeholder group, thus providing additional valuable insights.

> If current trends continue, [policy and regulatory risks] will have far more effect on businesses when compared to other issues.
>
> *Expert Panel member Bill Coley CBE, former President*
> *of Duke Power and CEO of British Energy Group*

The questions put to the Expert Panel members cover all the main issues associated with strategic stakeholder engagement:

- **Question 1** Where would you place policy and regulatory risk for organisations today and in the next five years when compared to the other issues (e.g., when compared to business development, new disruptive technology, skills and labour)?
- **Question 2** In your experience, what kind of organisations engage with decision-makers well and what kind of organisations engage less well (e.g., investors, supply chain, non-governmental organisations, trade associations, trade unions, think tanks, professional institutions)?
- **Question 3** Where would you place the greatest emphasis in the stakeholder spectrum (e.g., politicians, officials, independent public bodies such as regulators, third parties such as NGOs, investors and supply chain, local communities, media)?
- **Question 4** What are the most important organisational factors that contribute to a successful engagement programme (e.g., is it leadership, executive team commitment, resources, wider engagement within the organisation)?
- **Question 5** What are the most important factors that contribute to successful implementation of an organisation's engagement programme (e.g., is it a strong story, commitment by executives, use of expert external advisors, coordinated and concerted effort, forming alliances)?
- **Question 6** What constitutes success in a Government Affairs programme (e.g., is it number of risks mitigated, monetary value of risks mitigated and opportunities realised, access to decision-makers, representation in influential forums, benefits accrued compared to resources expended, number of positive mentions in the media)?

Stakeholder group covered by Panel member	Expert Panel member										
	1	2	3	4	5	6	7	8	9	10	11
Business	✓	✓	✓	✓							✓
NED business	✓										✓
Trade Association				✓					✓	✓	
Trade Union										✓	
Large NGO											✓
Small NGO		✓				✓					✓
Consultant								✓			✓
Parliament										✓	
Special Advisor							✓	✓		✓	
Civil Service				✓							✓
NDPB				✓							
NED NDPD				✓							
Institutions									✓		✓
Academia		✓									

Notes: NED, Non-Executive Director; NGO, Non-Governmental Organisation; NDPB, Non-Departmental Public Body.

Summary of Expert Panel views in relation to Question 1

Policy and regulatory risk can vary from sector to sector and country to country. Policy and regulatory risks are high on the agenda for:

- Organisations that operate in heavily regulated markets such as the financial services sector.
- Those sectors in the political limelight because of their impacts on consumers, such as the electricity or banking sectors.
- Issues where government action is needed to effect change, for example in climate change mitigation and skills development.

Policy can and does set trends and influence behaviour. For example, there have been new policies to address skills development, but the money committed by government itself, or on behalf of consumers, has been very low, with the burden being placed on business through a levy. But Government's role, in the main, is to establish the policy and regulatory framework for the long term, often beyond an organisation's business plans.

Policy and regulatory risk increases with developments at the national level, such as the decision of the UK to leave the EU (Brexit), or political changes on the international stage such as a more radical agenda following the inauguration of Donald Trump as President of the USA in 2017. Also, Government can change policy direction sharply and, worse, adopt a 'picking winners' approach. Such developments create policy uncertainty for business and discourage investment.

The indications are that Government intervention in markets will continue for most sectors of the economy for the foreseeable future and this means that policy and regulatory issues will be high on the agenda for organisations. There are other risks, and opportunities, for organisations such as the emerging disruptive technologies associated with the Internet of Things (IoT), and the role of social media in influencing consumer behaviour. However, a change in government policy is potentially as destructive as new technology is disruptive; without an understanding of how current and potential regulation could impact an organisation, other key drivers of success such as business development could be rendered redundant.

Summary of Expert Panel views in relation to Question 2

Large companies – and in particular those with a well-recognised 'brand' – tend to engage well because they understand that they must, and they devote resources to the activity. Trade associations have the advantage of representing broad swathes of their sector and this makes them attractive to decision-makers; however, they are sometimes less effective than they would otherwise be because they can only deliver messages that represent the lowest common denominator from their membership.

NGOs with large memberships can also engage well but only if their arguments are well rounded – there is a view that their messages tend to be simplistic and lacking in detail and evidence. Nonetheless, NGOs that represent high-profile constituencies often receive a sympathetic audience with politicians, and therefore tend to be able to influence the debate; consumer groups are also in this category. 'Think tanks' can be effective in engagement, but there are always concerns about their independence if their work is sponsored by third parties.

Small businesses and NGOs do not engage well because of the time and resources needed. Nonetheless there are instances in which smaller companies have engaged very well at the local level – for example, with their local politicians – and by doing so have gained a voice in the national forums.

Although there are notable exceptions, supply chain companies also tend not to participate in lobbying activities, in part because of their position in the value chain where they provide services to those companies that are impacted more directly by policy and regulation. They are also highly competitive and diverse, making it harder to galvanise action effectively. With some exceptions, investors also tend to leave engagement with decision-makers to those businesses they have interests in.

Those organisations that engage well do so because they support their arguments with information and facts, even if what they provide is in the service of their aims. Professional institutions are well-placed to do this but have been less effective than they could be, in part because they have a diverse membership, which makes it difficult to establish a collegiate approach.

Organisations that engage well, then, have a well-argued narrative and devote appropriate resources to the task, but they also recognise that it takes time to build relationships and trust with decision-makers. This is a long-term effort and often involves starting all over again with new decision-makers because of the relatively rapid turnover of people in political and Civil Service institutions.

Summary of Expert Panel views in relation to Question 3

The issue defines which stakeholders the organisation should engage with. Organisations need to focus on legislators if they wish to see a change in the regulations that govern their markets, or alternatively if they wish to see those regulations unchanged. Greatest emphasis should be placed on engaging with politicians and officials who are directly involved in the process, at the national or Devolved Administration levels; some issues require direct engagement with local politicians. It is also important to engage with those organisations that are closely allied to these groups and who may provide advice such as regulators.

There will be occasions when it is necessary to encourage discussion around a wider stakeholder group to reach a consensus view that can then be acted upon by government. It may be appropriate to engage with other third parties, including NGOs and institutions, since they too will contribute to the decision-making process. All stakeholders are important at one time or another.

Summary of Expert Panel views in relation to Question 4

There are three main organisational factors that contribute to a successful engagement programme:

- A clear vision of what the organisation is trying to achieve and the strategy to deliver it, a vision that has the capacity to engage both internal and external stakeholders.
- Leadership by the CEO and the Board, commitment by the executive team, and recognition that everybody has a role to play in developing relationships with decision-makers and key influencers, and networks that provide valuable intelligence and information. It is important that the leadership is credible with decision-makers and this depends on, for example, what can be delivered and the impression given in the discussions.
- A professional team with sufficient resources to deliver the programme; the latter will need to be constantly reviewed and refreshed in response to changing circumstances.

Summary of Expert Panel views in relation to Question 5

An engagement strategy should engender trust in the organisation and its representatives. A strong narrative is a default requirement; it should be well-thought through, presented in a simple and straightforward manner, and be of benefit to all interested stakeholders. The narrative needs to be supported with facts and data, and the messages consistent and coordinated. Commitment, perseverance and patience are also important because it takes time to deliver results.

The leadership of the organisation and executive team need to be fully involved in the engagement programme, and by doing so enhance the credibility of the organisation's narrative. Those that interface with decision-makers must want to engage, they must be open, available and supportive when needed; and they need to understand that different approaches are needed when interacting with politicians or officials. Without this approach, expending resources is less helpful.

Forming alliances, inside the organisation and externally, can be powerful but it has to be with like-minded partners otherwise it is a waste of time and effort. Strong political intelligence is important – the organisation should use external advice to support the engagement programme, particularly those with experience in the areas of interest.

Summary of Expert Panel views in relation to Question 6

It can be difficult to measure success when engaging with decision-makers and key influencers but what is important is to focus on measuring outputs rather than inputs; what is also true is that final decisions are subject to lots of factors outside the control of any one organisation. Nonetheless, success can be assessed with an eye to the 'tangible' benefits to an organisation:

- Those that result in monetary value; for example, by reducing financial risk, improving its competitive position and higher profits.
- Those that make the organisation's business easier; for example, reassured investors, improved product rating, greater consumer satisfaction or greater employee retention.

There are less tangible success factors; for example, invitations to participate in influential forums. Access to decision-makers is very important, but access should not be confused with influence. A good measure of success is if an executive makes a call to a decision-maker and that call is returned; a greater measure of success is if the decision-maker contacts the executive to discuss an issue or seeks information when formulating a policy.

1.3 Key questions for an organisation

Hindsight is a wonderful thing. There are many companies that struggle to make progress with stakeholder engagement, although they perhaps do not fail as spectacularly as British Energy in those early years following its privatisation in 1996. The purpose of this book is to highlight the many aspects of engaging with decision-makers and other key stakeholders. A private company does engage routinely with investors but often does not devote sufficient resources to a stakeholder engagement programme for the policy arena, or worse, neglects such engagement to the detriment of the business.

There are several important observations to be drawn from the views expressed by the small Expert Panel and the results of the very much wider McKinsey survey: policy and regulatory risk (and opportunity) is a priority for many organisations but that they need to improve their capability to carry out an effective engagement programme; and leadership in both the internal and external domains is an important contributor to successful programmes.

Irrespective of the sector or jurisdiction in which it operates, an organisation needs to establish what it wants to achieve in the policy and regulatory arena. It needs to ask a series of fundamental questions of the external world and within the organisation to ensure it is well-placed to engage, should it choose to do so.

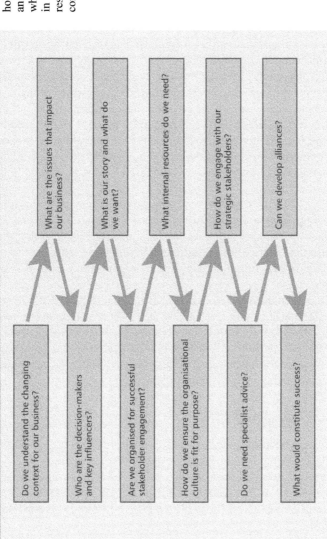

Some fundamental questions for an organisation

Do we understand the changing context for our business?

What are the issues that impact our business?

Who are the decision-makers and key influencers?

What is our story and what do we want?

Are we organised for successful stakeholder engagement?

What internal resources do we need?

How do we ensure the organisational culture is fit for purpose?

How do we engage with our strategic stakeholders?

Do we need specialist advice?

Can we develop alliances?

What would constitute success?

Illustration 1.4 Some fundamental questions for an organisation

The leadership of an organisation must want to carry out strategic stakeholder engagement, and this requires an understanding of the context in which it is operating, its ambition in this area, the organisation and resources needed, and what would constitute success.

It will need to understand who its stakeholders are, their concerns and their influence on the environments in which the organisation operates. This understanding is not restricted to decision-makers in Government but will include influential independent organisations, think tanks and consultants, and even individuals. An organisation will need to be innovative in the way that it addresses different stakeholder communities.

An understanding of the nature of formal and informal processes for engagement is important. Both types of processes offer important opportunities to influence the policy debate, the former by the organisation reacting to the government's agenda, while the latter requires a more proactive approach, and offers opportunities to help define the agenda and to propagate messages through influential third parties. Once again, those organisations that are innovative in the way they engage are more likely to be heard.

Successful organisations in stakeholder engagement are particularly well-organised internally. It is surprising, then, how many companies are not well-organised, sometimes because the leadership is not convinced of the merits of an engagement programme or committed to its implementation, or the culture of the company does not lend itself to a collegiate approach, or individual needs get in the way of an effective programme. The right resources are needed to match the organisation's ambition, whether it is limited or expansive, along with supporting tools and materials to provide the necessary 'glue' for those participating in the programme. All of these issues are explored in detail in the chapters that follow.

The question of what makes a successful engagement programme, the nature of the advice that is available from third parties, and the possibilities of alliances with other organisations are also discussed in detail. The value of a periodic review of the programme is discussed, and some potential success factors are highlighted to ensure the organisation is focused on the right activities.

It is important that practitioners take away some actions that will help improve their performance in this area. A few exercises are presented to help facilitate reflection by different levels in the organisation. These exercises will encourage participation, ownership and accountability in the engagement programme, by the leadership team and by the specialist team responsible for its implementation, and internal experts more widely in the organisation.

Summary key points

- Government intervention in markets can have a profound effect on the financial well-being of companies that operate in these markets.
- Executives see major risks to their businesses from government and regulator involvement in their markets, but there are also opportunities.
- External affairs issues are in the top three priorities for executives around the world.

- Organisations, commercial or otherwise, can and must improve their performance when dealing with decision-makers and key influencers.
- Leadership, organisation and an ability to draw on all the abilities available within a business are critical for a successful strategic stakeholder engagement programme.

2   Decision-makers

Chapter summary

This chapter begins by exploring what is meant by stakeholders and how they may be categorised. The main focus is on strategic stakeholders, the decision-makers in the political institutions at the national level, and in the increasingly important Devolved Administrations and Local Government; the EU institutions are also discussed because they will remain important during the Brexit process and beyond. An understanding of the way these institutions are organised and work is extremely important, as are the key actors and their roles in the decision-making process; without this knowledge, it is very difficult to develop and implement an effective strategic stakeholder engagement programme.

Stakeholder engagement practitioners in the UK will have to be familiar with the decision-makers discussed but perhaps not to the level of detail provided in this chapter. Practitioners in other countries can use the material presented to help in their stakeholder mapping exercises in relation to decision-makers.

2.1 Stakeholder spectrum

One of the most important activities involved in gaining a voice in the public arena is to recognise the many stakeholders across the political, economic and civil society landscape, and to understand the role they might play in an organisation's engagement programme, both internal and external. The main emphasis may well be on decision-makers and key influencers, but it very quickly becomes apparent that it is important to engage across the stakeholder spectrum for an effective programme.

It is possible to establish, broadly, four categories of stakeholders:

- **Primary stakeholders:** Those that an organisation, small or large, needs to make every effort to interact with directly on a regular basis; examples include Ministers and officials, Shadow Cabinet members, and those Members of Parliament that sit on influential Parliamentary Committees. Political advisors are also very important primary stakeholders.
- **Secondary stakeholders:** Those that an organisation tries to interact with in the knowledge that they have a good working relationship with decision-makers and key influencers; examples include the regulators, the professional

Stakeholder spectrum

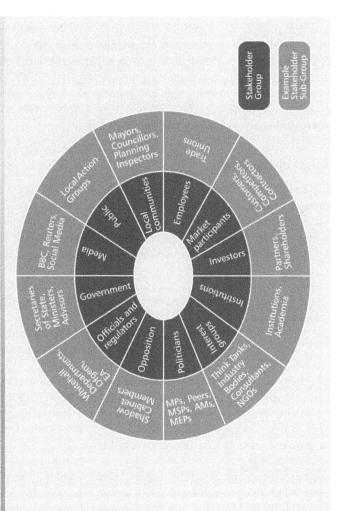

Illustration 2.1 Stakeholder spectrum

An excellent understanding of stakeholders is fundamental to an engagement programme. At one end of the spectrum lie the political decision-makers and other key influencers, while at the other end lie the public and the media that informs it.

Notes: BBC, British Broadcasting Corporation; NGOs, non-governmental organisations; MPs, Members of Parliament; MSPs, Members of the Scottish Parliament; AMs, Assembly Members; MEPs, Members of the European Parliament; EA, Environment Agency.

institutions, industry or sector trade associations, market participants and non-governmental organisations (NGOs).

- **Tertiary stakeholders:** Those that contribute to the general pool of knowledge and advice, or represent wider views from which decision-makers may seek to inform their policy development; examples include investors, think tanks and consultants, and the media.
- **Quaternary stakeholders:** Those stakeholders, such as local communities and the public, that decision-makers must engage with on issues to ensure their actions are well-informed.

Strategic stakeholders, then, are those covered by the first two categories and are the main focus of this book; tertiary and quaternary stakeholders are also discussed because under certain circumstances they too can influence the political process and policy arena. An organisation's leadership and its experts are internal stakeholders, and they too are important and are discussed in detail.

An organisation can be active or passive in its engagement. The first three categories require an active engagement programme; engagement with the fourth category can be active, for example with communities in which the organisation's assets are placed, or passive, perhaps by providing helpful information on the website that encourages interaction with the wider public.

2.2 Political institutions

A sound understanding of the political institutions of a country is essential if an organisation is to engage effectively with the Government's decision-making process. It is important to understand the roles of each institution, their responsibilities, how they are organised and go about their business, and the formal relationships between them; and, most important, where the decision-making power resides.

> In an age of unprecedented transparency, the reality of power can still remain obscure to the public.
>
> *Nick Clegg, former MP and Deputy Prime Minister,*
> Politics Between the Extremes, *2016*

It is also helpful to understand how the democratic institutions of the land came about, whether they are longstanding, mature and well-tested; alternatively, the institutions could be relatively new to a country and draw on the experiences of other nations. Such knowledge helps an organisation to understand the political context of a country's decision-making, and how best to engage with its institutions.

The first full 'Parliament' in the UK occurred in the reign of Edward I in 1275, but in reality, it had grown out of what were King's Councils made up of the lords of the land, both lay and spiritual, and later knights and prominent citizens who represented communities of ordinary people. Indeed, the Councils themselves were preceded centuries earlier by the Anglo-Saxon Witan, a gathering where the King sought the views of his nobles and bishops.

Parliament was an assembly summoned to fulfil several functions: a Court of Justice where petitions could be heard, tax-granting to help govern the country and a debating council where national policy could be discussed; in time Parliament would become a legislative body. Also in time, the representatives of the people drew apart from the Lords to form the 'House of Commons'.

Over the centuries, the relationship between the Monarch and Parliament changed markedly with an important milestone being the Civil War in the mid-seventeenth century, which led to the rise of Parliament as the key institution governing England. Today the Queen has a constitutional role in opening and dissolving Parliament, and in approving Bills before they become law.

The UK Parliament, then, has evolved over a long period of time, and its role and responsibilities continue to change, for example, with devolution of powers to the local level. It is important that an organisation understands the changing political context, and its implications, on the environment in which it operates; it will then be in a much better position to protect its interests through its strategic stakeholder engagement programme.

2.2.1 Westminster Parliament in the UK

The UK Parliament today consists of two Houses, the Commons and the Lords, the Lower and the Upper Houses, respectively, a system that prevails in many countries around the world. Members of Parliament (MPs) are elected to their positions by their constituencies in a general election, or subsequently in by-elections brought about by the resignation or death of a sitting MP. In England, MPs 'win' their seats through a simple majority in a 'first-past-the-post' process; in many countries, a system based on proportional representation is used to decide who enters Parliament.

Parliament has 650 elected members representing constituencies across the UK and Northern Ireland. The average constituency size in England is around 70,000, that for Scotland and Northern Ireland slightly less, and Wales about 80% of this average. However, the constituency size varies significantly, and there are proposals for a major change to make them more equal in size, and at the same time to reduce the size and cost of Parliament. The proposals, then, will reduce the number of MPs to 600, and every constituency size will be within 5% of the average.

The Coalition Government in 2010, involving the Conservative and Liberal Democrat parties, brought forward legislation to fix the lifetime of a Parliament to five years, ending the practice whereby a general election could be called by the sitting Prime Minister at any time up to five years, to suit their political aims.

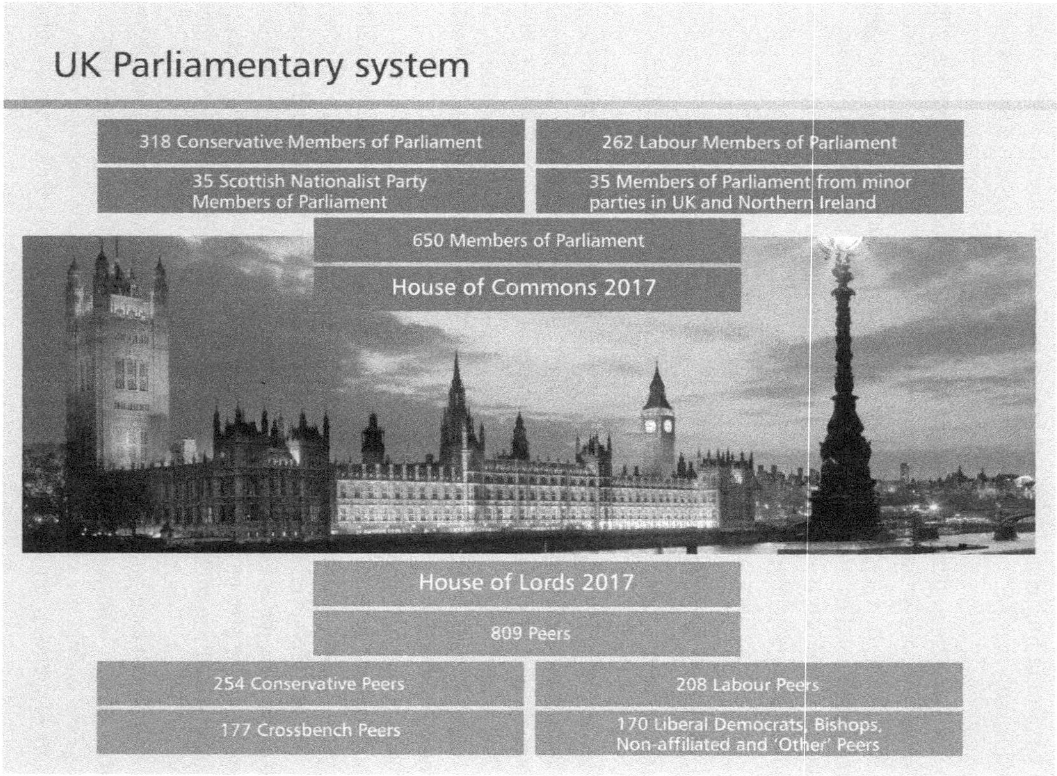

UK Parliamentary system

318 Conservative Members of Parliament

35 Scottish Nationalist Party Members of Parliament

262 Labour Members of Parliament

35 Members of Parliament from minor parties in UK and Northern Ireland

650 Members of Parliament

House of Commons 2017

House of Lords 2017

809 Peers

254 Conservative Peers

177 Crossbench Peers

208 Labour Peers

170 Liberal Democrats, Bishops, Non-affiliated and 'Other' Peers

Illustration 2.2 UK Parliamentary system

The UK Parliamentary system is an example of many around the world. It has two Houses, a Lower House, the Commons which is the legislative chamber, and an Upper House, the Lords, which contributes to the democratic process by providing valuable legislative scrutiny, views and comment.

Now, the only way an election can be called earlier than the five-year term is if two-thirds of MPs agree to this motion, or there is a vote of 'no confidence' in the Government; a simple majority then brings forward an election.

The House of Lords, the Upper House of Parliament, is populated by two major groups: those that have inherited their positions and those who have been appointed to the role, usually as Life Peers, as reward for services rendered to the UK. This House can be described in political terms with over 40% associated with the two main political parties: Conservatives and Labour. The vast majority of those Members who can participate in the business of the House of Lords are Life Peers, with just 92 Hereditary Peers remaining.

One of the benefits of appointing Peers who have genuinely added value to societal well-being is that they bring with them a wealth of knowledge and experience to draw on, which are sometimes lacking in the lower chamber. It is not uncommon for Peers to serve in the Government.

The two-tier model for a Parliament prevails in many countries around the world, although the respective roles and functions, and contribution to the decision-making process, may differ.

The Government

The Prime Minister makes appointments from their political party to serve in the Government's Cabinet. In the UK, the Cabinet, led by the Prime Minister, consists of the Chancellor of the Exchequer, and each Secretary of State appointed to lead all the major Whitehall departments, 25 in total in 2016. Other Cabinet attendees may include the Chancellor of the Duchy of Lancaster, the Chief Secretary to the Treasury, the Minister for the Cabinet Office and Paymaster General, the Attorney General and the Chief Whip.

The Chancellor and every Secretary of State are supported by a few junior Ministers. For example, the Secretary of State for Business, Energy and Industrial Strategy (BEIS) has three Ministers addressing different aspects of the Department's portfolio of activities; one or more Parliamentary Under-Secretary of State, junior to Ministers, may also be appointed to help with the Department's work programme.

A Prime Minister may choose to change the make-up of their Cabinet during a Parliament. They may do this for several reasons; for example, to reward those Ministers who have been particularly effective, or to remove those who have not, or simply to refresh the Cabinet with new ideas and energy. It may be a major reshuffle or involve a very few changes, but either way it is important for those wishing to engage with the decision-making process to be prepared to renew their engagement programme once a new Minister is in place.

For example, those working in the energy sector would have seen considerable turnover in Ministers in the Department of Energy and Climate Change (whose role is now covered by BEIS). The Department had five Secretaries of States,

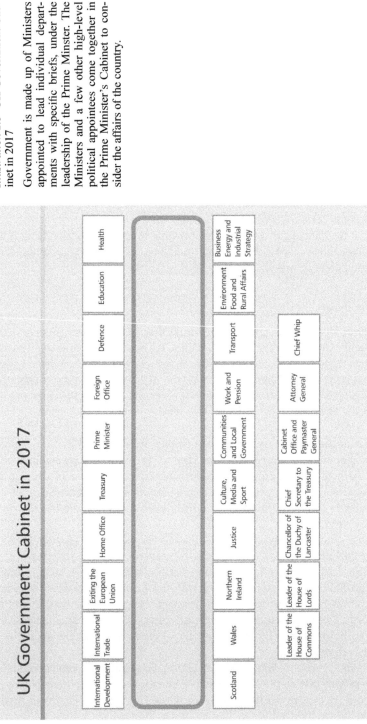

Illustration 2.3 UK Government Cabinet in 2017

Government is made up of Ministers appointed to lead individual departments with specific briefs, under the leadership of the Prime Minster. The Ministers and a few other high-level political appointees come together in the Prime Minister's Cabinet to consider the affairs of the country.

eight energy Ministers and two Climate Change Ministers in the period 2008 to 2016. Of course, part of the turnover was due to a change of Government in 2015, and a change of Prime Minister in 2016; nonetheless, organisations have had to work very hard to ensure that their concerns and messages are being heard by a changing political hierarchy.

Cabinet members will appoint one or more Special Advisors to aid their decision-making. These are political appointments and distinct from Whitehall; nonetheless, they will bring with them specialist knowledge and a wider experience helpful to Ministers. It is likely that such Advisors will have worked with Ministers in the past, perhaps in opposition, or are drawn from 'think tanks' who have helped with developing policy ideas for manifestos or election campaigns; they may also themselves be aspiring MPs. They can wield considerable influence over Ministers and are an important stakeholder group in their own right.

The opposition parties

The leader of the main opposition party, that is the political party with the second most seats after a general election, will appoint a shadow cabinet that largely mirrors that of the Government so that it is well placed to challenge the policies being developed. Its members will tend to have the same titles but prefaced with the term 'Shadow'. The pool from which the cabinet is drawn is naturally smaller, and the resources available for research, briefings and other support are also much more limited.

The leaders of other, smaller parties will also appoint MPs to specific briefs that cover the main areas of Government business; because the number of MPs available is relatively small, it is likely that some MPs will have more than one brief to cover and with little or no support except administrative.

An organisation should ideally develop relationships with members of the opposition parties as part of a wider engagement programme on specific issues; also, if the organisation takes a medium- to long-term view of policy, it can better position itself with those who may form the next Government.

The relationship between the two Houses

The two houses of Parliament have similar ways of carrying out their official business. For example, they play an important role in the development of new legislation, they carry out consultations and inquiries, and they have a number of Standing Committees that address some of the key issues in the economic and societal well-being of the country. However, in the UK the legislative power resides in the House of Commons; the Lords can effect changes to legislation as it passes back and forth between the two Houses, but it can only delay, not stop the legislation unless there is insufficient Parliamentary time to complete the process.

2.2.2   Devolved Administrations

An effective engagement programme needs to address stakeholders at both the national and Devolved Administration levels, and there needs to be a good understanding of their respective roles and the nature of the interactions between the two.

Viewed from within, the individual nations that make up the United Kingdom and Northern Ireland have always had some form of autonomy, which recognises differences in history and culture. Viewed from the outside, the United Kingdom is largely seen as a single entity presenting just one face to the rest of the world, particularly within the important global institutions. This is not unusual; many countries around the world have significant devolution of powers to its regions; for example, Autonomous Communities in Spain, the Cantons in Switzerland, the Provinces in Canada, and the States and Territories in Australia. It is important to understand a country's history and the drivers for devolution that will determine where political decision-making resides, today and in the future.

Emergence of the United Kingdom

The histories of England and Wales have always been interlinked, with enmity on both sides. Wales remained largely separate from England despite the Roman, Saxon, Danish and Norman invasions of the British Isles, being belligerent and independent and with its own language for centuries. Nonetheless, and despite attempts to have a barrier separating the two countries for periods, Wales has largely been 'overseen' or governed by English Kings, or Parliament when it emerged, for much of the last thousand years or so.

The history of Scotland is quite different. This is a nation that remained largely independent for most of its history, defying all invading forces until the Act of Union in 1707 when Scotland agreed to join with England and Wales to form Great Britain. Scotland retains its own legal and religious system to this day, but 300 years later, continued union with the rest of the UK is not certain, particularly with the rise of the Scottish Nationalist Party as a major force.

Ireland first came under English rule in the twelfth century but it was a difficult country to administer, and it was not until the mid-seventeenth century that it was secured through conquest by Oliver Cromwell. It remained difficult to oversee with natural and manmade disasters visiting the country at regular intervals. The Union with Ireland Act in 1801 was forced through Parliament but did not improve the circumstances of its people.

Following considerable action by nationalists, Ireland was divided in 1922 with the southern, largely Catholic community gaining independence, and the northern, largely Protestant community remaining part of the Union. There remain many who harbour ambitions for a united Ireland, although this has been discussed much less over the past 20 years or so; however, the difficulties of maintaining a border with Ireland in the south in a post-Brexit UK, and the fact that a majority in Northern Ireland voted to remain in the European Union may bring the idea of a united Ireland back on the agenda.

Despite the many rebellions, particularly in Ireland and Scotland, the Union has remained largely intact over the past few centuries. During this time the populations have intermingled and the fabric of societies knitted together through immigration and marriage, shared institutions and values, and new physical infrastructure. This period also covered the UK-led industrial revolution and the emergence of the British Empire, neither of which would have been as successful without the combined population and talents of all the regions of the British Isles.

If independence has been the desire of some in Scotland, Wales and Northern Ireland, most people appear to have been content to have been given more power to govern themselves through an active devolution process, particularly over the past 20 years or so. However, it is possible that the UK decision to leave the European Union (EU) in the 2016 referendum will provide a new drive for the break-up of the UK; there are many people in Scotland, Wales and Northern Ireland who believe it would be better to be an independent country within the EU rather than part of the United Kingdom and outside the EU.

The Scottish Government did in fact vote in favour of another referendum on independence in early 2017, arguing that there had been a significant change in circumstances brought about by Brexit which was detrimental to the people of Scotland who had voted by a significant majority to remain in the EU. From a legal perspective, another referendum can only go ahead if the UK Government agrees to it, and this it was not inclined to do until the negotiations with the EU were complete and any new relationship with the EU could be considered by the Scottish Government and the people of Scotland. Clearly, independence for any of the four nations of the UK would throw up many new challenges for those wishing to engage with their key stakeholders.

Scottish Parliament

The Scottish Parliament came into being in May 1999 following a referendum in 1997, which voted for devolution, and the Scotland Act 1998, which outlined its powers. It has an elected body of 129 MSPs, although unlike Westminster, it is based on proportional representation and runs for four years.

The Cabinet, led by a First Minister, is extensive and shows the breadth of activities in which the decision-making is devolved. In addition to nine Cabinet Secretaries, there are 13 Ministers with portfolios that span the economy. The current powers of the Scottish Parliament touch all aspects of health, education, tax and finance, economic development, rural affairs and natural resources (although offshore oil and gas remain a contentious issue), Local Government including services, and transport.

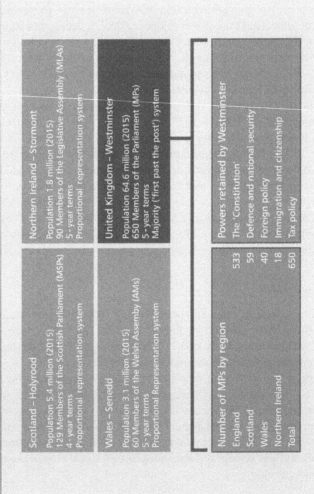

Illustration 2.4 Devolved Administrations in the UK

The devolution of power is an increasingly important part of the democratic process, allowing people at the regional level greater control and accountability of their own affairs. Each Devolved Administration is slightly different, reflecting its different circumstances and needs.

Note: Figures shown are for 2017.

Devolved Administrations in the UK

Scotland – Holyrood

Population 5.4 million (2015)
129 Members of the Scottish Parliament (MSPs)
4 -year terms
Proportional representation system

Wales – Senedd

Population 3.1 million (2015)
60 Members of the Welsh Assemby (AMs)
5 -year terms
Proportional Representation system

Northern Ireland – Stormont

Population 1.8 million (2015)
90 Members of the Legislative Assembly (MLAs)
5 -year terms
Proportional representation system

United Kingdom – Westminster

Population 64.6 million (2015)
650 Members of the Parliament (MPs)
5 -year terms
Majority ('first past the post') system

Number of MPs by region

England	533
Scotland	59
Wales	40
Northern Ireland	18
Total	650

Powers retained by Westminster

The 'Constitution'
Defence and national security
Foreign policy
Immigration and citizenship
Tax policy

Following the Referendum on Scottish Independence in 2014, which resulted in a clear majority to remain within the Union, there was a commitment by the three main parties – Conservative, Labour and Liberal Democrat – at Westminster to devolve further powers to Scotland. Following extensive consultation, the Smith Commission set out a number of recommendations and these were adopted in the Scotland Act 2016. The Devolved Administration now has its first law-making powers and new powers on tax and air passenger duty, welfare and licensing of onshore oil and gas extraction.

National Assembly for Wales

A referendum in 1997 approved the creation of the National Assembly for Wales and this came to pass through the Government of Wales Act in 1998. The Assembly has 60 Members elected through proportional representation with five-year terms. As with Scotland, the powers devolved to Wales have grown over time, although the nationalist movement is weaker than that in Scotland and there has not been a call for independence.

The Welsh Government is led by a First Minister, and the Cabinet consists of seven Cabinet Secretaries and three Ministers with portfolios that cover health, education, Local Government and its services, and rural affairs. The Welsh language remains a very important part of the culture of the country.

Northern Ireland Assembly

The Northern Ireland Assembly came about following a Referendum in 1998, and was brought into force by the Northern Ireland Act 1998. The Assembly has 90 Members elected through proportional representation, with five-year terms. The Assembly has had a troubled past, being suspended for periods during the first decade of its life, but has carried out its duties since it was restored in 2007 following a period of Direct Rule from Westminster. In 2017, new elections were needed to establish a fresh mandate following the resignation of the deputy First Minister.

The Northern Ireland Executive is made up of the First Minister, the Deputy First Minister, eight Departmental Ministers and two junior Ministers, and as in Scotland and Wales there are devolved powers that address health and education, finance and the economy, local communities, the environment and rural affairs.

Powers retained by the Westminster Parliament

Some powers are retained by Westminster, particularly those in which the UK faces the world: foreign policy, defence and national security, and immigration. The British 'Constitution', which is essentially made up Acts of Parliament, court judgments and conventions, is retained by Westminster, although aspects of this may be tested should there be further calls for independence in the Devolved Administrations.

Illustration 2.5 Devolved Administration Executives

Devolved Administrations are organised in much the same way as the National Government, with a First Minister and a group of Departmental Ministers, and have control over a range of matters.

Notes: In Holyrood, there are a further 13 Ministers with portfolios across the economy; in the Senedd, the Counsel General and Leader of the House and Chief Whip also attend Government meetings; in Stormont, two junior Ministers also attend the Executive.

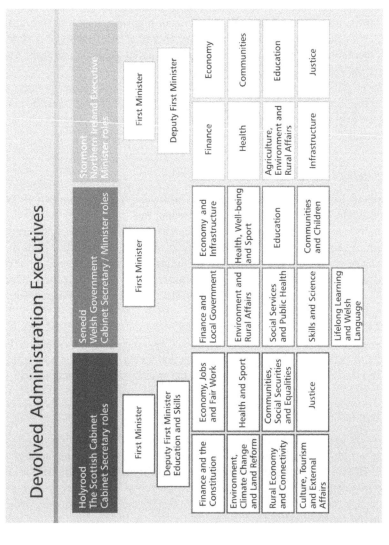

Devolved Administration Executives

Holyrood
The Scottish Cabinet
Cabinet Secretary roles

First Minister

Deputy First Minister
Education and Skills

Finance and the Constitution	Economy, Jobs and Fair Work
Environment, Climate Change and Land Reform	Health and Sport
Rural Economy and Connectivity	Communities, Social Securities and Equalities
Culture, Tourism and External Affairs	Justice

Senedd
Welsh Government
Cabinet Secretary / Minister roles

First Minister

Finance and Local Government	Economy and Infrastructure
Environment and Rural Affairs	Health, Well-being and Sport
Social Services and Public Health	Education
Skills and Science	Communities and Children
Lifelong Learning and Welsh Language	

Stormont
Northern Ireland Executive
Minister roles

First Minister

Deputy First Minister

Finance	Economy
Health	Communities
Agriculture, Environment and Rural Affairs	Education
Infrastructure	Justice

The ability to raise taxes has historically been a jealously guarded power by national government. The rates of income tax, for example, have largely been the domain of Westminster, although the Scottish Parliament has had the power to apply a small variation to the rates since 1999. However, since 2016, the Scottish Government has the power to set rates in Scotland different from the rest of the UK, although taxes will continue to be collected by HMRC and the revenues then sent to Scotland.

Other changes came into force in Scotland from 2017: the power to set the rates and bands of income tax on non-savings and non-dividend income, half the share of Value-Added Tax (VAT) receipts in Scotland to be assigned to the Scottish Government's budget, and power over Air Passenger Duty and Aggregates Levy. Two big sources of national income alongside income tax, national insurance and VAT, will continue to have their rates set by Westminster, as will Corporation Tax. Interestingly, Northern Ireland will be given the power to set Corporation Tax because of its unique competition with Ireland south of the border.

Some aspects of energy and the environment arena such as targets for renewables deployment and emissions of carbon, sulphur and nitrogen oxides are initially agreed at the European Union level; as such they are addressed at Westminster, although all countries are expected to contribute to the targets agreed. Further, implementation of polices and measures to deliver these targets are developed in Whitehall, in consultation with the relevant institutions in the Devolved Administrations.

The level of devolution in Scotland, and to a lesser extent in Wales and Northern Ireland, is now such that there are calls for England to also have a greater level of autonomy within the UK. One idea proposed is that only English MPs should be allowed to vote on policies and measures that impact England alone; this has yet to receive serious traction in Westminster as it could hasten the demise of the Union, something no Prime Minister would want to preside over.

There appears to be a desire for greater political and economic control at the local level in many countries across the world; devolution brings benefits in terms of making decision-making more responsive to local needs, and local politicians and civil servants more accountable for their actions. However, there are also tensions if the pace of devolution is either too slow or too rapid, and there will always be issues that can only be considered at the national level.

2.3 Parliamentary Committees

2.3.1 *Westminster*

It is important that organisations understand the work of Parliamentary Committees because their work can lead to changes in policy. Their prime role is to scrutinise the work of each of the Government departments, with an emphasis on policies, spending and administration. They do this by conducting inquiries in specific areas of interest, and these usually involve written and oral evidence and, if needed, fact-finding missions within the UK and overseas. Once completed, the inquiry findings are reported to the Commons and published so that they are available to all interested stakeholders. Government is then asked to respond to the Inquiry recommendations within 60 days.

For example, the Business, Energy and Industrial Strategy Committee carried out an Inquiry into the Government's Industrial Strategy; the stated aims of the Inquiry were:

> *The Committee will consider what the Government means by industrial strategy and question how interventionist in the free market it should be, such as whether it should prevent foreign takeover of UK companies.*
>
> *Priorities for the private sector, in terms of what businesses want from a revamped industrial strategy, the pros and cons of a sectorial approach and possible geographical emphasis will also be explored by the Committee.*
>
> *It will also look at the industrial strategies of previous governments and of other countries to see if there are any lessons to be learnt.*

These Committees are powerful Parliamentary institutions insofar as they may require Ministers, experts or individuals to give oral evidence to their inquiries. It is very difficult to decline an invitation to give evidence; oral evidence to the inquiries is held in public and transmitted on the Parliamentary television channel.

There are 52 Committees in the House of Commons, each with a Chair and, typically, around ten MPs drawn from across the political spectrum. Their work ranges well beyond the individual departments; some address issues that cover the work of more than one department such as the Audit Committee, and there are a small number of Joint Committees involving Members from both Houses of Parliament; some Committees address the Administration of Westminster itself.

The activities of the Committees are supported by a Clerk, and a Committee staff, and they in turn may use expert independent advisors whose role is to help provide inquiry questions and a substantive brief for Committee Members. Oral evidence is recorded and draft transcripts are sent to witnesses so that they can correct matters of fact, but not the text of what was said, before publication of the final report.

The House of Lords also holds inquiries. There are just six major Standing Committees but others can be formed to address issues as they arise. As in the Lower House, the make-up of the Committees will have representatives from different political parties. Again, the Government is usually obliged to respond to inquiry recommendations.

It is important that an organisation engages with the Clerk of a Committee, to better understand the kinds of issues the Committee may be considering in future inquiries, or to raise an issue that would benefit from an inquiry.

2.3.2 Devolved Administrations

The Devolved Administrations also have Committees carrying out valuable work; in some ways, they are more important because unlike Westminster, which has a second chamber in the House of Lords, the Administrations must rely solely on these Committees to provide the necessary scrutiny of policy and legislation.

Organisation of Local Government in the UK

	Council type	England	Wales	Scotland	Northern Ireland
England 353 Local Authorities Expenditure of £120.9 billion	Single tier (Unitary)	Unitary authorities in shire area	City	City	City
		London Boroughs	County	Regions	District
		Metropolitan Boroughs	County Boroughs	Island	
	Two tiers	County Councils			
		District, Borough and City Councils			
Wales 22 Unitary Authorities Expenditure of £8.0 billion	Governance	Mayor Elected Leader	Mayor Chairperson	Provost/Convener Elected Leader	Mayor Chairperson
		Elected Councillors	Elected Councillors	Elected Councillors	Elected Councillors
		Four-year terms	Four-year terms	Five-year terms	Four-year terms
Scotland 32 Unitary Authorities Expenditure of £15.7 billion	Delivery	Chief Executive	Chief Executive	Chief Executive	Chief Executive
Northern Ireland 11 Unitary Authorities Expenditure of £0.8 billion		Council Officers	Council Officers	Council Officers	Council Officers

Illustration 2.6 Organisation of Local Government in the UK

The term 'local' can be applied to a small region, a district, or a city or town. Local Government structures can be complex, not least because they have evolved over a long time.

Notes: Expenditure figures for 2014/15 financial year; in England, 353 Local Authorities made up of 27 County Councils, 201 District Councils, and 125 Unitary Authorities of which 32 are London boroughs and 36 are metropolitan boroughs.

Source: Local Government in England: Structures, Briefing Paper Number 07104, House of Commons, 29 January 2016, and *Commonwealth Journal of Local Government Handbook*, published 2016.

For example, in Scotland there are three types of Committees, those that are mandatory, those that address specific subjects and those that are set up to consider specific issues. Committees are established at the beginning of each session so that, for example, 16 Committees covered the work of Parliament in 2016, from Economy, Jobs and Fair Work, to Health and Sport. Each Committee has a Convener to lead it and between five and nine Members drawn from across the political spectrum. Committees in Wales and Northern Ireland are organised in much the same way, with the Standing Committees covering broadly the same areas.

2.4 Local Government

It has always been important for organisations to engage with local communities, particularly in relation to the traditional areas such as planning or public procurement; their level of engagement has grown as the portfolio of responsibilities of local decision-makers increased to include other areas of economic and social activity.

The framework under which Local Government operates is set at the national level by dedicated Departments: the Department for Communities and Local Government (DCLG) in England; the Department of Local Government and Community Empowerment in Scotland; the Department of Local Government and Local Government Business in Wales; and the Department of the Environment in Northern Ireland. These departments are led by a Secretary of State in England and someone of equivalent rank in the Devolved Administrations, indicating the importance attached to Local Government matters.

The drive for greater decision-making, and accountability, to the regional level has also driven changes in Local Government, in the belief that they are best able to deliver the needs of their constituents. England has the greatest variety of councils and due to its size by far the largest number: 353 Local Authorities in 2016. Many parts of England have two tiers of Local Government while some have a single (unitary) tier serving their local communities; below these are around 10,000 Parish, Community and Town Councils, demonstrating the long tradition of local activism and decision-making in most parts of the country. Local Government in Scotland, Wales and Northern Ireland is organised in a simpler way with a single tier of operation. The average size of a community is similar across the UK and, except for Northern Ireland, so is the average spend per person, although there are variations across the UK.

In many ways, the political process at the local level mirrors that at the national level, with elected councillors taking on the responsibilities of Local Government. Councillors are elected for four-year terms compared with five-year terms of the national Government, the exception being Scotland which has the reverse, with five-year terms for local elections and four-year terms for its Parliament. The main difference between national and local politics is that councillors tend to be part-time whereas national politicians are full-time, and both are paid accordingly.

As occurs at the national level, there is an executive team that will ensure that policy is implemented, services delivered and budgets managed. There are small differences in the way authorities organise this aspect of their work, but there is

Local Government responsibilities

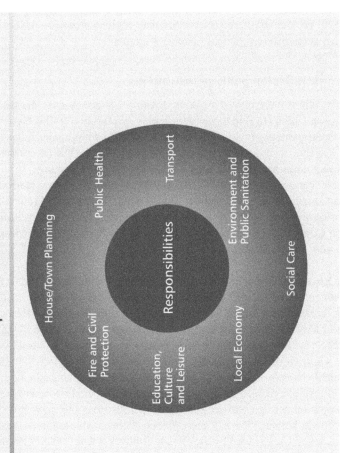

House/Town Planning

Public Health

Transport

Fire and Civil Protection

Responsibilities

Environment and Public Sanitation

Education, Culture and Leisure

Local Economy

Social Care

Illustration 2.7 Local Government responsibilities

Local Government is responsible for a range of services that affect ordinary people's daily lives: health, education and transport to name a few. The public and private sectors work closely at the local level to deliver many of the community services.

a leader of the Council, perhaps the Mayor for example, and an elected deputy, who run the Council meetings; if one political party has a clear majority, it will provide those elected to these positions, otherwise it will be the person who can gather support from across the political spectrum.

The activities of the Council are important to the local communities that they serve; the Council must be able to deliver the services they are responsible for when they are needed and at an affordable cost. To achieve this requires good management and professional Council officers. A Chief Executive will work closely with the Council leadership team to ensure the effective delivery of services to the community.

In general terms, Council-level responsibilities cover planning, education, transport, social care, public health and the environment, local economy and council tax collections. In those regions where a single-tier system exists, the council will provide all these services; in other regions provision of services will be split between different tiers of Local Government.

2.5 European Union political institutions

Many institutions have played a role in defining UK policy over the years, from the European Union (EU) to those representing 'grassroots' civil society. The former has been particularly active in defining policy development in the UK over the past 40 years or so, and this will continue even after the UK leaves the EU; yet the EU institutions and the way they work remain opaque to many.

An understanding of the roles of the key EU institutions, then, is necessary to inform an organisation's stakeholder engagement programme. From a political and decision-making perspective, there are three main European institutions: the European Council, the Council of the European Union and the European Parliament. In very simple terms:

- **The European Council:** Has the role of defining the political agenda for the EU, in particular its direction and the priority issues that need to be addressed; it deals with foreign policy issues, including security. It is made up of the Heads of State of EU Member States; the European Commission President and High Representative for Foreign Affairs and Security Policy also attend Council meetings.
- **The Council of the European Union:** One level down from the European Council; its role is to coordinate policies, amending and adopting laws. It develops policy based on the guidelines given by the European Council, for example on foreign and security policy; it also has the power to conclude agreement between the EU and other countries or international institutions. This Council is attended by the relevant Ministers from each EU country and the actual attendees depending on the policy area being discussed. Ministers are expected to have the authority to commit their governments to action on decisions agreed at Council meetings.
- **The European Parliament:** Has a strong legislative role, passing laws together with the Council of the European Union. It also decides on potential EU enlargement and international agreements involving the EU. It can

instruct the executive arm of the Union, the European Commission (EC), to propose legislation and reviews its overall work programme. It has a supervisory role; for example, it can scrutinise the performance of the various EU institutions, or it can set up inquiries in response to petitions; and working with the Council of the EU, it establishes the overall budget.

There are 751 elected Members of the European Parliament (MEPs), grouped by political persuasion and not by nationality. The number of MEPs for each Member State is determined, roughly, by the size of its population. For example, the UK has a population of around 65 million and is represented in the Parliament by 73 MEPs – the country is divided into 12 regions from an EU perspective, and each region has between three MEPs (Northern Ireland and the North-East England) and ten MEPs (South-East England).

MEPs participate in the 20 Standing Committees (and two Sub-Committees) that cover all aspects of social and economic activity in the EU, from Foreign Affairs to Petitions; there are also ad hoc temporary (12-month) Committees of Inquiry formed to cover specific issues. They play an important role in the legislation process, interacting strongly with the other arms of EU governance. They can, for example, hold expert hearings in public and report their findings, recommendations and, where appropriate, amendments to potential legislation to the Parliament in plenary sessions. Committees are large, consisting of between 25 and 71 full members, with an elected Chair and a political make-up reflecting the plenary assembly.

These three institutions have worked together to deliver policies that have had profound effects on EU citizens, from the way they work to the environment they enjoy. For example, the targets agreed in response to the climate change issue – a 20% reduction in greenhouse gas emissions, 20% of energy to come from renewable energy sources and a 20% reduction in primary energy use compared with projected levels, all by 2020 – have had a profound impact on the way Member States produce and consume energy. Heads of State had to agree, collectively, to these EU targets and to further agree the burden-sharing by each Member State in the Council of Ministers. The European Commission, the EU's politically independent executive arm, working with the Parliament, brought forward policies to enable these targets to be met; national governments had some flexibility on how they would be implemented in their jurisdictions.

The EU has not always led new policy development; new legislation can be led at the national level and have a strong influence on the rest of Europe. For example, the UK led the liberalisation of energy markets by privatising and deregulating state entities and this led to increased competition and lower costs for consumers; this approach to markets has now been adopted in the rest of Europe, albeit at a slower pace. More recently, the UK has seen some major government interventions into the market to ensure that decarbonisation of the economy and security-of-supply objectives were met; these also required successful passage through the EU's State Aid process, which scrutinises new policy developments for potential anti-competitive outcomes. Other European

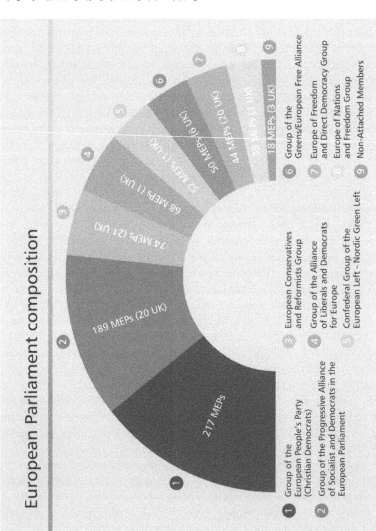

European Parliament composition

1 217 MEPs

2 189 MEPs (20 UK)

3 74 MEPs (21 UK)

4 68 MEPs (1 UK)

5 52 MEPs (1 UK)

6 50 MEPs (6 UK)

7 44 MEPs (20 UK)

8 33 MEPs (1 UK)

9 18 MEPs (3 UK)

1 Group of the European People's Party (Christian Democrats)

2 Group of the Progressive Alliance of Socialist and Democrats in the European Parliament

3 European Conservatives and Reformists Group

4 Group of the Alliance of Liberals and Democrats for Europe

5 Confederal Group of the European Left – Nordic Green Left

6 Group of the Greens/European Free Alliance

7 Europe of Freedom and Direct Democracy Group

8 Europe of Nations and Freedom Group

9 Non-Attached Members

Illustration 2.8 European Parliament composition

The European Union, and its institutions, is a very important global entity. It is made up of 28 countries, with an estimated 510 million people in 2016, and a GDP of €14.6 trillion (PPP, purchasing power parity) in 2015. To put this into context, the USA had a population of 323 million in 2016 and a GDP of about €13.8 trillion (PPP) in 2015.

Notes: MEP is a Member of European Parliament of which there are a total of 715 elected; numbers are as of January 2017.

countries are now following suit and they are doing so under European Commission guidance.

2.5.1 UK decision to leave the EU (Brexit)

It would be wrong to suggest that there is a shared political view of the future of the EU. The pillars of the modern EU 'state' are enshrined in the Treaty of Rome in 1957 and maintained in subsequent Treaties agreed in the intervening period to date. Four basic freedoms are enshrined in the original Treaty, maintained in subsequent Treaties and apply to all EU Members: the free movement of labour, capital, goods and services. The creation of the Eurozone involving most of the Member States was a major step in the integration process, although a number of countries, including the UK, opted out of the zone.

Some Member States see a natural progression to greater integration and 'political union'; others have a different vision for Member States in the EU, one based more on the original idea of a 'common market' with considerable political power retained at the national level. The tension between these two visions of the future of the EU led to the UK's referendum on its membership of the EU in June 2016; the referendum result was for the UK to leave the EU by a small majority.

The political process to leave the EU began with the Prime Minister 'triggering' Article 50 of the Lisbon Treaty in March 2017. There follows a two-year period in which the details of the future relationship between the UK and the EU can be agreed.

Whatever the nature and scope of the UK's future relationship with the EU, it would be naïve to think that developments in one will not affect developments in the other. For organisations in the UK, a prudent stakeholder engagement programme will need to include the political and executive arms of the EU; whether that is simply a watching brief or a more proactive approach will depend on the issue.

Summary key points

- Strategic stakeholders are all those in Government, Parliament and the Civil Service that influence the policy-making arena.
- A two-tier model for a Parliament prevails in many countries around the world, although the relative contribution of the two tiers to the decision-making process differs.
- There is increasing devolution to the regional and local levels with the relationship between national governments and their Devolved Administrations differing markedly.
- An effective engagement programme needs to address stakeholders at both the national and Devolved Administration levels, the nature of that engagement dependent on the issue.
- An organisation's level engagement with local decision-makers will need to grow as the latter's portfolio of responsibilities increases to include other areas of economic and social activity.

Case Study 2.1 Government policy can be transformational

The activities of Parliament can often seem a long way from the day-to-day business of organisations. Although it is not always apparent, government policy initiatives can lead to dramatic changes in the environment in which organisations operate. Organisations need to engage with the political process to protect their interests. A good example of this is a reform of the electricity market in the UK, which had a major impact on incumbents and potential new entrants.

Background

The UK has enjoyed significant benefits from the political decision to liberalise its markets over the past 20 years or so, with competition delivering, for example, low electricity prices for consumers. But more recently, Government concluded that the market alone could not deliver the new electricity infrastructure needed to replace ageing plants and to deliver the low-carbon technologies needed for the UK to meet its European Union 2020 climate change targets. Other important considerations were security of supply and cost to the consumer. An investment by the industry of £100 billion was needed.

Government decided that it needed several interventions in the market to incentivise new build. Various policy initiatives were developed by civil servants and implemented over several years, but always under the scrutiny and involvement of politicians. The overall programme was called Electricity Market Reform (EMR).

Delivering Electricity Market Reform

EMR is essentially made up of four individual instruments: the Carbon Price Support Mechanism, the Contract for Difference Feed-in Tariffs scheme, the Capacity Mechanism and the Emission Performance Standards:

- The **Carbon Price Support Mechanism** provides a minimum carbon price for fossil electricity generators.
- The **Contract for Difference Feed-in Tariffs** scheme provides a guaranteed subsidy for each unit of electricity produced by low-carbon technologies, for a set period.
- The **Capacity Mechanism** provides an incentive for existing plants to remain operating and to encourage new plants onto the electricity system to maintain security of supply.

- **Emission Performance Standards** for fossil generation are set to limit emissions from this sector.

To these was added the Levy Control Framework (LCF), which essentially capped the overall budget available for the deployment of low-carbon technology.

Outcomes

Government consulted extensively over an extended period, from policy concept to the passage of legislation through Parliament. There was ample opportunity for organisations to engage with the process, from formal consultation responses to informal roundtable discussion and workshops.

Not surprisingly, organisations were very interested in participating in the process because the risks and opportunities, and the monies involved, were significant; the projected future cost of low-carbon projects under the LCF was £8.4 billion for 2020/21, while the cost of the Capacity Mechanism for 2018/19 was just under £1 billion. What is also true is that there were 'winners' and 'losers' in the market, and crucially, that the Government now determined who they were.

Case Study 2.2 Devolution increasingly important in policy development

Organisations must increasingly take note of developments and be prepared to engage with decision-makers and key influencers in the Devolved Administrations and Local Government. Politicians at the regional and local levels can distinguish themselves from their neighbours by implementing national policy to suit their agendas, and this offers risks and opportunities for organisations. The ambitious Climate Change targets in Scotland are a good example of policy development at the regional level.

Background

The Scotland Act 1998 created a Scottish Parliament with powers to make laws on a range of issues including the environment. In 2009, the Climate Change (Scotland) Act was passed unanimously by the Scottish

Parliament, committing the country to ambitious targets for greenhouse gas (GHG) reductions: at least 80% in 2050 relative to 1990 levels, with a target of at least 42% by 2020. The Scottish Government had legislative powers to help deliver the changes proposed by the target – for example, planning and Scottish renewables incentives (albeit paid by consumers across the UK) – and it was also able to provide grants to stimulate new developments.

Next steps

The GHG target of 42% by 1990 was reached in 2014, some six years earlier than planned. There were significant reductions in the power generation, industry and waste sectors but very little movement in the transport, building and agriculture sectors. For example, power sector decarbonisation was accelerated by significant renewables deployment brought about by generous incentives and an encouraging planning process; the transport sector, on the other hand, relies more heavily on global developments in new technologies to deliver lower emissions and the consumer response is slow, even when local incentives are available.

In early 2017, the Scottish Government came forward with ambitious new targets to accelerate the transition to a low-carbon economy; it proposed a target of 50% reduction by 2020 relative to 1990 levels and 66% reduction by 2032. It also signalled which parts of the economy would need to be addressed: it wanted to see, by 2032, a fully decarbonised electricity sector, 80% of domestic heat to come from low-carbon heat technologies and 40% of registered cars and vans in Scotland to use ultra-low emission technology.

Outcomes

Market participants responded positively to the 2009 Act because of the opportunities associated with high targets and a relatively benign planning process. The Committee on Climate Change (CCC), an independent advisory body set up by the UK Government, suggested in its advice to the Scottish Government that their new targets should be transparent, stable, feasible and evidence-based. The risks and opportunities involved with the new target proposals ensures that market participants will once again actively engage with the Devolved Administration's stakeholder engagement programme.

Case Study 2.3 Europe an important influence on national policy

Organisations must take note of potential policy developments at the national level, but they should also consider what is happening at the European level. The European Union (EU) has been very success-ful in promoting action by its Members in relation to economic activ-ity, social well-being and environmental protection. It has done this through a series of policies and measures to help the EU meet targets agreed by Member States, with widespread implications for business and consumers.

Background

In 2009, the European Commission (EC) adopted the '2020 Framework package' as a step in the process of decarbonising the economies of EU Members by 2050. The package involved targets for greenhouse gas emissions, renewable energy and energy efficiency in 2020. Each national Government negotiated their country's contribution to the EU target and was then required to develop policies, including intervention in markets, to deliver on their promises.

The political and policy processes at the European and national levels used for the 2020 package were repeated in Member State discussions on targets for 2030, the next meaningful milestone on the path to the longer-term EU targets for 2050.

Delivering the 2030 EU Climate and Energy Package

EU countries agreed a new 2030 Framework for climate and energy. This included EU-wide targets and policy objectives for the period between 2020 and 2030 that involved further major reductions in greenhouse gas emissions and ambitious new targets for renewables and energy efficiency.

To meet the targets, the European Commission proposed several measures to apply across Member States. These included a reform of the carbon market, new indicators for competitiveness and security of energy systems, and a new governance system that draws on national plans for competitive, secure and sustainable energy. This strategy sent a strong signal to the market on the EU's path of travel, encouraging private invest-ment in new pipelines, electricity networks and low-carbon technology.

Outcomes

The business and NGO communities welcomed the greater clarity given by the EU political process leading to the agreed targets for 2030, with many organisations contributing to the EC's consultation exercise individually or through their trade associations. Member States also held consultation exercises as they developed policies to meet their individual targets and, where appropriate, organisations took the opportunity to present their views.

The UK's decision to leave the EU does not affect its individual targets since all EU laws will be transposed into UK law in the first instance. Over time, however, there will be a re-evaluation of EU policies through a purely UK prism and changes made to the legislation as appropriate. It is also probable that there will be an ongoing relationship with Europe on certain issues, with climate change mitigation high on that list. On these issues, the EU will continue to influence UK policy, and organisations will continue to engage with the appropriate institutions.

3 Key influencers

Chapter summary

There are many outside Government who can influence policy, from institutions to eminent individuals; this chapter describes key influencers beyond political circles. The Civil Service plays a fundamental role at all levels of government, mainly as an executive to Ministers, but they also provide advice and options for their political masters. Also, close to the decision-making process are Special Advisors who are appointed by individual Ministers and as such have considerable influence over policy. In addition, independent public bodies such as regulators, although tied to specific Civil Service Departments, have considerable power to influence policy debate. Independent views by professional institutions, notable NGOs and high-profile individual commentators have also demonstrated they can affect government policy. These key influencers must be included in an effective engagement programme.

Stakeholder engagement practitioners in the UK will be familiar with many, if not all the key influencers highlighted in this chapter. As was the case in Chapter 2 for decision-makers, practitioners in other countries can use the material presented in this chapter to help in their stakeholder mapping exercises in relation to key influencers.

3.1 Key influencers on Government and Parliament

The work of decision-makers in Governments around the world is influenced by a range of stakeholders, from bodies that encourage policy direction and support and scrutinise Parliamentary processes to those who represent a variety of different interests in civil society. These influencers play an important role at the national, Devolved Administration and local levels.

There are broadly three tiers of influence. The first tier is made up of those institutions that support the work of Government and Parliament: the Civil Service and other public bodies. Organisations in the second tier are at a distance from the political policy-making process but nonetheless carry influence because of the constituencies they represent; for example, the professional institutions, trade unions and large membership non-governmental organisations (NGOs). The third tier includes organisations such as business associations, think tanks and

Influencing UK political institutions

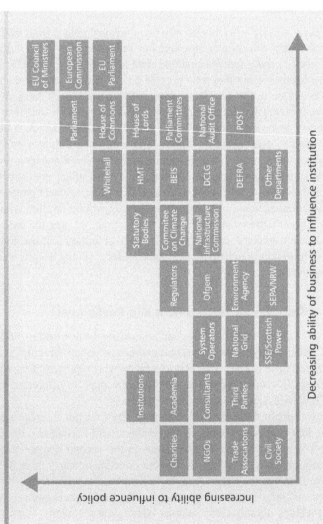

Increasing ability to influence policy

Decreasing ability of business to influence institution

Illustration 3.1 Influencing UK political institutions

A range of stakeholder groups can influence national policy development and, depending on the issue, some will play a more important role than others.

Notes: NGOs, non-governmental organisations; SSE, Scottish and Southern Energy; Ofgem, Office of Gas and Electricity Markets; SEPA, Scottish Environment Protection Agency; NRW, Natural Resources Wales; HMT, Her Majesty's Treasury; BEIS, [Department for] Business, Energy and Industrial Strategy; DCLG, Department for Communities and Local Government; DEFRA, Department for Environment, Food and Rural Affairs; POST, Parliamentary Office of Science and Technology; EU, European Union.

consultants, and prominent individuals. The relative contribution of each tier to the decision-making process may differ in different countries and by issue, but it is important that all are considered in a stakeholder engagement programme.

There are many different public bodies that support the work of Government and Parliament: those employed by Parliament itself, the Civil Service, and executive agencies and public bodies. The first of these consists of the National Audit Office (NAO), the Parliamentary and Health Ombudsman, the Electoral Commission and the Parliamentary Office of Science and Technology (POST). The NAO is perhaps the most visible of these since it scrutinises public spending by Government departments, agencies and other bodies, reports its findings to Parliament and by doing so encourages improvement in the services they provide.

The Parliamentary and Health Ombudsman investigates complaints about public services while the Electoral Commission, as the name implies, ensures that all matters related to elections and referenda are well run. The role of POST is to brief Parliamentarians on all matters related to public policy in science and technology; its POSTnotes are very well researched, balanced and authoritative, ensuring Members of Parliament and others in the political arena are well-informed on topical issues.

Government continually consults representatives of business, professional institutions and civil society to ensure its decisions are evidence-based and robust. These representatives include, for example, trade associations, academia and the various technical institutions, and NGOs and charities; there will also be action groups who will seek to influence the agenda of local politicians.

3.1.1 Civil Service in the UK

The Civil Service that supports Parliament in Whitehall is made up of several thousand professionals, the vast majority of which work in the 25 departments led by Ministers. The Civil Service is not political; rather, it supports the Government of the day by helping it develop and implement its policies and by providing valuable continuity across Parliaments. It is led by the Cabinet Secretary and Head of the Civil Service, who is the Prime Minister's most senior policy advisor.

> Civil servants, in particular, wield considerable influence over decisions that affect every aspect of society – from local planning to taxation, from building regulations to the case for war – but they act, or at least should act, accountably to those who have political authority derived from a democratic mandate.
>
> *Nick Clegg, former MP and Deputy Prime Minister,*
> Politics Between the Extremes, *2016*

The organisational structure of the Civil Service continues to evolve, and although there is a common template for departments, there are differences reflecting the nature of the work carried out. Each department is led by a Permanent Secretary that reports to the Head of the Civil Service. Each department has a few major themes of work, perhaps between four and eight, each led by a Director-General;

each theme is broken down into specific areas, again between four and eight, led by Directors, and below them Assistant Directors and Team or Policy Leads who manage different strands of the overall work programme.

For example, the Department for Transport has an executive team of five Director-General roles covering the following themes: Rail, Roads, Devolution and Motoring, High-Speed Rail, Resources and Strategy, and International, Security and Environment. The groups within the Rail theme, for example, include Passenger Services, Network Services, Major Projects, Rails Strategy and Security, and Rail Corporate Services and Portfolio Office; and one level further down, there are six teams that make up the Major Projects Group with the following responsibilities: the Thameslink Programme, Intercity Express, Crossrail, Crossrail 2, Programme Management Office and High Speed 2 Interface.

One further department worth mentioning is the Cabinet Office. The stated aim of this department is primarily to support the Prime Minister and Cabinet and to drive efficiencies and reforms; it is also to create a more united country through political and constitutional reform, and to make the United Kingdom secure.

Organisations need to identify which level of Civil Service department they need to engage with and this will depend on their interests. They will also need to identify which executive or internal expert is best placed to lead its engagement.

In the Cabinet reshuffle of 2016, there were a number of changes to the Whitehall Departments including the bringing together of the Department of Energy and Climate Change (DECC) and the Department for Business Innovation and Skills (BIS) to form a new Department for Business, Energy and Industrial Strategy (BEIS); this means a changing environment for stakeholder engagement and reflects the emphasis placed on issues by politicians.

Also of note was the creation of two new departments to implement the UK's complex withdrawal from the European Union following the Referendum in May of that year; they were the Department of International Trade (DIT) and Department for Exiting the European Union (DExEU). These new departments were created by drawing on resources from across the Civil Service and, in some specialist areas, from external consultancies, accountancy firms, project management specialists and individual experts. Also, existing departments set up their own Brexit teams so that they were better positioned to support the main 'Brexit' departments as needed.

3.1.2 Civil Service support for the Devolved Administrations

Scotland has historically had strong institutions, particularly those related to law and justice. But there are others: the Scottish Executive supports the Scottish Government's activities, just as Whitehall supports the UK Government programme

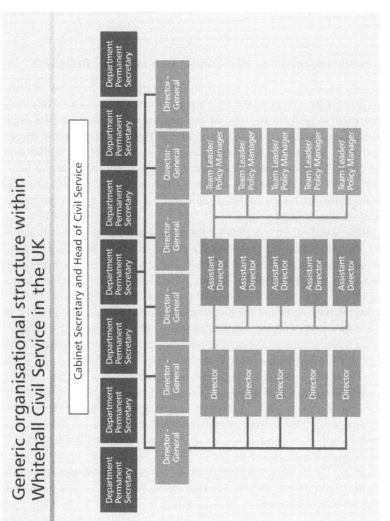

Generic organisational structure within Whitehall Civil Service in the UK

Cabinet Secretary and Head of Civil Service

| Department Permanent Secretary | Department Permanent Secretary | Department Permanent Secretary | Department Permanent Secretary | Department Permanent Secretary | Department Permanent Secretary | Department Permanent Secretary |

Director-General | Director-General | Director-General | Director-General | Director-General | Director-General

Director | Assistant Director | Team Leader/Policy Manager
Director | Assistant Director | Team Leader/Policy Manager
Director | Assistant Director | Team Leader/Policy Manager
Director | Assistant Director | Team Leader/Policy Manager
Director | Assistant Director | Team Leader/Policy Manager

Illustration 3.2 Generic organisational structure within Whitehall Civil Service in the UK

The Civil Service is organised in much the same way as any other organisation with, for example, a Departmental Permanent Secretary whose role is similar to a CEO of a major organisation, a Director-General has a role similar to that of an executive, and Directors are the equivalent of middle managers.

at Westminster. There are a number of other executive agencies of the Scottish Parliament set up to address, for example, the transport or environment needs of the country.

As with Whitehall and the Scottish Executive, the Welsh Civil Service is the executive arm of the Welsh Government; their stated aim in the future is to deliver the Assembly programmes and to help in the next stage of the devolution process. And the Northern Ireland Civil Service provides support to the Northern Ireland Executive.

The Scotland Office, as the custodian of the devolution settlement, remains an important institution. It supports the Secretary of State for Scotland, and its remit is simply to look after the interests of Scotland in Westminster and Whitehall, particularly in relation to the reserved powers. It also seeks to promote a strong Union. The Wales Office and Northern Ireland Office have similar mandates.

3.2 Influential independent Non-Departmental Public Bodies

Executive agencies are set up by individual departments to carry out specific functions, and are known as Non-Departmental Public Bodies (NDPBs); they are treated separately from the rest of the department with their own management, staff and budget. In total, there are 347 such bodies across the 25 Ministerial and 21 non-Ministerial departments; the number associated with each department varies significantly, from a single public body at the Scotland Office to 47 bodies at the Department for Business, Energy and Industrial Strategy. The creation, review and dissolution of such bodies follow guidelines set out by the Cabinet Office.

These bodies touch all aspects of UK civil society, and they are not only essential but highly influential, not least because they are seen to be independent of Whitehall and Government. They include some of the most recognisable organisations in the UK such as the British Broadcasting Corporation (BBC), the Meteorological Office, the Forestry Commission and the Crown Estate.

Some executive agencies and public bodies are particularly influential by helping to set the direction of policy and the country's ambition in an area, as well as providing concrete proposals on how that ambition can be met. For example, the Committee on Climate Change (CCC) was set up under the Climate Change Act in 2008, and its role is twofold: to set a series of five-year carbon budgets that will lead to an 80% reduction in greenhouse gas emissions in the UK by 2050 and to report to Parliament on progress. Each five-year budget is agreed in Parliament. However, what is not clear is what sanctions are possible on the UK Government if their policies are not sufficient to deliver the carbon agreed budgets; this is unlikely to be tested in the near future.

The CCC has been very influential, then, in defining the Government's energy policy through its decarbonisation agenda. Many of the economic instruments that are currently in play, such as the Carbon Price Floor and Contracts-for-Difference scheme, are options supported by the CCC;

these instruments are transformational for the industries involved and affect everybody in the UK through higher energy prices. Of course, Governments change and so do their priorities, but the remit of such bodies is established in an Act, and as such they have a life of their own, unless there is a change in the appropriate legislation.

Another body arose from the Armitt Review, commissioned by the Labour Party led by Ed Miliband and published in 2013, which highlighted the need for a body broadly like the CCC to take a long-term view of UK infrastructure needs, particularly in relation to transport, communications and power. Such a body, the National Infrastructure Commission (NIC), was set up in 2015 by the Chancellor of the Exchequer, albeit in 'shadow mode' until the required legislation could be passed in 2016. The NIC has adopted an evidence-based approach, as occurs with all policy initiatives developed by the Civil Service, provides recommendations to Government, scrutinises Whitehall plans to meet these recommendations, and carries out and publishes annual assessments on progress.

Although still in 'shadow mode', the NIC carried out three early studies in 2015, two on transport-related issues and one on power and these were well-received by Government. The Chancellor asked for two further studies in 2016, one a specific regional development study to explore greater connectivity across the corridor between Oxford and Cambridge linking two world-class universities and innovation centres, and one on communications related to the deployment of 5G technology. The NIC will also carry out the first formal comprehensive assessment of infrastructure needs for the UK. There are good indications that Governments, today and in the future, will commit additional significant resources to improving the UK's infrastructure in the decade post-2020, which is fundamental to economic growth right across the country.

It is important that those organisations that have an interest in the climate change initiatives and infrastructure in the UK take the opportunity to engage with the CCC and NIC while they carry out their various studies. In this way, they will be more aware of emerging developments and perhaps influence the policy outcomes.

The Competition and Markets Authority (CMA) is another important independent body that has arguably carried out two of the most significant investigations in recent years, the outcomes of which touch people's lives in the UK: competition in retail banking and in energy markets. The former was prompted by perceived weaknesses in the retail banking sector to the detriment of customers; the latter occurred because the energy industry – and electricity and gas utilities in particular – were thought to be profiteering, and there was a perceived lack of transparency in the way they were operating.

Their reports, published in 2016, are in two parts: they highlight potential problems in these markets that are particularly detrimental to consumers, and suggest remedies that would improve their circumstances. It is incumbent on the regulator to bring forward proposals that address these outcomes.

In terms of process, the CCC, NIC and CMA carry out their work in broadly the same way: they gather evidence from across the stakeholder spectrum through a variety of approaches, from a request for information to bilateral discussions. Stakeholders are not obliged to provide such information, or engage with the CCC and NIC studies; it is purely voluntary. However, this is not the case with the CMA, where companies must provide the information, in the format requested and to a strict timescale, otherwise they may be subject to legal action. The CMA data request is extensive and can go back many years, covering activities across the operational spectrum from basic trading data to information on company strategy and decision-making, and from management structure to governance arrangements.

The main difference between these bodies is that the CMA analysis largely focuses on past information to draw its conclusions, while the CCC analyses past performance in terms of greenhouse gas reductions and looks ahead to what needs to be done to achieve the UK targets; the NIC is largely concerned with looking at the future, beyond current activities and policies.

What they do have in common is considerable analytical capability to draw on: from within their own organisations, from the mainstream Civil Service and beyond to private organisations. Following extensive and detailed analysis of the information provided, they publish their findings formally for consideration and action by Government and the regulators.

A further important group of independent bodies that have considerable influence over market environments is the regulators. These have been set up to look after the interests of consumers and public more widely across the economy: in education, health, transport, the environment, utilities, financial services and many others. For example, a number of regulators were formed following the privatisation of the public utilities in the 1980s and 1990s including the Office of Gas and Electricity Markets (Ofgem), the Office of Water Services Regulation Authority (Ofwat) and the Office of Communications (Ofcom). Their role is to protect the consumer by encouraging competition in the market, by ensuring that utilities fulfil their obligations as set out in their licences including Government schemes, to initiate appropriate corrective action if they fail to do so, and to carry out reviews so that services to customers are improved.

Once again, organisations must include regulators in their strategic stakeholder engagement programme and be prepared to be asked to provide data and information on their operational activities.

3.3 European Institutions supporting the political process

Being part of the Europe Union (EU) for more than 40 years has meant the UK has often had to take a collegiate view of policy development, sometimes following proposals put forward by others and sometimes taking a lead role with its own initiatives. Power resides within the Council of Ministers, and to a lesser extent with the European Commission (EC), which is charged with

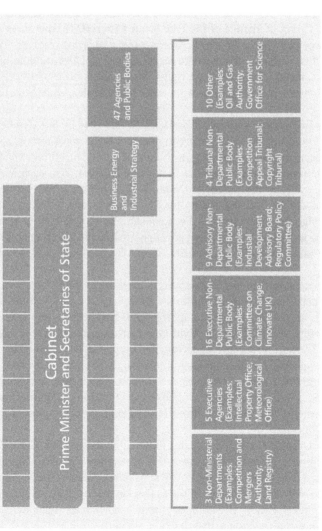

Executive agencies and public bodies

Cabinet
Prime Minister and Secretaries of State

Business Energy and Industrial Strategy

47 Agencies and Public Bodies

| 3 Non-Ministerial Departments (Examples: Competition and Mergers Authority; Land Registry) | 5 Executive Agencies (Examples: Intellectual Property Office; Meteorological Office) | 16 Executive Non-Departmental Public Body (Examples: Committee on Climate Change; Innovate UK) | 9 Advisory Non-Departmental Public Body (Examples: Industrial Development Advisory Board; Regulatory Policy Committee) | 4 Tribunal Non-Departmental Public Body (Examples: Competition Appeal Tribunal; Copyright Tribunal) | 10 Other (Examples: Oil and Gas Authority; Government Office for Science) |

Illustration 3.3 Executive agencies and public bodies

There is considerable focus on the work of mainstream Civil Service departments but each department will also have a significant number of influential, independent executive agencies and other public bodies that have been set up to address an issue.

Note: Information presented in www.gov.uk/government/organisations, 2016.

bringing forward new proposals, for example in areas identified by the Council; the EU Parliament also plays an important role in setting the ambition for the EU, and through its Member representatives provides an important direct link to the UK.

There are, then, several bodies that support the political institutions across the EU, each with its own sphere of influence:

- The **European Commission (EC)** is the independent executive arm for the EU, proposing and enforcing legislation and implementing policies; it also draws up and implements the EU budget. The EC is made up of a Commissioner from each of the Member States, led by the Commission President who is appointed by the European Council. There are 53 Departments or Executive Offices that carry out the Commission's work-programme.
- The **Court of Justice of the European Union (CJEU)** ensures that EU law is applied in the same way across Member States and resolves disputes when needed; organisations can take action against an EU institution, if they feel it has somehow infringed their rights. The Court is made up of one judge from each Member State plus 11 Advocate-General roles, with incumbents providing expert advice to the Court.
- The **European Investment Bank (EIB)** is owned by the Member States and was set up to provide funding to progress the aims of the EU; for example, its projects can encourage growth and jobs, mitigate climate change and promote policies outside the EU. It has one Director from each Member State, and one from the European Commission. The role of the European Central Bank (ECB) is responsibility for EU economic and monetary policy, and to manage the euro currency by, for example, setting interest rates. An ECB President and Vice-President are supported by the governors of national central banks from all EU countries.

There are several bodies that scrutinise the work of the EU institutions and supporting departments. For example, the European Court of Auditors ensures that EU funds are collected and used appropriately and helps to improve EU financial management; the European Ombudsman considers complaints against EU institutions, bodies, offices and agencies; the European Data Protection Supervisor addresses people's right to privacy in relation to their personal data.

There are two advisory bodies: the European Economic and Social Committee (EESC), which represents workers' and employers' organisations and other interest groups, and the Committee of the Regions, which represents regional and local authorities.

The EU has an outward-looking diplomatic service, the European External Action Service (EEAS). This institution is responsible for foreign and security policy, and delivering a coherent story in its relations with other countries. Its purpose is to extend the influence of the EU on key issues such as conflict resolution, security, development and climate change, and human rights across the world through political, economic and practical support.

It is possible to engage with officials in these institutions, by seeking bilateral meetings, through third-party advocates such as trade associations, particularly those that are pan-European, and in discussion forums where key officials are present. It is also possible to bring issues to the attention of key influencers by briefing national Members of the European Parliament (MEPs) and, when appropriate, civil servants who support the national governments.

The UK has always been influenced by developments in its European neighbours, and vice versa. The UK's decision to leave the EU will naturally change the relationship between the two entities but in two important respects there will be less change: first, much of the EU-driven legislation adopted over the past few decades will be transposed into UK law, although it will subsequently be reviewed; and second, the UK will want to continue to work with the EU institutions in the future, particularly on issues related to trade, and this means adhering to EU regulations, standards and practices, much as countries such as Norway and Switzerland do today. In this sense, the EU will continue to be an influential group for the UK Government.

It is incumbent on organisations, then, to ensure they have a good knowledge and understanding of these important institutions as they go about their stakeholder mapping exercises and develop their engagement programmes.

3.4 Influential third parties

Each country will have its prominent voices that are heard by decision-makers. They can be powerful allies for organisations or fearsome foes; they are rarely ignored. An effective engagement programme will engage with key influencers to help get an organisation's views, arguments and messages through to decision-makers.

A number of third parties are influential with Government by virtue of the constituents they represent and the specialist knowledge they bring to the debate. International institutions provide valuable context to the work of Government, highlighting emerging trends and drivers, and comparing, for example, a country's economic well-being or the health of key sectors with those elsewhere. Such comparisons, released into the public domain, can encourage Governments to bring forward polices and measures to improve their relative performance in the global market.

The UK's professional institutions can be hugely influential if they choose to engage. There resides in the institutions considerable knowledge, experience and a deep-rooted desire to safeguard the disciplines they represent. It is always helpful for Government to receive authoritative reports from institutions such as the Royal Society of Engineers or the Institutes of Civil, Mechanical, Chemical and Electrical Engineers; also in this group is the Royal Society, whose members represent the keenest technical and scientific minds in the country. There are always opportunities for organisations to work with and influence the work of, professional institutions, particularly in the innovation and skills arenas.

There are a few representative organisations in the business sector, with trade associations particularly prominent. The latter can be 'broad church' organisations such as the Confederation of Business and Industry (CBI) or narrower, sector-specific

Informing UK political decisions

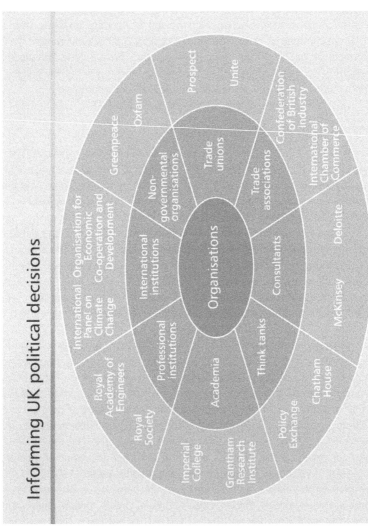

Illustration 3.4 Informing UK political decisions

There are many institutions that play an important role in helping to inform policy development, and by doing so, help influence the outcomes. An effective stakeholder engagement programme will include many of these institutions.

organisations such as Energy UK. They can be useful to Government, the Civil Service and the NDPBs because they can provide a first point of contact when consulting on issues; an association can provide a view on how the sector is positioned. The difficulty is that it is often difficult for an association to represent all the views across its membership, but it is nearly always possible, nonetheless, to provide some helpful comments. Perhaps most important is that the association can facilitate cross-sector, sector–government and sector–third party discussions, and help its members to understand and implement policy.

Trade unions are also important institutions for Government, although perhaps much less so than a generation ago; in 2015, there were 6.5 million members of trade unions in the UK, just over 20% of country's workforce of 32 million workers; of the 6.5 million, 2.7 million were in the private sector and 3.8 million were in the public sector. Unions can have partisan views and tend to support left-of-centre Governments but nonetheless bring much to the discussion table, representing as they do key sectors of the economy. They can be powerful partners on certain issues, such as the training and skills agenda.

Government has always relied on academics to provide valuable independent views, ideas and analysis in policy development. In the main this is highly beneficial, although it should be recognised that academics may also have an interest in promoting an agenda, as do other interested stakeholders. They can make a genuine contribution by developing new concepts, by highlighting the potential of new developments and by describing possible futures in which new policy can be tested; however, they are less able to inform on economic, financial and other business-related aspects of such developments. It is always helpful to engage with academics because they are able to take a more holistic and detached view of issues.

Non-governmental organisations (NGOs) play an important role in civil society, giving voice to groups of common interests. NGOs such as Greenpeace, Friends of the Earth, World Wildlife Fund for Nature and the Royal Society for the Protection of Birds are highly visible with the public through their effective campaigns on issues such as climate change, where they have pushed, cajoled and shamed governments and industry into positive action on this important issue. And they go further by presenting their view of what such action should entail; for example, by placing a high emphasis on renewables and energy efficiency measures. They present a clarity of argument and single-minded commitment that makes them effective in gaining the moral high ground; they are trusted by Governments and the public alike.

NGOs, then, find themselves with considerable power. They are often at the high table of political decision-making, an enviable position for lobby groups. In some ways, they have joined the 'establishment' of government and industry and this makes it more difficult for them to challenge conventional thinking and behaviour, possibly their most important contribution to civil society. But NGOs remain important stakeholders in the policy arena. Organisations need to understand NGO positioning on issues that may impact its activities; they can be allies, for example, on the environment, or adversaries, as in the nuclear debate. Either way, an organisation must decide how best to engage with this powerful stakeholder.

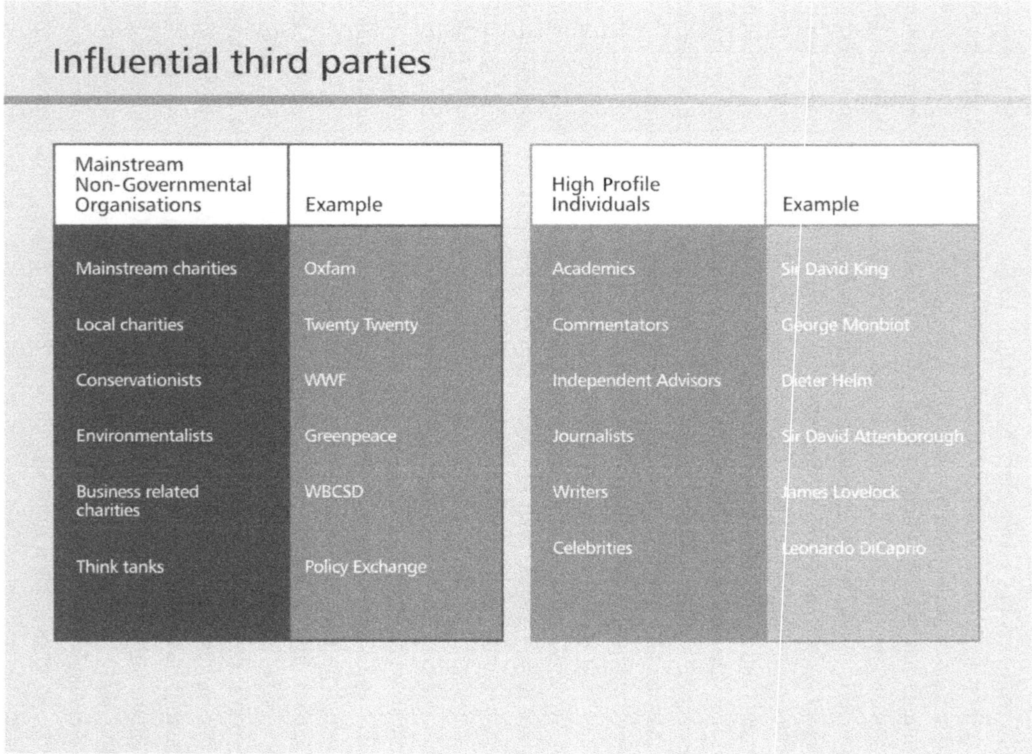

Influential third parties

Mainstream Non-Governmental Organisations	Example
Mainstream charities	Oxfam
Local charities	Twenty Twenty
Conservationists	WWF
Environmentalists	Greenpeace
Business related charities	WBCSD
Think tanks	Policy Exchange

High Profile Individuals	Example
Academics	Sir David King
Commentators	George Monbiot
Independent Advisors	Dieter Helm
Journalists	Sir David Attenborough
Writers	James Lovelock
Celebrities	Leonardo DiCaprio

Illustration 3.5 Influential third parties

Non-governmental organisations and prominent individuals often represent others when discussing an issue and can therefore lobby decision-makers without being seen to be self-interested.

Notes: WWF, World Wildlife Fund for Nature; WBCSD, World Business Council for Sustainable Development; Twenty Twenty, a Leicestershire-based education charity working with young disadvantaged people.

High-profile individuals also have a strong voice in the policy arena. They may be independent consultants or commentators, journalists and writers, and some are prominent celebrities holding strong views about an issue. Some, like naturalist Sir David Attenborough and scientist and writer James Love-lock, played very important roles in bringing climate change into the main-stream of politics, using their ability to reach the wider public. Others, like the leading economist Dieter Helm, bring a keen analytical mind and strong communications skills to debate the issues of the day, be they in small expert roundtables, the media or through their specialist books. If they can be con-vinced that a particular stance on an issue has merit, such individuals will always be heard by decision-makers.

Summary key points

- There are broadly three tiers of key influencers, those in the Civil Service and other public bodies, those that represent large constituency groups, and those with narrower but high-profile interests in civil society.
- All Governments around the world rely on a Civil Service to help them deliver their policies, and this places officials in a unique position of influence.
- There are many other organisations that are set up as independent bodies to provide valuable scrutiny of the public policy arena, and their observations and recommendations are highly influential.
- Third parties can be highly influential, particularly on issues where they have recognised credibility and legitimacy.
- Developments in neighbouring countries can be influential, in part due to proxim-ity, but also because there are longstanding agreements that are beneficial to all concerned.

Case Study 3.1 The importance of expert reviews

Organisations must have a view of what the Government's vision is for their industry or sector if they are to prepare for potential new developments. Expert reviews by independent bodies or eminent individuals, at the request of Government, can often provide such insights. Crucially, they also provide an opportunity for organisations to influence the recommendations by contributing their views and ideas at an early stage.

Background

Government often asks highly qualified individuals to carry out a review of an issue. It does this for a few reasons, but particularly to provide a truly independent view of an issue, making it easier for Government to act on the recommendations. The Marshall Report and the Stern and Armitt Reviews have all proved highly influential in the evolution of the electricity market, the environment in which many companies operate.

Three important reviews

In March 1998, the Government appointed Lord Marshall to investigate ways in which economic instruments could be used to make effective reductions in greenhouse gas emissions. Marshall reported in November 1998 and made several policy recommendations that would reduce emissions while maintaining the competitiveness of the UK economy. In July 2005, the Government asked Nicholas Stern, later Lord Stern, to review the economics of climate change; he reported his findings in October 2006. This was an important study because it highlighted that action was necessary and affordable.

It is not always Government that initiates important reviews. In 2013, the leader of the Labour Party, then in opposition, asked Sir John Armitt to carry out a review of UK infrastructure needs for the twenty-first century.

Outcomes

Lord Marshall's recommendations led to the creation of two economic instruments to help the UK meet its climate change obligations. Lord Stern's Review led to a step change in the UK's climate change activities, and the creation of the Committee on Climate Change, which has proved to be highly influential in raising the profile of an important issue across the stakeholder spectrum. Sir John Armitt's report was adopted by the Conservative Government that came into power in 2015 and led to the creation of a new body, this time in the National Infrastructure Commission, charged with providing independent advice to Government.

The implications of these reviews may not be immediately apparent because the recommendations can take time for Government to implement, and organisations tend to focus on the short term. However, this approach by organisations is short-sighted because the evidence is that these reviews can lead to profound changes in the environments in which they operate; organisations need to engage with such initiatives and take the opportunity to influence review outcomes by contributing their knowledge and ideas.

Case Study 3.2 Non-departmental public bodies can be highly influential

Organisations should take a keen interest in the activities of the mainstream Civil Service departments, but they should also pay attention to the activities of public bodies set up by the departments; such bodies are often set up to fulfil a particular role and to be independent of Government departments. The Committee on Climate Change (CCC), for example, is one such body that is free to engage with organisations to deliver the best evidence-based advice; equally, if an organisation wants to be proactive on the issue, it should engage with the CCC.

Background

The Stern Review on the Economics of Climate Change, published in October 2006, gave impetus to the decarbonisation agenda in the UK. The CCC was set up to advise the Government on how best to meet its national and international climate commitments. It does this by preparing a series of five-year carbon budgets, the latest being the fifth budget covering the period 2028 to 2032, supported by a series of recommendations. The Government can formally accept, or reject, the CCC budgets and recommendations, but once it accepts the advice, it has a legal requirement to do everything it can to meet the carbon budget targets.

The first report

The first report by the CCC titled *Building a Low-Carbon Economy* was published in December 2008 and provided recommendations on the country's emission reduction target for 2050. It presented the first three carbon budgets covering the periods 2008–2012, 2013–2017 and 2018–2022, and indicated where policies and measures could make the greatest reductions.

The report placed great emphasis on decarbonisation of the electricity sector, suggesting there should be financial incentives to promote the deployment of low-carbon technologies. It also suggested there should be renewed emphasis on energy efficiency measures in buildings and industry, and that transport emissions would need to be tackled through new technology.

Outcomes

The report and the Government's acceptance of the recommendations had far-reaching implications across the economy, particularly for the electricity sector, which saw a number of transformational policy initiatives brought forward over the next few years. Almost a decade later it is possible to see the impact of the work of the CCC: the electricity sector is indeed being transformed, with major renewable penetration into the market, there is an accelerated withdrawal of fossil generation from the mix, and contracts for the first new nuclear build have been signed by the Government and the companies involved.

However, there have been mixed results elsewhere with limited progress in the crucial areas of energy efficiency in buildings and industry, and transport where electric vehicles have yet to make the breakthroughs into mass productions. What is clear is that the work of the CCC has been highly influential, affecting the investment decisions of organisations in many sectors across the economy. Crucially, they have, at every stage, carried out extensive stakeholder consultation and this has allowed organisations an opportunity to express their views.

Case Study 3.3 A role for strong independent voices

The role of high-profile commentators is often underestimated. Decision-makers will always listen to credible and independent voices, for example, those of James Lovelock and David Attenborough. Their interventions can have a profound impact on an issue such as nuclear or shale gas, and because of this, it is important to engage with them whenever possible.

Background

James Lovelock is a world-renowned independent scientist lauded for his scientific work, from developing an instrument to monitor chlorofluorocarbons which are harmful to stratospheric ozone, to creating the concept of the earth as a single self-regulating living organism in his Gaia Theory. He is revered as someone who has spoken powerfully on environmental issues throughout his life.

Lovelock believes that man's influence on the climate is real and that without a meaningful response by the international community, the consequences for mankind could be catastrophic.

An influential voice

In 2004 Lovelock gave voice to these concerns in a Memorial Lecture titled *Global Heating from an Engineer's Viewpoint*, on his receiving the John Collier Medal, an award jointly sponsored by British Energy, the nuclear operator, and several technical institutions. Lovelock suggested that except where electricity is powered by abundant water flow or geophysical heat, there was no alternative to nuclear energy.

Lovelock's comments were picked up by national newspapers and he continued to voice his thoughts on the threats of climate change and the importance of nuclear as a meaningful response for many years. In 2012, he moved away from supporting nuclear because he believed new power stations had become expensive and would take too long to build.

More recently he has voiced his support of shale gas. As always, Lovelock's message on this is clear: it is that viewed holistically, the benefits of shale gas outweigh the detriments.

Outcomes

The fact that such an eminent scientist and environmentalist was happy to embrace nuclear in 2004 had a profound impact on the immediate future of nuclear in the UK. By providing an appropriate platform for James Lovelock, British Energy encouraged discussion and debate about what had been a pariah technology for decades. Another notable environmentalist very much in the public eye, David Attenborough, followed suit and his positive messages about nuclear reached a new part of the stakeholder spectrum.

There is little doubt that without the intervention of these powerful independent voices, nuclear would have taken much longer to reach the mainstream. It is possible that James Lovelock's more recent support for shale gas may encourage stakeholders to debate the issue more openly.

4 Stakeholder engagement processes

Chapter summary

In order for an engagement programme to be effective it is crucially important that an organisation has a sound understanding of the formal and informal processes in play, and that it focuses on how and when to engage. There are a significant number of formal processes for organisations to consider, from consultations and inquiries to Parliamentary Questions and Judicial Review. There are also many informal avenues to explore, from bilateral briefings of Ministers to expert round-table discussions, and from conference speeches to hospitality events. An organisation's engagement with formal processes follows a clearly defined government programme; an organisation's informal engagement will be determined by a variety of factors, including how proactive it is in seeking opportunities to present its views on issues. Both formal and informal processes are helpful in raising the profile of organisations, making it more likely that their messages will be heard in decision-making circles. The following sections explain these vital processes.

The level of detail on processes presented in this chapter is needed for practitioners in the UK to maximise the potential for successful engagement with strategic stakeholders. There will be similar processes in play in other countries, but it is incumbent on practitioners to establish all the potential engagement processes in their jurisdictions.

4.1 Understanding engagement processes

There are many opportunities to engage with decision-makers both formal and informal, and it is important to understand the nature of the activities involved and the key players in both areas. The formal activities are the easiest to access, not least because the Government and its executive bodies set the agenda and organisations can be reactive; the activities involved range from consultations and inquiries to task forces and missions. The formal processes do allow an opportunity to place 'on the record' an organisation's position on issues that may impact the environment in which it operates. The transparency involved also offers an opportunity to influence not only those developing policies but other stakeholders who also have an interest in the policy outcomes.

Engaging in the Government's formal processes, then, raises the profile and credibility of an organisation with decision-makers, in addition to providing an opportunity for relaying its key messages further afield.

Parliament and its officials are prominent in the formal processes. However, others in the stakeholder spectrum can also play important roles; for example, private and civil society organisations, and individuals, are able to challenge Government and influence outcomes directly by using the Judicial Review process and more generally through the law. These avenues are increasingly being explored by stakeholders in response to Government intervention in their markets, interventions that create winners and losers.

There are also informal processes by which it is possible to engage with decision-makers, although there may be few forums to do this; rather it is incumbent on organisations or individuals to be proactive in seeking opportunities to present their views on topical issues and, whenever possible, to support their arguments with evidence. Officials are also increasingly seeking opportunities to have discussions with individual organisations to help inform their decision-making. The advantage of informal processes is that they provide opportunities to deliver messages to decision-makers directly; the disadvantage is that it can be difficult to get access to the right decision-makers.

4.2 Formal processes

4.2.1 Consultations and Inquiries

The most common and popular forms of engagement with policy are through consultations. These tend to be the domain of the Whitehall Departments and to a lesser extent some of its executive agencies and public bodies such as the regulators Office of Gas and Electricity Markets (Ofgem), Office of Water Services (Ofwat) and Office of Communications (Ofcom). The purpose of these consultations is twofold: to inform stakeholders that Government aims to make changes to the environment in which they operate and to seek views on a set of specific issues or proposals. By using this process, the Government departments and their independent public bodies can be confident that their potential outcomes and actions are less likely to be challenged later. The consultations can focus on single issues or they can be broad, landscape-scanning and open-ended. They set out proposals that make clear the nature and scope of the changes being proposed, and the detailed questions posed attempt to elicit views and opinions; there is an expectation that such views and opinions will be supported by evidence. A response to a consultation is purely voluntary.

Consultations may be open from four to twelve weeks with a deadline set in the document, but it is possible for organisations to gain a small extension if there is good reason to do so. The number of submissions can run into thousands when the topic is particularly high-profile. In some cases, it is possible that non-governmental organisations (NGOs) run campaigns encouraging activists and other individuals to submit a response to the consultation, and facilitate the process by providing a pro forma; however, the Department running the consultation will likely place these in one box and apply an appropriate weight to this group of submissions.

The names of all those who have provided written submissions are listed for public view, although their actual submissions may not always be available for scrutiny. Officials may also seek views in meetings with interested stakeholders, with the discussion captured in meeting notes for the record. It is very helpful to an organisation if it is on a list of stakeholders to be consulted by officials on issues related to its sector.

An analysis of the submissions and any other evidence provided is carried out by the department, sometimes with the help of consultants if the consultation is particularly long, or if the material requires more expert knowledge. A summary of the findings and an interpretation of what was submitted during the consultation process are published by the department in question some time later, the time depending on the urgency of the policy, the length of the consultation and the complexity of the proposals.

The strength of formal consultations is that they are in the public domain; unfortunately, this does not mean that the analysis and interpretation of the submissions are also in the public domain. This part of the process can be, in effect, a 'black box' that gives Government considerable latitude when putting forward its views of what has been gathered; in the extreme it can ignore large parts of the stakeholder spectrum if their views tend in a different direction from the Government's proposals. If that is a potential weakness in the process, it is also fair to say that there have been clear cases where Government has 'listened' to stakeholder views and modified its original position.

Detailed proposals for the introduction of an Apprenticeship Levy scheme by the then Business, Innovation and Skills (BIS) Department in 2015 is an example of a formal consultation. The Government's objective with this new initiative was threefold: to increase the number of apprenticeships significantly; to help small and medium-sized enterprises (SMEs) take on apprentices by providing financial support; and to keep the cost of the initiative off the public purse, with the money instead coming from businesses with a wage bill over £3 million. The overall sum of money involved in the scheme was significant, some £3 billion each year to help fund millions of apprentices through their training programmes. It was critically important, then, that organisations were very active in presenting their views on the scheme, to ensure that they could participate in the scheme in the most cost-effective manner.

As in all such documents, the Government set the scene by presenting several proposals and questions relating to these proposals. These covered issues such as eligibility and ensuring the levy was simple and fair, payment of the levy and when it would come into force, and how it would interact with training initiatives. The consultation ran for a period of six weeks from 21 August to 2 October 2015. There were 711 responses from a wide variety of interested parties including employers, private training providers, colleges, schools and universities; a significant number of responses, 119, were from bodies such as Trade Unions, professional bodies and Trade Associations.

The Department also engaged with stakeholders informally, meeting with more than 200 businesses, representative bodies and Whitehall departments. Although skills policy is a devolved matter, the levy would apply across the UK so the Consultation was

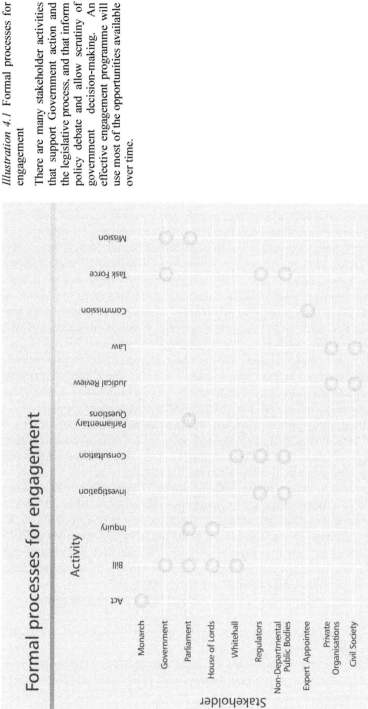

Formal processes for engagement

Illustration 4.1 Formal processes for engagement

There are many stakeholder activities that support Government action and the legislative process, and that inform policy debate and allow scrutiny of government decision-making. An effective engagement programme will use most of the opportunities available over time.

treated likewise. BIS analysed all the submissions and published a summary of its findings and conclusions in November 2015, with the levy coming into force in April 2017.

Formal consultations, then, follow a clear and predictable process although the timescales can differ. All consultations are listed on the Government's website along with any supporting material. They provide a simple and effective way for organisations to engage with Government policy as it is being developed.

Inquiries are usually carried out by Parliamentary Committees, both in the Commons (Lower House) and the Lords (Upper House). They differ from consultations in that they tend to address decisions, policy or otherwise, that may already have been implemented. The inquiry questions are prepared by the Clerk to the Committee, often with the help of an external expert advisor such as an academic. The timescale involved is decided by the Clerk and will depend on the nature and scope of the inquiry and the stakeholders involved.

Inquiries involve both written and oral evidence, and if necessary, site visits to help inform the Committee Members. As with consultations, providing a written response is purely voluntary, but an organisation or individual is expected to accept an invitation to provide oral evidence to a Committee. To make efficient use of time, a panel of up to four or five stakeholders may be invited for any one session. This approach means that the Committee can hear a range of stakeholder views on an issue but it does limit the number of questions because more than one panellist may want, or be required, to respond; it also means each panellist is afforded less time to contribute to the proceedings.

Each Member of the Committee will have been allocated a different question to ask the panel, prepared by the Clerk and advisor, with some follow-up questions as needed; these questions may seek to clarify written evidence in a submission if it has been provided, or they may address different aspects of the summary in the original call for evidence. The Clerk will provide an indication of the kind of issues the Committee will probe in the oral sessions, affording panellists time to prepare their evidence. Oral evidence in the UK is usually, but not entirely, taken in public and broadcast on the Parliamentary TV channel.

An example of an inquiry is that by the Energy and Climate Change Select Committee (ECC) on energy efficiency in the domestic sector, launched on 16 September 2015. Government had announced it would end two existing policies in this area, while a third policy was also coming to the end of its lifetime in March 2017. The Committee was keen to investigate the lessons learned from these energy efficiency schemes and to use this information in their scrutiny of energy efficiency policies over the course of their Parliament (2015–2020).

Interested stakeholders were asked to respond to just three broad questions:

- *Why have previous approaches to energy efficiency failed to deliver significant results?*
- *What lessons can be learnt from current and previous schemes including Green Deal, Green Deal Home Improvement Fund and Energy Companies Obligation (ECO)?*
- *How does the UK's performance on home energy efficiency compare with other countries? What lessons can be learned from these countries on energy efficiency?*

The Committee asked for responses to be no longer than 3,000 words, and reserved the right to extend the list of questions as it got into the inquiry. The Committee received 99 written submissions by the deadline of 12 October 2015; it also held five oral evidence sessions between November 2015 and January 2016. On 8 March 2016, it published its report, which contained a summary of the findings, its recommendations and a list of all those stakeholders who provided written and oral evidence, the latter kept on record.

Once again, inquiries follow a clear and predictable process in terms of providing written evidence to Parliamentary Committees; what is less clear is which organisations or experts will be invited to give oral evidence. Inquiries are effective because they require the relevant Government department to respond to their findings; they do, then, provide good forums for organisations to have their views heard. As with consultations, all inquiries are listed on the Government's website, and as with consultations they provide a simple and effective way of engaging with Government policy, although not with the decision-makers themselves.

4.2.2 Legislation

A changing environment requires Government to modify existing legislation or to bring in new legislation; the former can be carried out by the Government department and made possible under delegated authority specified in an Act of Parliament, while new legislation requires a full Parliamentary process.

The process to modify existing legislation is relatively simple because provisions for making potential changes are usually written into the relevant Act. Nonetheless, it is common practice for departments to go through a formal consultation process to inform interested stakeholders of potential changes and to elicit their views on what is being proposed. It is possible then for organisations to influence the legislation by making a formal response to the consultation, and by participating in any forums the Government is using to canvass opinions.

New legislation begins with the identification of a need, for example, a need to change the market structure for the electricity sector to incentivise deployment of new, low-carbon technology. In this case, the need was originally highlighted by stakeholders who wanted Government to bring forward new instruments to encourage investment. One particularly influential stakeholder was the Committee on Climate Change, which is charged with advising Government on how the UK can transition to a low-carbon economy. Other influential stakeholders were commercial organisations interested in deploying low-carbon technologies and bringing much-needed new investment into the electricity sector.

The next stage involves one or more formal consultations carried out by the department, in which proposals are put forward for comment by all interested stakeholders. The consultation outcomes are used to inform a draft Bill, which contains the proposed legislation, and this is then presented to Parliament for debate and amendment. Organisations can seek changes to the Bill by asking Members to propose amendments when the Bill is debated in the Lower and Upper Houses. The role of the officials during this period is to support the process by preparing revised text as amendments are brought forward.

The Bill can begin its passage through Parliament in the House of Commons or the House of Lords; it has a clearly defined process beginning with the First Reading, whose purpose is to have the Bill formally printed, followed by a Second Reading that affords Members of Parliament (MPs), once it has begun its journey in the Commons, a first opportunity to debate the proposals in the Bill.

The Committee Stage that follows the second reading of the Bill is a crucial step in the process in which the text of the Bill is scrutinised line-by-line by Committee Members. The Committee can seek expert evidence, both oral and written, from outside Parliament if needed and amendments to the text by MPs are discussed and voted on by the Committee.

The amended Bill then returns to the House of Commons for the Report Stage, providing MPs a further opportunity to debate the Bill content and to propose further amendments. There follows a Third Reading, which allows debate on the content but no further amendments. The House then votes on whether to approve the Bill and if it does, it is then sent to the House of Lords to go through much the same process, the only substantive difference being the possibility of bringing forward amendments at the Third Reading Stage.

In the unlikely event that the House of Lords has proposed no amendments by the end of the Third Reading, the Bill can be sent directly for Royal Assent and becomes an Act of Parliament. Much more likely is that there are amendments proposed by the Lords and the Bill is then sent to the Commons for further consideration; it is possible that the Bill goes back and forth ('ping-pong') until both Houses agree on the final version of the Bill. Once this has happened, it can be sent for Royal Assent and the legislation in the Act can come into force at a set time.

There are ample opportunities, then, for organisations or individuals to engage with the process, particularly during the period when ideas are being considered by the department seeking to bring forward new legislation and more formally by responding to any consultations. It may be possible to present further evidence if the Bill Committees decide on gathering further evidence beyond Parliament and Whitehall; it is also possible to seek changes to the bill by briefing MPs and Peers who may then table amendments at the appropriate times.

As the agreed, final version of the Bill emerges, organisations can more easily establish the full implications for their activities and begin their preparations to implement any changes to their operations once the Act become law.

4.2.3 Using Parliamentary Questions and the Freedom of Information Act

There are occasions when organisations seek clarity on particular issues and there are two formal processes available to them: they can use Parliamentary Questions (PQs), and the Freedom of Information Act (FOI). PQs are an essential part of House business, allowing Members to seek clarity from and put pressure on Ministers on specific issues. They can table questions for oral or written answers, the former in the House of Commons. There are clear guidelines for such questions, for example, they must seek information or press for action, avoid expressions of opinion and have a factual basis; they must not ask for information readily

Illustration 4.2 Legislation process through Parliament in the UK

There is a clear legislation process in the passage of a draft Bill through Parliament and several opportunities for stakeholders to engage with this process.

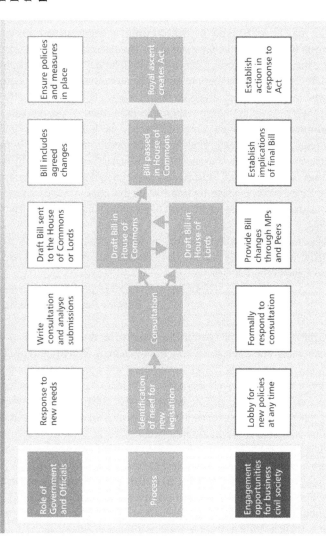

Legislation process through Parliament in the UK

Role of Government and Officials	Response to new needs	Write consultation and analyse submissions	Draft Bill sent to the House of Commons or Lords	Bill includes agreed changes	Ensure policies and measures in place

Process	Identification of need for new legislation	Consultation	Draft Bill in House of Commons / Draft Bill in House of Lords	Bill passed in House of Commons	Royal ascent creates Act

Engagement opportunities for business civil society	Lobby for new policies at any time	Formally respond to consultation	Provide Bill changes through MPs and Peers	Establish implications of final Bill	Establish action in response to Act

available elsewhere, nor must they be hypothetical or about opposition policy. PQs must be drafted concisely and conform to existing Parliamentary conventions.

Officials are charged with providing draft answers for their Ministers, the latter having the final say on the response. Once the Minister has provided an oral response to a question in the House, the Member who tabled the question is able to follow up with supplementary questions to elicit more information; other Members who have an interest in the issue are then invited to ask supplementary questions. All the questions and answers are recorded and available for public scrutiny; the numbers involved are significant, with oral questions running into the thousands and written questions into the tens of thousands.

Organisations can have concerns raised in the House of Commons by, for example, a Member of Parliament whose constituency includes the organisation's operations; alternatively, a question may be placed with a Member from the opposition parties who may have the issue in their portfolio of interests and for whom it is in their interests to challenge the Government's Minister. Building relationships with these MPs, then, is an important part of the stakeholder engagement programme.

Governments are always under pressure to be more transparent and accountable in their actions. In the past, they could do this by releasing information into the public domain of their own volition or in response to public and media pressure. The Freedom of Information Act, which came into force in the UK in 2005, formalised these activities, requiring public authorities to publish certain information as part of their normal business and to respond to specific queries on information held by these bodies from members of the public. Public bodies can withhold some information in certain categories; for example, requests for information that consume excessive resources, or involve sensitive commercial information or are simply thought to be frivolous.

> [FOI] acted as a weathervane for the wider principle: how is power made transparent to the wider public? How can the powerful be held to account for the decisions they take?
>
> *Nick Clegg, former MP and Deputy Prime Minister,*
> Politics Between the Extremes, *2016*

FOI has proved a popular and powerful instrument for disclosure. In the years following the Act coming into force, there have been hundreds of thousands of FOI requests processed, the majority at the Local Government level, confirming the popularity of this disclosure mechanism with the public. Around 100,000 organisations are now covered by the Act, including private companies that deliver public services. Although sometimes onerous and time-consuming, the use of FOI has been welcomed by the public bodies who believe the greater transparency involved has led to them being more trusted than before; the public have also welcomed an initiative that confirms their legal right to certain information and established a process to gain access to this information.

FOI, then, can be a powerful tool to aid stakeholder engagement. Prominent NGOs such as Greenpeace have used information gained under the FOI Act routinely to nourish their various campaigns against developments in, for example, the energy sector.

4.2.4 Recourse to the Judicial Review and law courts

An organisation or an individual can challenge decisions made by the Government and the public bodies through the courts using the Judicial Review (JR) process. The court does not have the power to remake the decision but can examine how the decision was made. There are three categories to consider: whether the decision was unlawful, irrational or unreasonable. If the court finds that the decision falls into one of these categories, it can quash the decision and require the public authority to make the decision again. The court will provide a judgment setting out why the decision should not stand and may give guidance about how the decision should be made.

A claim for Judicial Review has two stages: the permission stage and the final hearing stage. A claimant is required to obtain the permission of the court to bring the claim; the initial decision of the court is dealt with on the papers and then, if it has not been given permission, a claimant can renew the application for permission at an oral hearing. Once permission has been granted, the claim will then proceed to a full hearing. When issuing a claim for Judicial Review, a claimant is required to identify and serve any parties who would be affected by the decision of the court.

> Judicial oversight and an increasing litigious culture have clipped the wings of governments, too.
>
> *Nick Clegg, former MP and Deputy Prime Minister,*
> Politics Between the Extremes, *2016*

Organisations, and on the odd occasion individuals, have increasingly gone to the courts to challenge Government decisions. Greenpeace for example has taken the UK Government to Judicial Review on more than one occasion, particularly in relation to nuclear power, and proved successful in ensuring that an adequate process was followed by Government before a decision was made. Gina Miller, an individual, was one of the lead claimants who challenged the Government's right to trigger Article 50 of the Lisbon Treaty, a necessary first step in the process for the UK to leave the European Union, without the explicit consent of Parliament. She won that case and was also successful in the UK's Supreme Court, which upheld the original ruling when the Government appealed the decision. In her words, 'No Prime Minister, no government can expect to be unanswerable or unchallenged. Parliament alone is sovereign.'

Others have acted against the UK Government but been less successful. In 2014, Drax Group won its case against the Government in the UK Court of Appeal in relation to the non-allocation of a contract under a new incentive scheme for one of its biomass units; this contract was worth around £1.3 billion and was an important step in the conversion of several units of coal plant to biomass. Ultimately Drax did not prove successful because the Government then appealed against that decision and won. This did not deter Drax, which in 2016, and in alliance with another energy company Infinis Energy, challenged the Government again, this time with a Judicial Review in relation to the sudden removal of Climate Change Levy exemption for renewable energy. The two companies lost this case because Government had not given specific assurances that the exemptions would continue. Dorothy Thompson, the CEO of Drax, said: 'This hearing has raised a number of important issues regarding the way in which the government encourages private sector investment in UK energy infrastructure.'

At the local level, Fish Legal, on behalf of Seiont, Gwyrfai and Llyfni Angling Society in North Wales, filed a case for Judicial Review against Natural Resources Wales (NRW). Fish Legal believed NRW's investigation into their concerns about pollution of Llyn Padarn lake, a Site of Special Scientific Interest (SSSI), which they believed was causing a decline in the population of rare Arctic charr fish, was inadequate. Fish Legal failed with its request for Judicial Review but the process did put pressure on NRW and those using the lake to review, and where possible improve, their activities to ensure there was no damage to fish stocks.

It should be said that when organisations or individuals challenge the Government on its decisions, the chances of success are low. However, such challenges, even when unsuccessful, serve to maintain both the integrity of the decision-making process and stakeholder confidence that their concerns will continue to be heard.

4.2.5 Royal Commissions for ad hoc Inquiries

Government has the option of setting up Royal Commissions to address specific issues that are of public concern and cross political boundaries. They can be ad hoc in nature or created as Standing Commissions; the Royal Commission on Environmental Pollution, for example, was set up in 1970 to produce reports on a range of topical environmental issues. Whether ad hoc or Standing, they can be highly influential, although Government is not obliged to accept their advice or recommendations.

The Chair and its members are appointed by the Government with a clear remit and timescale for delivering their conclusions; they are supported by a secretariat. As with other inquiries, Commissions invite both oral and written evidence and can make site visits as needed. They then deliberate and report their findings, usually between two and four years after their creation.

As with Parliamentary Committee inquiries, organisations and individuals are invited to provide written and oral evidence and this affords an opportunity for them to engage with the process, with their key messages placed on the record for the Commission.

4.2.6 Task forces and Missions

The Government uses independent task forces to address particular issues. For example, the Better Regulation Task Force was established in 1997 to ensure that regulation and its enforcement adhere to certain key principles they had developed: proportionality, accountability, consistency, transparency and targeting. It has influenced Government by publishing reports on a variety of policy issues.

Task force members can be drawn from across the stakeholder spectrum, from business and academia to trade unions and representatives of civil society; the only criterion is that members bring knowledge and experiences of the issue involved and adopt a non-partisan view. There are opportunities to contribute to the work of these task forces, directly if invited to join them following a formal application process, or indirectly through the provision of information as they go about their business.

Task forces are also created to oversee implementation of government priority areas; for example, the Digital Infrastructure and Inclusion Task Force was established to drive the roll-out of universal broadband and better mobile phone connections for the benefit of all parts of society. Task forces are different insofar as membership is normally composed of Ministers from across the departments that have an interest in the issue.

Occasionally Ministers will have a mission to another country, perhaps on a fact-finding exercise or to promote their department's activities in a particular area. It is common for relevant experts from organisations to be invited to contribute to such missions by providing briefing material or participating in the mission itself. These are excellent opportunities for organisations for a variety of reasons: they are being recognised as expert in the area of interest, they can have their views heard, and their participation engenders valuable goodwill for the organisation with the Minister and their officials. They also offer an opportunity to network with other key influencers and to establish contact with politicians and officials in other countries.

Such missions have taken added on significance since the decision by the UK to exit the European Union because the UK needs new relationships in general, and trade agreements in particular. Government then will rely on business organisations to come forward with their views on what is needed in such trade agreements; this will be an ongoing activity and organisations, then, should ensure they are on departmental stakeholder lists, to be consulted on relevant trade issues and to participate in formal trade missions.

4.2.7 Exiting the European Union

There is a question as to whether European policy is relevant when the UK has opted to leave the European Union (EU). There are good reasons why organisations should continue to engage with the relevant institutions in the UK and Europe:

- The UK Government will need to repeal the European Communities Act of 1972. Much of the existing EU regulation will pass directly into UK law in the first instance. Each Government department will then carry out a case-by-case examination of policy and determine whether that policy should remain in the same form or whether there are good reasons to amend or even abolish it; the Government, then, will be actively seeking views from stakeholders before it comes to a conclusion. This policy review process, which could last several years, offers a unique opportunity for organisations to seek changes to existing policy and regulation.
- A new relationship between the UK and the EU will emerge following negotiations, and whatever the nature of this relationship, Europe will continue to have an influence on UK policy. For example, there will continue to be cooperation in the security area, or the aerospace industry, which relies heavily

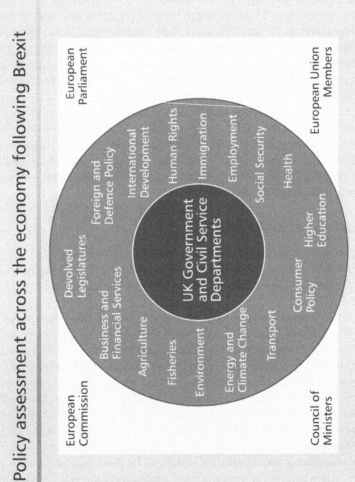

Policy assessment across the economy following Brexit

European Commission

European Parliament

Devolved Legislatures

Foreign and Defence Policy

International Development

Human Rights

Immigration

Business and Financial Services

Agriculture

Fisheries

Environment

Energy and Climate Change

Transport

UK Government and Civil Service Departments

Employment

Social Security

Higher Education

Health

Consumer Policy

European Union Members

Council of Ministers

Illustration 4.3 Policy assessment across the economy following Brexit

Government departments have a whole raft of policy issues they will need to revisit, once the European Communities Act 1972 has been repealed and the regulations initially incorporated into UK law.

on partnerships across national borders; developments that impact such areas will have to be considered by UK and EU policy-makers.
- Many organisations have operations in both the UK and EU and will need to continue to engage with the relevant institutions to protect their interests in EU markets.
- The Government will be seeking new trade agreements with countries around the world and, once again, will actively seek views, comment and information from organisations whose businesses are impacted as it prepares its negotiating position. This offers organisations a good opportunity to build relationships with and to influence decision-makers.

There are, then, ample opportunities for organisations to engage with Government initiatives. Most interactions will support Government activities by providing ideas, comment and information, but on occasion organisations may need to challenge the Government on its decision-making. Similar formal processes will be available in other countries, and a good understanding of what is available in this arena and how to engage is fundamental for an effective stakeholder engagement programme.

4.3 Informal processes

In a formal process of engagement, an organisation is required to respond on issues that have a clearly defined scope; there are opportunities to go beyond the scope but with no guarantee that the views expressed or information provided will be taken into account in the decision-making process. The informal processes of engagement, on the other hand, require a proactive approach that focuses on issues of direct interest to the organisation; however, it can be more difficult to gain traction with decision-makers through informal processes. An important consideration for an organisation when it is involved in informal processes is to maintain the trust of its stakeholders, and this is best achieved through a strong ethical policy and always adhering to it.

4.3.1 Informal engagement opportunities

There are at least four categories of activity for informal engagement: bilateral meetings, third-party forums, proprietary events and specialist awards. The first, and perhaps most important, are those involving bilateral meetings where it is possible to focus on issues of most interest to the organisation. Decision-makers welcome briefings, particularly on issues that will help them deliver their programmes more effectively, and the provision of up-to-date information and data is particularly welcome. It is relatively easy to organise bilateral discussions with Members of Parliament, officials, regulators and other public bodies; it is harder to gain audience with Ministers unless there is a particularly urgent issue that requires their attention, one that could potentially place the Government in a difficult position; in this case, a meeting with the Minister's Special Advisor is an important first step and, if the issue is indeed critical, the Advisor will be able to facilitate a meeting between the organisation's executives and the Minister.

Visits to operational sites by those in Government, and their Special Advisors and officials, are an important part of an informal engagement programme. Such visits provide an opportunity to educate an important group about the business and to convey key messages; they are also popular with Ministers who use the visits for photo opportunities and blogs. One common use of site visits is to celebrate events; for example, a launch of a new initiative, the opening of a facility or the recognition of an important milestone. All are good reasons to have events where Ministers, and their Advisors and officials, meet with an organisation's executive team and employees; local community leaders and the media can also be involved. Employees enjoy such visits by Ministers because their work is recognised and it is an experience they can share with colleagues, family and friends.

Another approach to delivering key messages is the commissioning of studies by expert commentators such as academics or consultants. They can be commissioned by an individual organisation or by a group and they have the benefit of being independent and authoritative. They can be launched formally and the results can be disseminated widely, particularly if the media are present. These studies can be sent to decision-makers for their consideration as they develop new policy or regulations.

Organisations can also participate in high-profile activities that assess annual performance in, for example, sustainability and Corporate Social Responsibility (CSR). A good performance raises the credibility of an organisation with external stakeholders, and once again is a source of enormous pride for employees.

Hospitality events provide an opportunity to interact with a select group of key influencers, although these events will not normally include those in Government or politicians more widely. However, it is possible to interact with advisors, experts from think tanks, academics and colleagues from other organisations in the sector, and even the media. Sporting and musical events, for example, provide an environment for informal discussion, perhaps on generic rather than specific issues, but are very useful in placing the organisation at the forefront of people's thinking, engendering goodwill and developing relationships.

4.3.2 Trade Association activities

Nearly all organisations, belong to one or more trade associations; for example, organisations may be members of the Confederation of Business and Industry (CBI) that represents large sections of the business community in the public arena, and a second trade association that represents the more specific needs of their sector. Trade associations are important because they provide a focal point for decision-makers when they need to canvas sector views on issues; they also provide forums for discussion, both formal and informal, between its members and Government Ministers, officials, regulators and other public bodies such as the influential Committee on Climate Change. The benefits of such forums for trade association members are regular contact with decision-makers and key influencers, who provide up-to-date information on policy development and implementation, and wider networking opportunities; on the other hand, organisations will sit alongside their competitors at these meetings, and this means the organisation's messages may be diluted, which makes it more difficult for them to influence the debate.

Illustration 4.4 Engagement through informal processes

There are many opportunities for an organisation to engage with its stakeholders in an informal environment, and these complement the formal processes used by Government to consult on policy issues.

Notes: Energy UK is the Trade Association for the electricity industry in the UK; Marketforce is a conference provider; Westminster Energy Forum organises specialist policy seminars; the British Management Data Foundation organises roundtable discussions.

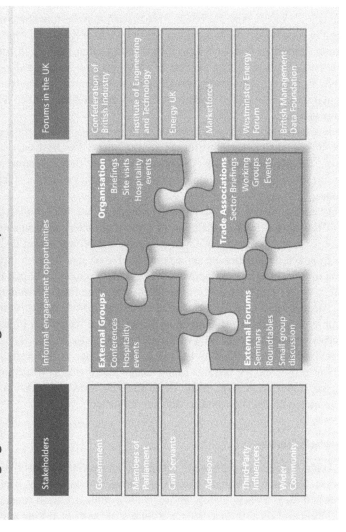

Engagement through informal processes

Stakeholders	Informal engagement opportunities	Forums in the UK
Government	**Organisation** Briefings Site visits Hospitality events	Confederation of British Industry
Members of Parliament	**Trade Associations** Sector Briefings Working Groups Events	Institute of Engineering and Technology
Civil Servants	**External Groups** Conferences Hospitality events	Energy UK
Advisors		Marketforce
Third-Party Influences	**External Forums** Seminars Roundtables Small group discussion	Westminster Energy Forum
Wider Community		British Management Data Foundation

Trade associations rely on their membership to provide support for their activities; for example, CEOs participate in Board meetings and member organisation experts populate their Committees and Working Groups. These are important activities since they set the agenda and positioning of the association in its outward-facing engagement programme, not only with decision-makers but also with the media and wider public.

Trade associations can offer other networking events, for example, in the form of an annual conference or dinner or both. It is possible to raise the profile of the company in several ways; for example, by sponsoring the conference and perhaps having the organisation's CEO make a speech on a topical issue, or simply taking a table at the lunch or dinner mixing company executives with political advisors, officials and influential commentators.

Trade associations may have a 'broad church' membership and this means an organisation's views may not be heard; worse, it may be that some members dominate the running of the association and its work programme. Nonetheless, it is usually helpful to remain within a trade association because it offers certain benefits, such as providing regular briefings on new policy and regulatory developments, a forum for sharing knowledge and capabilities when dealing with implementation of new policy initiatives, and an opportunity to keep abreast of competitor views.

There is a subscription fee as a member of an Association, and it is incumbent on the organisation to ensure this money is well spent. The best way to do this is to ensure the organisation is well represented on the Board, Committees and Working Groups, and always to have a presence when key external stakeholders are present.

In some cases, it may also be helpful to organise another smaller grouping outside of the formal trade association to provide an alternative voice to decision-makers. Such a grouping will naturally have a narrower scope and be held together by a shared positioning on a number of issues; it may be informal in nature and involve little cost in comparison to a trade association. Experience suggests that such groupings are a welcome alternative voice for Government and its officials, particularly if together they form a significant part of the sector involved. For example, the Independent Generators Group (IGG) had seven organisations that together contributed over 20% of the electricity sector's capacity; crucially, these organisations represented all the major technologies in the sector, brought employment and economic benefits to the local commutates in which they operated, and had major investment plans. These attributes were important in the IGG gaining a voice with decision-makers and key influencers.

4.3.3 Specialist forums

Beyond Trade Associations, there are organisations and individuals that provide independent forums to facilitate discussion between stakeholders. The forums vary from half-day seminars involving up to 150 people, to small roundtables of perhaps 20 experts coming together for a couple of hours to debate and discuss an issue. In some cases, the seminars are facilitated by a specialist organisation such as the Westminster Energy Forum (WEF), which delivers excellent policy seminars at regular intervals during the year. The seminars usually have several speakers who bring the audience right up to date on different aspects of the chosen theme. They also offer a good opportunity to network with professionals across the stakeholder spectrum.

Ad hoc seminars are also organised by professional institutions or by academics, to address an issue. Here also, a small number of speakers may be used to inform the audience, although it is more common to have a single speaker to promote discussion.

Specialist roundtables are popular and offer advantages over the larger forums: greater scope to delve into an issue; opportunities to present the organisation's messages; and becoming informed on the positions being promoted by officials, regulators and competitors. A good example is the British Management Data Foundation (BMDF), which has been facilitating meetings since 1979, bringing together decision-makers and the business community to discuss topical issues using a well-established format that ensures a voice to everybody who attends.

Well-known experts in a field also provide forums for discussion, with the advantage that they have a deep knowledge of the subject and a good understanding of stakeholder concerns, which makes them excellent facilitators. These roundtables also require an annual subscription fee and, once again, the way to get good value is for the right experts to participate in these forums. It is also important that a note of the meeting discussion is circulated within the organisation.

There are also organisations that specialise in large conference forums; these tend to follow set themes every year, although the detailed content and most of the speakers may be different. These events offer several opportunities: a platform for the CEO to make a speech alongside a keynote speech or address by a decision-maker, a Minister for example; there may also be an opportunity for the CEO to be interviewed by the specialist media; and there are excellent opportunities to network more widely.

Summary key points

- An organisation can engage with decision-makers in a wide range of formal processes, from consultations and inquiries to task forces and missions.
- Participation in formal processes tends to be reactive in nature, with Government and its agencies defining the agenda, although there are some processes in which organisations can take a lead role, for example, by seeking Judicial Reviews and Freedom of Information requests.
- Engaging in the Government's formal processes raises the profile and credibility of an organisation with decision-makers, in addition to providing an opportunity for relaying key messages.
- Organisations can take a more proactive role in informal processes, some of which can be proprietary while others are facilitated by expert third parties.
- An organisation must maintain the trust of its stakeholders, and this is achieved through a strong ethical policy and adhering to it at all times.

Case Study 4.1 Participating in Select Committee inquiries

Select Committees serve a very important role in the democratic process by scrutinising Government policy. Their inquiries treat decision-makers and expert commentators with equal respect, and organisations should take the opportunity to comment on Government policy that affects their markets and operations. Inquiries can be influential, as shown in the Energy and Climate Change (ECC) Select Committee's inquiries into the reform of the electricity market.

Background

The ECC Select Committee conducted several inquiries into the Government's market reforms that would transform the sector. These were complex reforms with a few new economic instruments brought forward to deliver different objectives. The electricity sector was intimately involved in the process, not least because it was understood that there would be winners and losers when the reforms were implemented.

Engaging with the formal process

GDF SUEZ (now ENGIE) was invited to participate in three oral sessions in the period February 2011 to October 2012, the first on the reforms themselves, the second on the draft Energy Bill that included the market reforms and the third on new nuclear build. In each case, the company had formally responded to the inquiry with a written submission that addressed a series of questions from the Committee.

Outcomes

The oral sessions ran for about an hour on each occasion, with evidence provided by a panel of four representatives from the sector; this meant that the actual time afforded each panellist to make their contributions was quite short. But on each occasion the organisation could get across its views and these were captured in the final report. For example, there was a proposal to include an Emission Performance Standard on coal-fired power stations that could have compromised their running.

Dr Steve Riley of GDF SUEZ said: 'I think we're already on record as saying that we think the emissions performance standard is an unnecessary regulation. Certainly, existing coal plant has enough constraints on it through the Large Combustion Plant Directive, the Industrial Emissions Directive and the Emissions Trading Scheme to ensure that there's a fairly low level of generation unabated going forward. Given the level at which the Emissions Performance Standard is set in this document, it's very much a back-stop and probably an unnecessary piece of legislation.'

The Committee report stated: 'We conclude that neither of the Emissions Performance Standard options proposed in the Electricity Market Reform consultation would promote decarbonisation of the power sector and that introducing regulation in the form proposed would not only be pointless but could even create uncertainty among investors.'

The Committee understood the arguments, and its recommendation not to go further with the Emission Performance Standard was influential. Participating in this formal activity, then, was a success.

Case Study 4.2 Recourse to the law

If an organisation is unhappy with a Government decision, it can challenge that decision through the law. One way to do this is to seek a Judicial Review whereby an organisation can ask a law court to examine the process by which Government, or one of its public bodies, came to its decision on an issue. Greenpeace has used the Judicial Review process very effectively on several occasions in its opposition to nuclear power.

Background

Greenpeace and other prominent non-governmental organisations (NGOs) have long opposed the building of new nuclear power stations in the UK. They argue that they are expensive, take a long time to build and produce long-lived radioactive waste streams for which a solution has yet to be found, and that more benign alternative technologies exist; and this even though nuclear generation is a very low-carbon technology that has contributed and continues to contribute significantly to climate change mitigation.

In 2003, an Energy White Paper essentially 'parked' nuclear, focusing instead on other low-carbon sources and energy efficiency measures to address climate change. In 2006, the Government carried out an Energy Review in which it signalled it wanted to see a new generation of nuclear power stations built, alongside the deployment of renewable technologies and the promotion of energy efficiency.

Response through a formal process

Greenpeace challenged the Government through the Judicial Review process. It argued that the White Paper in 2003 indicated nuclear was not then on the agenda and that there would need to be full public consultation before a decision was made on further deployment of this technology. Greenpeace argued that such a consultation had not been carried out and that the Review carried out was fundamentally flawed.

Greenpeace won the case; the Court agreed that the consultation process before the Government decision had been 'misleading', 'seriously flawed' and 'procedurally unfair'.

Outcomes

The Government was obliged to go back and conduct a more comprehensive consultation with stakeholders, which it duly did and once again concluded that nuclear should be part of the UK's generation mix.

Greenpeace, emboldened by this success, sought a further Judicial Review in 2011 arguing that Government had not taken full account of the disaster at the Fukushima nuclear power station in Japan, when addressing potential new nuclear build at eight sites in England and Wales in the Nuclear National Policy Statement. It lost this case, but does not hesitate to use the Judicial Review process or the law if it feels that decision-makers are not fulfilling their obligations as they see it. Judicial Reviews, then, offer organisations a public forum to have their views heard.

Case Study 4.3 Using assets to deliver strong messages

An organisation must use all its attributes to raise its profile with decision-makers. Its operations, for example, can be used to showcase an organisation's products and services, employment and skills, and wider benefits to the local economy. A visit by the UK's Energy Minister to ENGIE's Dinorwig Power Station is a very good example of an organisation educating an important decision-maker on the importance of its asset to the UK.

Background

Ffestiniog and Dinorwig pumped storage power stations in North Wales have a combined capacity of just over 2GW. The principle of these stations is relatively simple: off-peak electricity is used to pump water from a lower lake to an upper lake; power is then generated by passing water from the upper lake through a turbine in times of system need. Both these plants play a very important role in the UK's electricity system by providing ancillary and other support services to National Grid, the system operator.

Dinorwig is the site for the company's foremost visitor centre, also known as Electric Mountain. It has about 175,000 visitors each year, and a total of about five million visitors since operations began. The power stations and the visitor centre have brought much economic benefit to the local communities and raised the profile and credibility of the company.

Raising the profile of the organisation in decision-making circles

There was considerable ignorance in Government circles on the importance of these two plants to the UK's electricity system. To help correct this situation, an invitation was extended to the then Energy Minister Charles Hendry to visit the Dinorwig plant.

The Minister and his Advisor visited the site where he was escorted by an enthusiastic Plant Manager and his team. The site visit was comprehensive, with the Minister taken through all parts of the plant and to the operations room where he could observe at first hand the way both Dinorwig and Ffestiniog plants supported National Grid in its operation of the electricity system.

Outcomes

There was little doubt that the Energy Minister was hugely impressed with the plant and the engineers who operated and maintained it. He was left with a sense of pride that the UK had such a magnificent pumped hydro facility and recognised that these plants were important for the company, the local community and for the UK. There were ample opportunities for photographs, and these were displayed on the Department of Energy and Climate Change website.

For the company, it was crucially important that at a time of a changing market it was possible to remind the highest levels of Government of the importance of these two plants to the operation of the electricity system. This made it easier to engage with politicians and officials on issues related to the plants that arose at a later time.

Case Study 4.4 Building relationships with Devolved Administrations

The devolution agenda means organisations need to engage with politicians and their officials at the regional level. This is important because they may need political support for initiatives that affect their operations, their employees or the local communities in which they operate. Every opportunity, then, to build relationships with decision-makers in the Devolved Administrations is important, and a milestone event in which the Welsh Energy Minister was the Guest of Honour at a 50-year power station celebration was such an opportunity.

Background

Ffestiniog Power Station was the UK's first major pumped storage power station. It was commissioned in 1963 with a combined output of 360MW of electricity, which is enough to supply the entire power needs of North Wales for several hours.

In 2013, the plant had successfully operated for 50 years, and it was decided to hold an event for employees and the local community to celebrate and for the organisation to raise its profile with political audiences.

The celebratory event

The event was scheduled for 6 August. Hundreds of people were invited, representing employees past and present, suppliers who supported the plant, representatives from the local community, and executives from the two international companies who own the plant: the French company GDF SUEZ (now ENGIE) and the Japanese Company Mitsui. Also invited were Welsh Government officials with Carwyn Jones, the First Minister of Wales, as guest of honour; the local media and journalists from specialist magazines were also invited.

Outcomes

Although the location of the power station was difficult to get to, being in the mountains of North Wales, the event was very well attended and a great success. There was clear recognition of the importance of this groundbreaking plant to the local community and the North Wales economy, over the 50 years of operation. The speeches by the First Minister of Wales and ENGIE's CEO were very well received by those present and by the media.

The event raised the profile of the organisation's activities in the area and its executive team. In particular, it provided an opportunity for the company to build relationships with those in high office in the Welsh Government; it also afforded an opportunity to interact with other important stakeholders in the local community and supply chain. The media interviewed key decision-makers in Government and in the business who were able to discuss not only the future of the power station but also developments in Wales and in the wider UK market.

Case Study 4.5 Raising credibility of the organisation with key stakeholders

There are a few ways an organisation can raise its profile and credibility with key stakeholders in the public domain, and one way is to report its performance in an annual Corporate Social Responsibility (CSR) report. An organisation can raise its credibility further by participating in, for example, the Business in the Community (BiTC) initiative, which scrutinises and assesses an organisation's performance across its operations.

Background

Each year the BiTC carries out a survey of companies' Corporate Responsibility (CR) activities, and uses this information to compile its index. The top 100 performers in the CR index are listed in a *Sunday Times* supplement (*Companies that Count*) and are published on BiTC's website. The main opportunity from involvement in the BiTC initiative is to gain a better understanding of internal CR performance through BiTC feedback and benchmarking against other company performance; this feedback also shows where performance would need to improve in the period to the next assessment.

Engaging with the BiTC process

British Energy, a nuclear operator, decided to participate in the BiTC process. The company's objectives were to raise its profile in this important area by carrying out a review of its performance in four key areas: marketplace, workplace, environment and community. It was also hoped there would be opportunities to improve performance in the future by learning from comments and questions on its CSR-related practices, and by being exposed to new and innovative initiatives by others.

The BiTC process seeks evidence of good practice across a company's activities, from corporate structure to the way in which CR activities are integrated into the business. Information was sought on management practice in the key areas of marketplace, workplace, environment and community. Considerable internal resources and commitment were needed to ensure all the information was made available, and an external consultant provided guidance and advice.

Outcomes

This was a very successful exercise for British Energy. The company received a silver award in its first participation in the BiTC process, demonstrating that it had a very good bedrock performance on which to improve further; also, participation in the BiTC process demonstrated that a nuclear company was prepared to be judged in the mainstream.

There were additional benefits to participating in this exercise; for example, the leadership of the company was seen to be involved at all stages of the project, and indeed the Board and CEO had to sign off on the final submission. The exercise encouraged managers and employees to greater efforts to improve performance in their area of influence. It also encouraged the company to consider participation in other similar processes such as FTSE4Good and the Dow Jones Index.

5 Organising for stakeholder engagement

Chapter summary

An important aspect of an effective engagement programme is the question of where to position and how to organise the Government Affairs function within the business; also important is what resources this function can draw on and what influence it has with the CEO and the leadership team. This chapter addresses these questions because they determine the success or otherwise of the engagement programme. The tools available to make a programme effective, such as an assessment of political and regulatory risk, is addressed, and the importance of developing an organisation's 'story' and key messages are highlighted; crucially, this chapter also makes the case for the 5Cs: a *coherent 'story'*, *clarity of message*, a *consistent approach*, a *concerted effort* and the need for *coordinated action*. The chapter also explores the various options for gaining external advice, from political advisors who provide essential support for the stakeholder engagement programme, to high-level Boards that provide independent advice to the leadership team.

5.1 Context for an organisation's stakeholder engagement

5.1.1 Defining the activity space for an organisation

An organisation can choose to adopt a passive approach to its engagement. By this is meant that it keeps a relatively low profile in public space, by communicating the minimum information required to keep key stakeholders such as investors informed about the company's operations and performance. There will be a web-site to deliver basic information about the company and perhaps some high-level messages. It will not necessarily engage with the formal or informal decision-making processes, perhaps relying instead on its trade association to protect its interests.

At best this approach can lead to an organisation being better-informed than it might otherwise be; more likely it will miss threats and opportunities until it is too late to act and will simply have to live with the consequences. Organisations that have grown over time, like small independent generators or suppliers in the energy sector, tend to adopt a passive approach to engagement, which is perhaps

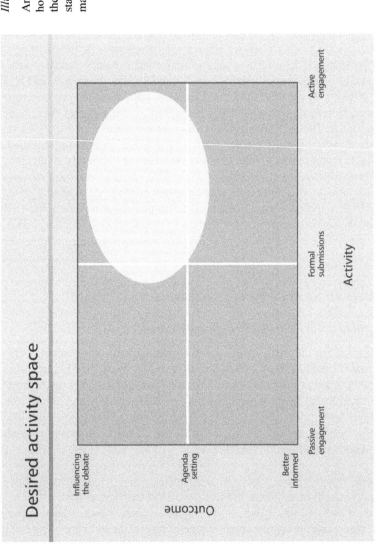

Illustration 5.1 Desired activity space

An organisation can define where and how it wishes to be active, and it will then be in a good position to develop a stakeholder engagement programme to match its aspirations.

not surprising since their focus is naturally on developing their business. Some larger companies also do not see the benefits of engaging more fully in decision-making circles, devoting relatively small internal resources to what is a critical activity; they may instead rely purely on public relations specialists to drive their agenda; some foreign companies investing in the UK are examples of this group. Public relations firms can advise and support but they do not have the detailed knowledge of the organisation needed, or the commitment of an employee who may have engagement with decision-makers as their core activity.

> Even among the most successful companies that excel at both shaping decisions and managing their reputations, many have a long way to go toward strengthening their capabilities in three areas: organising the company's external-affairs work, engaging with stakeholders, and setting the external-affairs agenda.
>
> *'How to reinvent the external-affairs function',*
> *McKinsey, July 2016*

At the other end of the spectrum is an organisation that is very proactive in public space, using all the tools at its disposal to help set the agenda and to influence the debate. An example of a highly successful lobbying effort is that of EDF Energy when making the case for new nuclear build in the UK. This company committed considerable resources to this activity and they were successful, as shown by the UK Government's response of changing the market structure to help, among other priorities, to facilitate new nuclear build through new economic instruments. Interestingly, the Government's interventions in the market also benefited EDF Energy's existing nuclear generation and all those who invested in renewable generation.

It may be appropriate for an organisation to adopt a passive approach to stakeholder engagement in some cases. However, it is very likely that Government intervention in markets will continue, and the risks and opportunities involved suggest organisations should commit resources to protect their interests; they can do this by developing their internal Government Affairs capability and implementing an active strategic stakeholder engagement programme.

5.1.2 Licence to operate

All registered companies need to adhere to certain legal requirements as part of their 'licence to operate'; for example, an energy company has:

- Formal 'licence to operate' requirements: the company must have a production licence, a supply licence and must adhere to industry codes and agreements.
- National legal requirements: the company must respond to 'mandatory' economic instruments (e.g., environmental taxes), 'voluntary' economic instruments (e.g., renewables support schemes, if it chooses to develop projects in

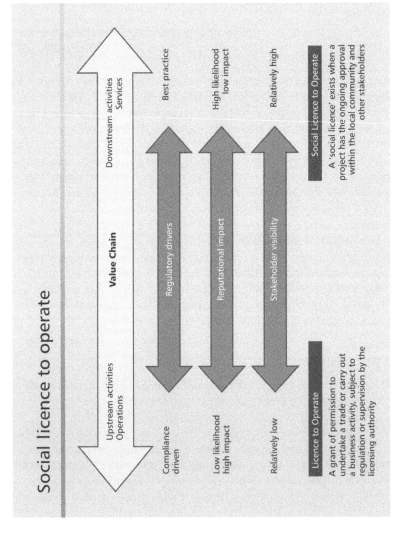

Illustration 5.2 Social licence to operate

The social licence to operate provides an organisation with the opportunity to show that it is always striving for best practice and that it wants to engage with the wider stakeholder community

Note: Definition of 'licence to operate' from *Dictionary of Banking Terms*, TP Fitch, Barron's Business Guides 2017.

this area) and obligations (e.g., there may be requirement for a company to pay for energy efficiency measures).

- To adhere to European Union (EU) laws – these include regulations (e.g., trading regulations) and directives that are transposed into national laws (e.g., environmental targets).

In addition to these, companies are keen to demonstrate best practice through their Corporate Social Responsibility (CSR) programmes, which are largely voluntary in nature. These programmes may include:

- Adhering to voluntary standards (e.g., Institute of Customer Service).
- Providing benefits to the local communities in which they operate, beyond providing jobs (e.g., training schemes for local people, the provision of community centres and so on).
- Supporting employees in their activities for charities (e.g., by providing match-funding schemes).

The annual CSR Report summarises performance in selected areas – for example marketplace, workplace, environment and community – and is an important document for external stakeholders because it provides the evidence that the company is at the forefront of best practice, going beyond 'licence to operate' to 'social licence to operate'.

Going beyond minimum compliance can not only enhance the reputation of an organisation but can also create business opportunities. In any event, it is also true that today's voluntary initiatives are tomorrow's obligation. Active communication with internal and external stakeholders helps to safeguard the 'social licence to operate'.

5.1.3 Ethical considerations associated with lobbying

The practice of trying to influence decision-makers (lobbying) has been going on for centuries in the UK, albeit in different guises. Today, society appears to be more accepting of the practice than it has been in the past, recognising that organisations have the right to express their views and to protect their interests. Non-governmental organisations (NGOs) and other pressure groups that represent civil society interests can lobby decision-makers without being seen to be unethical. Unions likewise can lobby politicians, particularly those to the left of centre, without being frowned upon. However, there remains some difficulty for companies engaging in this practice, because in most cases it is the organisation itself that is seen to benefit, perhaps to the detriment of others in their sector or at the expense of the consumer.

Where people try to exert influence or power without being open about it (corporate lobbying is an obvious example), there should be the maximum amount of transparency about who is trying to influence whom, and to what end.

Nick Clegg, former MP and Deputy Prime Minister,
Politics Between the Extremes, *2016*

Decision-makers likewise may have greater difficulty in responding to the concerns of commercial entities than they do to those of NGOs and other pressure groups; but there are checks and balances in the system that mitigate the possibility of unethical behaviour. For example, the Freedom of Information (FOI) process allows stakeholders the opportunity to question Ministers and other decision-makers on specific meetings held and to seek clarity on the issues discussed; Parliamentary Questions also offer a route to eliciting information on key issues from decision-makers.

The question for companies, then, is how to position themselves in this arena. Companies tend to have ethical policies that include, for example, the following high-level principles:

- Complying with laws and regulations.
- Establishing a culture of integrity.
- Behaving fairly and honestly.
- Respecting others.

These policies also make clear how employees must behave in the external domain in which they operate; for example, they must:

- Not defraud or deceive anyone or act dishonesty.
- Not engage in bribery and corruption.
- Only use agents and other third parties that share the same values.
- Not offer 'facilitation' payments in any country in which they operate.
- Ensure that any gifts and hospitality are reasonable, transparent and open to scrutiny, and do not influence business decisions.
- Engage in open and fair competition.

These are strong principles, applicable around the world. They should give confidence to stakeholders that the company will always behave ethically as it goes about its business of engaging in discussion on issues that affect the future well-being of the business, its shareholders and its employees.

An organisation must be transparent, credible, and honest in all its efforts to inform and influence decision-makers, the public, shareholders and so on.

Expert Panel Member Bill Coley CBE, former President of
Duke Power and CEO of British Energy Group

In addition to ethical policies, companies must have strong governance protocols to ensure these policies are adhered to. Regular audits and reviews within an organisation ensure that it continues to strive for the highest standards in this important area.

5.2 Developing an engagement programme

Effective lobbying has four main elements: a clear understanding of the issues that affect the business and the stakeholders involved; a 'story' to share with stakeholders; an engagement strategy; and organising the internal capacity of the business to deliver the engagement programme.

All organisations have issues to address, some sector-specific, and some more generic in nature. For example, the markets in which organisations operate are subject to change, brought about by new Government regulation, competition, disruptive technologies and so on; in some cases, there will be distortions like subsidies that may benefit some companies more than others, and the tax regime may change. Different stakeholders will play a role in defining these issues, and all of this and much more require attention if the organisation is to flourish.

The organisation will need to have a coherent story it can share with different stakeholders and to do so using different vehicles for optimum effect; it will also need a clear strategy, robust and thorough. And crucially, it will need to mobilise all the talents that reside within the organisation, supported by external specialist groups, if it is to be effective, for example, in addressing the risks, and opportunities, associated with new developments in the markets.

5.2.1 Getting organised internally

Effective stakeholder engagement needs to have a well-organised team. Chapter 1 summarised the spectacular failure of a company, British Energy, and highlighted that a contributory factor was the lack of effective engagement by the company, particularly with decision-makers in Government and Whitehall. This failure begins with the culture of the company and the observation that an organisation based on technical excellence and in the public sector for most of its life is used to having access to its masters in Whitehall. It does need to engage with the technical regulator because this is essential to its operations, but does not necessarily need to engage with other decision-makers; and if that organisation operates a 'pariah' technology such as nuclear, the desire to engage more widely may simply not be there.

> To succeed in external affairs, organisations need the right structure and people to support it. For many companies, this requires a rethinking of the function's setup, so its work is more visible in the organisation and more strategic, too.
> *'How to reinvent the external-affairs function',*
> *McKinsey, July 2016*

British Energy had other problems that made stakeholder engagement less effective than it should have been: the way in which it was organised and the attitude

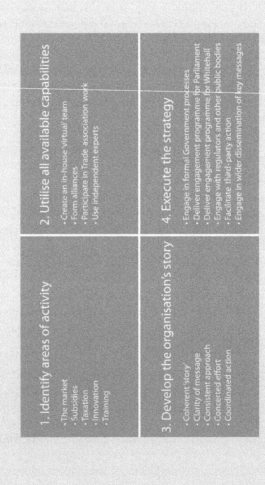

Elements of an effective lobbying programme

1. Identify areas of activity
- The market
- Subsidies
- Taxation
- Innovation
- Training

2. Utilise all available capabilities
- Create an in-house 'virtual' team
- Form alliances
- Participate in Trade association work
- Use independent experts

3. Develop the organisation's story
- Coherent 'story'
- Clarity of message
- Consistent approach
- Concerted effort
- Coordinated action

4. Execute the strategy
- Engage in formal Government processes
- Deliver engagement programme for Parliament
- Deliver engagement programme for Whitehall
- Engage with regulators and other public bodies
- Facilitate third-party action
- Engage in wider dissemination of key messages

Illustration 5.3 Elements of an effective lobbying programme

An organisation's engagement programme relies on an understanding of
the key issues that affect its environment, a compelling 'story', a clear
strategy, and the provision of sufficient
resources to carry out that strategy.

of its employees. The company was created by fusing together Nuclear Electric, which operated six nuclear power stations in England, and Scottish Nuclear, which operated two nuclear power stations in Scotland. There were four centres of activity outside of the power station sites: the technical centre at Gloucester, the Head Office in Edinburgh, a second Corporate Office near Glasgow and a small London office that housed the Chairman and Head of Government Affairs. There was a belief among different groups in these various locations that they were best placed to interact with decision-makers in Government and Whitehall; this belief was based on their expert knowledge of the industry, or through their past association, or because of their ongoing contacts. A company approach to stakeholder engagement was difficult in these circumstances.

Also, the absence of clear leadership in this area was harmful to the efforts of a small Government Affairs group that tended to be reactive in nature, did not take a holistic or far-sighted view of policy, and overly relied on the cooperation and goodwill of others in the organisation, who were mainly focused on their own work programmes.

There is little doubt that an organisation that was responsible for the operation of the UK's main nuclear fleet and delivered a quarter of the country's electricity supplies should have been able to protect its interests more effectively than it did, and the fact that it did not contributed to the spectacular demise of the company.

5.2.2 *The importance of leadership*

There are many instances where good leadership is crucial to a successful stakeholder engagement programme. Leadership in this area begins with a clear indication by the CEO and the executive team that Government Affairs is an important activity for the business; they will need to show that they will support the programme with the appropriate resources and devote their time to the engagement programme. Finally, the leadership must make clear that all those in the organisation who can contribute to the programme must work together, in a coordinated manner, to further the ambitions of the company in this important area.

The Chairman and CEO of an organisation have a crucial role to play in stakeholder engagement involving decision-makers and key influencers. This is particularly true when interactions involve Ministers, CEOs of regulators and other public bodies, and Chairs of Select Committees. Meetings with the first two groups should happen on a quarterly or half-yearly basis and afford opportunities to raise key issues and concerns for the business at the highest decision-making and advisory levels. Such meetings tend to be short, typically less than an hour, so it is important that a compelling 'story' is presented, with a clear indication of why it is important for decision-makers, and what is being asked of them.

> To get access requires building long-term relationships and it is these long-term relationships that contribute most to success.
>
> *Expert Panel Member Bernie Bulkin OBE,*
> *former Chief Scientist of BP and Chair of the UK's*
> *Office for Renewable Energy Deployment*

Organisations are occasionally called upon to provide evidence to a Parliamentary Select Committee and it is customary for the CEO to take on this task, and by doing so, to demonstrate respect for the Committee and its work. Providing evidence affords an opportunity to place the organisation, its operations and its views on the issues being discussed in the public arena. It is also important for employees to see their CEO perform well, giving them confidence that the organisation is doing all it can to safeguard its activities.

Leadership is not simply the domain of the Chairman and CEO; the executive team and their managers also have an important role to play, sometimes in support of the CEO in high-level meetings but mostly at the operational level, forging relationships with officials and regulators. They must also devote their time, and that of their experts, to this activity when needed.

5.2.3 A professional Government Affairs, Policy and Regulatory team

It is crucially important that the organisation is represented by an individual or team of expert practitioners in stakeholder engagement. The individuals involved need to be unusual in terms of the range of qualities they must exhibit; unusual also because no single quality is more important than the others; rather, all these qualities are needed to be successful when dealing with decision-makers and key influencers. They must:

- Have a strong interest in politics, policy and regulatory issues, and current affairs. A good understanding of the political arena at all levels of government is needed; also important is knowledge of the formal legislative processes in play and the roles of the key actors, so that the organisation can engage effectively and in a timely manner.
- Have a good knowledge of all aspects of the business. The individuals will need a good understanding of the business they are representing, and to have sufficient knowledge to be able to field questions on a range of issues as they emerge: technical, financial and so on.
- Have good analytical skills. They must have strategic thinking ability, and be able to analyse and interpret legislation and policy documents so that they can inform the business and prepare the organisation's formal responses.
- Have good facilitation skills. Delivering the organisation's engagement programme relies on the views and comments from experts across the business and it often requires excellent facilitation skills to get agreement on an issue, and in a format that is suitable for external consumption. There will also be occasions when facilitation is required across industry actors with their own competing views and ideas; here also, expert facilitation can often result in common messages that can be shared with decision-makers.
- Have excellent networking and interpersonal skills. The individuals must demonstrate integrity and the ability to inspire trust and confidence in stakeholders; they must be able to develop and maintain relationships with public

officials and their staffs, and with all those within the organisation who contribute to the engagement programme. They must be able to work with people from diverse academic, cultural and ethnic backgrounds.

- Have good communication skills. It is essential that stakeholder engagement practitioners are able to present concepts, ideas and arguments through oral and written media. They must be strong advocates for the organisation, and able to negotiate and persuade external stakeholders; they must be able to communicate effectively with external individuals and groups, and, internally, with all levels of management, directors and employees. Practitioners will also be expert at preparing essential written material including consultation and inquiry responses, reports and briefing material.
- Have attention to detail and strong follow-through. The provision of accurate data and information is crucial to the credibility of the organisation's narrative to the outside world; the material shared with decision-makers must be robust to scrutiny. It is also important that experts in this area seek all opportunities to convey the organisation's messages, in a consistent and well-coordinated approach.
- Be flexible in approach. Experts in this area will have to take a lead role on some occasions – for example, by representing the organisation's interests in specialist forums or meetings – and a subordinate role on other occasions when the CEO or an executive is present; in either case, the material presented will normally be prepared by the Government Affairs professional, drawing on the knowledge of other experts in the business. Team members must also be able to step in for each other at forums when the need arises.
- Have strong management skills. An ability to work independently and within teams is an essential quality. Project management is important, as is careful consideration of the time of others within the organisation, particularly those executives and organisation experts who contribute to the engagement programme.

5.2.4 Drawing on all the organisation's capabilities

There is sometimes a mistaken view that an organisation's communications function should be at the heart of its external engagement programme, and that Government Affairs should be a part of that effort. That may be correct if an organisation simply wants to manage its public relations, but if a key objective is to protect its interests in the marketplace, then the Government Affairs function needs to play a central role in the organisation, ensuring a coordinated approach to its outward-facing activities. It must also have regular access to the leadership of the organisation and clear recognition that it can draw on resources from other specialist functions when needed.

There are several internal departments that Government Affairs will need to engage with as it goes about its business of influencing its strategic stakeholders and the external debate. These departments can be split into those that contribute

Drawing on organisational capabilities

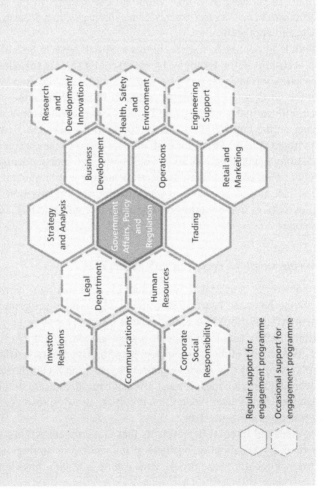

Illustration 5.4 Drawing on organisational capabilities

An effective engagement programme will draw on the knowledge and expertise that reside in many different parts of an organisation; the nature and timing of each department's contribution depends on the issue and activity involved. What is important is that the there is a willingness to contribute to the programme, and recognition for doing so; an organisation's executive team play a very important role in establishing the right culture for engagement.

regularly to the engagement programme by providing data, information and analysis, and experts to help with briefings and presentations; and those departments that are called on less regularly but tasked with providing up-to-date information about its operations. Examples of departments that can make a good contribution to the engagement programme include:

- **Strategy and analysis:** This department will play a key role in defining the direction of the organisation and as such is well placed to help develop the 'story' for decision-makers and key influencers; once the organisation's strategic aims are established, the policy and regulatory needs of the business will follow. It is crucially important that what is presented externally is evidence-based so that it is credible to external observers.
- **Business development:** This department will implement an important part of the organisation's strategy going forward, and it can define what is needed from decision-makers in the policy arena to support its development programme.
- **Trading, retail and marketing:** It is likely that new policy and regulation will come to affect the market environment in which the organisation operates; it is important then that the implications of changes to the market framework and structure are assessed, and if they are detrimental to the business, that this information is shared with decision-makers.
- **Operations:** A high level of credibility is important when meeting with strategic stakeholders, and this is best illustrated by performance in the ongoing operations; it is important to share meaningful metrics with external stakeholders in an open and transparent way.
- **External communications:** This department is primarily responsible for dealing with the media and wider public; key messages will need to be aligned to ensure a consistent approach to informing all stakeholders.

There will be occasions when other departments will contribute to the organisation's 'story'. For example, Members of Parliament (MPs) whose constituencies include the organisation's operational sites or offices will be interested in the welfare of employees and local communities; so, it will be important to have Human Resources and Corporate Social Responsibility professionals involved in the engagement programme to brief MPs accordingly. Regulators will need assurance that health, safety and environment performance adheres to best practice and the operations team is well placed to provide this comfort. Investors also will need confidence that the company's financial performance remains strong and this is provided by the Investor Relations team.

There will also be occasions when the advice of the legal department is sought, for example, if the company is required to deliver confidential data and information to a Government body such as the Competition and Mergers Authority in one of its inquiries, or if it wishes to get involved in a Judicial Review.

A successful engagement programme will draw on these departments to a greater or lesser degree. It is crucially important that all are aligned and committed to the programme, that a collegiate approach is adopted and that there is recognition for all those involved by the executive team. An appropriate governance

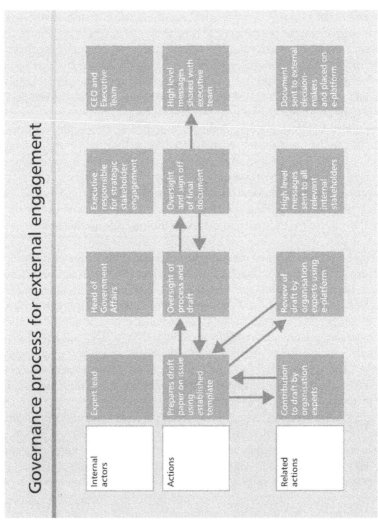

Governance process for external engagement

Internal actors	Expert lead	Head of Government Affairs		Executive responsible for strategic stakeholder engagement	CEO and Executive Team
Actions	Prepares draft paper on issue using established template	Oversight of process and draft		Oversight and sign off of final document	High level messages shared with executive team
Related actions	Contribution to draft by organisation experts		Review of draft by organisation experts using e-platform	High level messages sent to all relevant internal stakeholders	Document sent to external decision-makers and placed on e-platform

Illustration 5.5 Governance process for external engagement

A robust governance process is essential if an organisation is to be confident that the messages, and the supporting data and information that are communicated to the external domain, are accurate and well-founded.

process will help the internal organisation and delivery of the programme; it will, for example, ensure that a well-established procedure is followed in the preparation of material for external stakeholders.

5.2.5 The role of internal experts

Organisations are often blessed with experts without whom they could not function. The Government Affairs team needs these experts to help develop the organisation's position on issues that impact the business, and to provide the underpinning logic, information and analysis. The team will then share the organisation's position, and its evidence, with those decision-makers and officials charged with developing new policy or regulation.

It is often said that there are some very bright people in Government and the Civil Service. But it is also true that civil servants often have no real-life experience of the markets and sectors they are responsible for. Worse, civil servants change roles, sometimes without seeing a project through to completion, and are replaced by new officials that do not have the necessary deep knowledge of the area they are responsible for. It is important, then, that organisations help educate these officials, so that they will make better-informed decisions; this will be in the best interests of the sector and the organisations involved.

5.3 Developing the internal infrastructure

5.3.1 Resources fit for purpose

The appointment of a specialist Government Affairs team tends not to be high on the agenda of many businesses. Often the person charged with engaging with government is a 'singleton' expert, usually with a public relations or communications background, and provided with limited resources to deploy. This is not necessarily a bad thing if there is expertise and resources to draw on from other parts of the business, and the engagement programme is focused on a few issues.

> Without resources, effective stakeholder engagement won't happen.
>
> *Expert Panel Member Robert Armour OBE,*
> *Former Deputy Chairman, NuGeneration*

However, a 'singleton' expert cannot cover all the risks and opportunities that may have an impact on the business; worse, there may be periods when the 'singleton' is not available for various reasons and misses important announcements, meetings and other activities. Nor may the 'singleton' have the detailed knowledge needed to discriminate between what is more important and less important for the business, and this can make them less effective. Of course, a small organisation that is growing may not see this as a priority, but the potentially high monetary value associated with the impact of new policy and regulation warrants serious consideration of the nature and scale of resources needed in this important area.

The creation of a 'virtual' team of experts from different parts of the business to support the Government Affairs effort is very important. Each member of the team needs to be able to devote the time needed to this activity, with their contributions, however small, formally recognised as part of their work programme. There are several benefits to this approach: 'virtual' team members are committed to the programme, the capacity of the organisation in this important area is increased, and individuals can be rewarded through the annual appraisal system.

An appropriate budget is also needed, to pay for:

- Subscriptions to the appropriate trade association that represents sector interests.
- Political advisors to support the engagement programme.
- Subscriptions to specialist providers of roundtable discussion forums.
- Subscriptions to specialist providers of daily and monthly updates on developments in the policy and regulatory arena.
- Ad hoc projects; for example, specialist studies that can be used to underpin arguments and provide evidence to strategic stakeholders.

There are several options when assessing what resources are needed for a stakeholder engagement programme and the choice is dependent on the organisation and level of ambition. It is possible to use the traditional base measure, the cost of a 'man-year', to estimate the overall cost of a stakeholder engagement programme for the following three options:

- Level of ambition 1: *'Do we really need this?'* This option involves a part-time 'singleton' expert and a total cost of around 1 man-year equivalent. This assumes the expert devotes half their time to the Government Affairs role (i.e., 0.5 man-year cost) and draws on expertise from around the business totalling about 0.25 man-year costs; subscriptions to specialist providers of up-to-date information cost 0.1 man-year equivalent and expenses equivalent to around 0.05 man-year costs.
- Level of ambition 2: *'Make sure we don't get caught out.'* Here, to meet the level of ambition requires a full-time 'singleton' expert and a total programme cost of around 2 man-years equivalent. This assumes the expert devotes all their time to the Government Affairs role (i.e., 1 man-year cost), and draws on expertise from around the business totalling about 0.3 man-year costs; the programme is supported by political advisers who provide basic support equivalent to 0.5 man-year costs, subscriptions to specialist providers of up-to-date information at 0.1 man-year costs and expenses equivalent to around 0.1 man-year costs.
- Level of ambition 3: *'Making a difference.'* Meeting this level of ambition requires a small team of experts and a total cost of around 5 man-years equivalent. This assumes the team consist of three to four experts each addressing different aspects of the Government Affairs, Policy and Regulation programme (i.e., 3 to 4 man-year costs). The programme draws on expertise

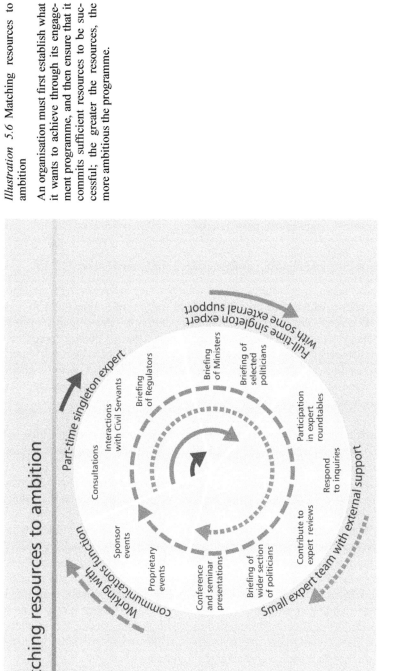

Matching resources to ambition

Illustration 5.6 Matching resources to ambition

An organisation must first establish what it wants to achieve through its engagement programme, and then ensure that it commits sufficient resources to be successful; the greater the resources, the more ambitious the programme.

from around the business totalling about 0.3 man-year costs and is supported by political advisers who provide significant support, equivalent to 0.8 man-year costs; subscriptions to specialist providers of up-to-date information, at a cost of 0.1 man-year equivalent and expenses equivalent to around 0.2 man-year costs complete the resources needed for this level of ambition.

If a man-year cost is, for example, £50,000, then the budget for a small team and its support, as described in Option 3, could be around £250,000 each year; if the man-year costs are higher, say £100,000, the cost for the team would be around £500,000. These illustrations are relatively small when compared to the monetary value associated with policy and regulatory risks (and opportunities) which could be worth tens of millions of pounds to the business; these risks (and opportunities) could easily be missed without an effective internal capability and an active strategic engagement programme.

5.3.2 Developing and applying a stakeholder management 'tool'

A stakeholder mapping exercise is an important first step in developing an engagement programme, whether the programme addresses a single project or a broader policy-related issue. The exercise need not be onerous but does require research and analysis for it to be effective; what is important is that the process forces 'virtual' team members to think through the full spectrum of stakeholders and to rank them with regard to key issues for the business. The exercise also draws on all the knowledge and intelligence that naturally reside in an organisation but may not necessarily have been exploited.

> Overall, a comprehensive stakeholder map needs to be developed with a full spectrum of stakeholders identified and an assessment made on who and when to engage.
>
> *Expert Panel Member David Beamer,*
> *CEO Brevia Consulting*

The mapping exercise can be at a high level with the objective of identifying stakeholders and their roles in general terms, providing a common knowledge base for the internal experts taking part in the exercise. The exercise can then focus on areas of direct interest to the organisation and on those stakeholders that may contribute to the decision-making process; internal experts would gain a deeper understanding of stakeholder roles. Going one step further, it may be most helpful to identify specific organisational issues or developments and map all the stakeholders that would impact these activities; this would provide a practical starting point for an effective engagement programme.

There are a few 'tools' available, some highly sophisticated, to aid a stakeholder mapping exercise and it may be appropriate to adopt one of these; alternatively, an organisation could develop a proprietary tool that may better serve its needs than commercial, off-the-shelf, generic software. The 'tool' used for the mapping exercise

Illustration 5.7 Stakeholder mapping options

Each stakeholder will have a role in the decision-making process and they will want to influence the debate on issues that interest them. An organisation will need to carry out a detailed stakeholder mapping exercise, drawing on knowledge from inside the organisation and from the external world.

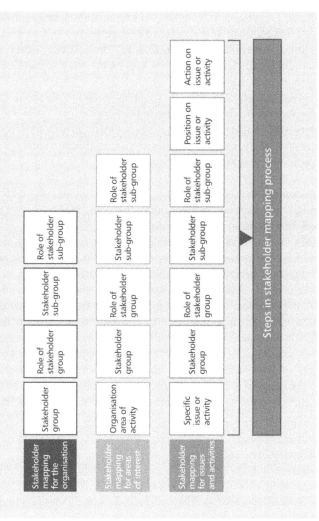

should solicit responses from internal experts in the relevant areas; some prompts or lists for each area within the 'tool' would help the process. For example:

- **Issue or activity of interest to the organisation:** brief description of an issue or activity; for example, a new business development project, a policy development, an awareness-raising or Corporate Social Responsibility initiative.
- **Stakeholder group:** establishes the broad stakeholder group being considered; for example, government, interest groups or market participants.
- **Stakeholder sub-group(s):** identifies stakeholder sub-group; for example, Special Advisors would be a sub-group of Government, and contractors would be a sub-group of market participants.
- **Stakeholder sub-group roles(s):** summarises in simple terms the role the group plays in relation to the issue; for example, think tanks provide valuable analysis and comment to aid policy development.
- **Individual stakeholder(s):** identifies key individuals within a particular stakeholder group; for example, the lead on the issue within Government or the industry trade association.
- **Individual stakeholder role(s):** summarises in simple terms the potential role the individual plays in relation to the issue.
- **Priority stakeholders:** ranks the stakeholders as primary, secondary, tertiary or quaternary, to allow effective resource allocation and the appropriate approach in the engagement programme.

Such an exercise then would result in a holistic view of stakeholders and their roles, highlight overlaps and potential omissions, and make the engagement programme easier to develop and implement.

It is very important that all members of the Government Affairs 'virtual' team understand what the organisation is trying to achieve and their role in the stakeholder engagement programme. A common electronic 'platform' is needed for members to consult, update and review progress; such a stakeholder management 'tool' is populated by an expert internal team from across the organisation in the first instance, and a person from the core Government Affairs team is made responsible for keeping it up to date.

The stakeholder management 'tool' can be a simple spreadsheet with a series of 'prompts' addressing two aspects: the external and internal domains. Stakeholders in the external domain are categorised, and their position and actions on issues of interest to the business are established by responding to the 'prompts'. This exercise will help identify those stakeholders that hold contrary views to the organisation and to those that could prove allies in the engagement programme.

The organisation's position on the key issues identified is established and the potential mitigation actions highlighted and implemented. The resulting outcomes may or may not be successful, and if they are not, further mitigation actions will

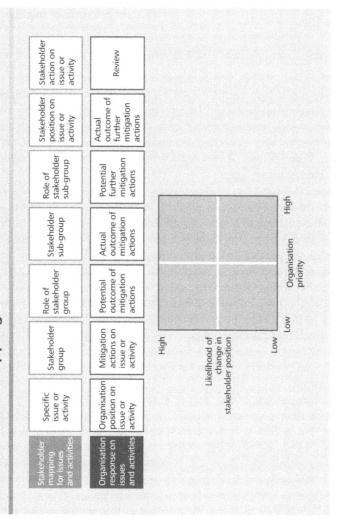

Illustration 5.8 Stakeholder mapping

A detailed mapping exercise that involves internal experts is an essential activity for an organisation so that it can establish which stakeholders to meet, and with what objective; such an exercise produces a 'live' document, one that evolves as the programme proceeds and the results of engagement are included.

be identified and the outcomes reviewed. The stakeholder map is a live document, to be reviewed and updated at regular intervals as more information becomes available.

Personal networks play an important role in stakeholder engagement. Such networks grow and evolve over time and require attention, particularly in relation to decision-makers, since they tend not to be in the role for any length of time. Each person involved in the engagement programme has their own network, and if all the networks were brought together, they would cover a large part, if not all, the stakeholder spectrum. An understanding of the positions of stakeholders through these networks is helpful in the mapping exercise.

It is important that resources are allocated where they can deliver the best results. The organisation should establish its priority issues and evaluate the relative likelihood that they can affect the views of decision-makers and other key stakeholders; effort can then be focused on those issues with a high chance of success.

5.3.3 Carrying out a political risk analysis

Organisations are less likely to undertake a formal analysis of political risk than policy risk, in part because there is little opportunity or desire by companies to influence the political landscape. Nonetheless, such an analysis is important as it can, and often does, have a profound influence on the market in which companies operate. If nothing else, it will lead to a much better understanding of some of the key political drivers that, like ripples in a pond, have ramifications further away in policy and regulatory space.

The political context can change at every election, now every five years in the UK unless there is a two-thirds majority in Parliament for an earlier election, or a negative outcome to a vote of confidence in the Government of the day; a detailed analysis on this timeframe is simply good practice. But it is also important to revisit the political risk analysis on a more regular basis as the company's strategy evolves, and because the political context and priorities, and the key political actors within Government, can change.

An analysis of political risk will be a qualitative assessment that draws on the views and opinions of informed commentators. A simple scenario approach that explores a range of political options is often very helpful; the potential policy implications for the organisation's sector associated with each of these political options can be considered, and an assessment of their implications for the business is possible.

There are several approaches that can be adopted to get a well-informed analysis. The exercise could be given to political advisers, although their knowledge of the market and the business may not be sufficient to provide the level of detail needed; an analysis within the organisation may likewise not be sufficiently informed to provide the political richness needed. Perhaps the best approach is the one adopted by Shell in their scenario development programme. The strength of their approach is a confidence to bring together both external experts and internal specialists to debate and argue the issues, leading to outcomes that are both well-informed and useful. In this way, a deep knowledge of the political context and the implications

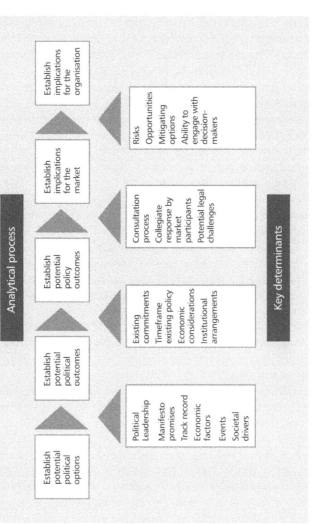

Illustration 5.9 Dealing with political risk

It is important that an organisation carries out an assessment of political risk in relation to its interests and activities. It can achieve this through a simple analytical process where it can explore the implications of key determinants.

Dealing with political risk

Analytical process

| Establish potential political options | Establish potential political outcomes | Establish potential policy outcomes | Establish implications for the market | Establish implications for the organisation |

Political Leadership
Manifesto promises
Track record
Economic factors
Events
Societal drivers

Existing commitments
Timeframe existing policy
Economic considerations
Institutional arrangements

Consultation process
Collegiate response by market participants
Potential legal challenges

Risks
Opportunities
Mitigating options
Ability to engage with decision-makers

Key determinants

is provided to internal stakeholders, making them much better able to engage more widely as they seek to influence the external debate on issues that are important to their business.

Of course, it may not be possible to devote major resources to such an exercise, but an abridged version of this approach has proved possible; those working in the Government Affairs, policy and regulation arena would be very well served by carrying out such an exercise.

5.3.4 The importance of a Risk Register

Policy and regulatory risk (and opportunity) has risen significantly in recent years and is now a priority issue in boardrooms; it is essential that a methodology is established that records and quantifies these risks. The creation, then, of a regulatory Risk Register captures and consolidates in one place the high-level risks and opportunities that are faced across all aspects of the company in relation to policy and regulation. The register provides a very good way of demonstrating to the CEO, executives and managers the importance of engaging with decision-makers, and the need for them to devote time and resources to a strategic stakeholder engagement programme.

While many of the risks and opportunities can be expressed in qualitative terms, the approach should ideally be a quantitative one based on informed assessment, so that the materiality of the risk or opportunity can be better understood and effort targeted appropriately. Each risk or opportunity should have the following information captured in an appropriate table:

- **Owner:** This shows who in the policy and regulation team has been assigned primary responsibility for the issue.
- **Risk or opportunity:** An issue is classified as a risk where a policy is deemed to pose a threat to earnings or impose additional obligations on the company. Opportunities occur when an initiative can add monetary value to the business.
- **Description of risk or opportunity:** Summarises the key threat or opportunity and assumes a level of understanding of the issues.
- **Timeframe and urgency:** Timeframes can be rated as short-, medium- or long-term and relate to how soon the event will start to impact the business. Likewise, urgency is rated high, medium, low and relates to how soon action should be mobilised.
- **Annual value:** This is the estimated annual value to the business as assessed by the policy and regulation team and relates to the total impact on the relevant UK activity, assets or portfolio.
- **Lifetime:** The lifetime indicates the duration of the policy initiative in relation to how it will impact on the assets or portfolio. For example, a new policy may typically have a lifetime measured in years; however, the lifetime of the impacted assets may be shorter, in which case the shorter period is a better lifetime. Alternatively, the timeframe assumed would be better aligned with the organisation's medium-term plan, for example, 3–5 years.
- **Total value:** This represents the annual value multiplied by the lifetime adopted.

- **Start dates:** The start date indicates the date at which the policy or initiative comes into force, or the best indicative date.
- **Probability and impact:** The *probability* of occurrence for each issue can be scored from one to five depending on the chance of the issue coming to fruition; for example, a value of '1' is the least likely (<20%) and '5' is the most likely (>80%). The *impact* can be banded according to the cost to, or opportunity for, the business, ranging from, for example, '1' (insignificant <£5 million) to '8' (extreme >£300 million).
- **Probability and impact (initial):** Both the *probability* and *impact* are assessed in relation to the starting position prior to any intervention or mitigation by the organisation. These are best displayed graphically.
- **Mitigation:** Mitigation describes the actions proposed by the policy and regulation team to counteract the identified risks or measures to realise opportunities. Where collaborative action is required, this is identified along with the partner involved; for example, the partner may be the relevant trade association or other organisations and commentators that have an interest in the issue.
- **Probability and impact (potential outcome):** The *probability* and *impacts* of the potential outcome are assessed and rated according to the same methodology described above; the probability and impact scores indicate the forecast or target outcome that would occur should the mitigation actions or measures taken to realise opportunities be successful. The difference between the initial and outcome scores gives an indication as to the potential value added by the organisation's intervention on the issues in question.
- **Rating:** An overall rating can be used to quantify the risk posed by each issue. It is calculated as a simple metric of the initial *probability* value multiplied by the initial *impact* value. This rating is created to help inform executives and help prioritise action.

Illustration 5.10 provides a valuable overview. The y-axis represents the cost/benefit *impact* on the company for each of the risks or opportunities identified; the x-axis represents the *probability* of occurrence. Each risk or opportunity is placed according to the combination of these; each box indicates the starting point in line with the initial *probability* and *impact*. Arrows depict the effect of mitigation and the arrowhead indicates the potential outcome should the risk be mitigated or the opportunity realised, i.e., the best outcome that can be reasonably expected. Colour coding can indicate the severity of the issues according to a combination of their probability and impact.

This analysis forces a detailed consideration of the risks involved and provides a priority list so that the organisation can focus its resources; the analysis can be wide-ranging and cover a cross-section of activities. The number of risks can be significant, in some cases more than 20 at any one time; the value at stake can be tens of millions of pounds, perhaps hundreds of millions in some sectors, when considered over the policy lifetime or against an organisation's medium-term plan.

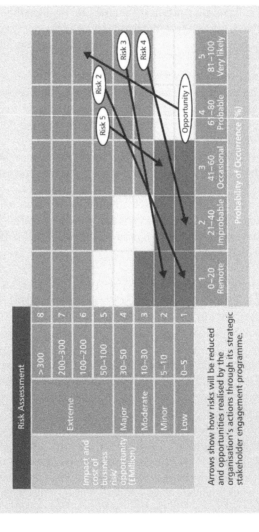

Illustration 5.10 Quantifying risks

It is possible and necessary to quantify policy and regulatory risks. Applying a simple methodology ensures that internal experts and their executives have a good understanding of the risks and opportunities in their area.

Note: Based on an original methodology and template developed by British Energy Group.

There is a clear need to work closely with Government, officials and regulators to mitigate risks or realise opportunities. On some occasions, it is necessary for an organisation to work unilaterally, and on other occasions it may be appropriate to work with other interested key stakeholders. It is also important that the Risk Register is updated as new risks and opportunities arise, and that progress is reported to the CEO and the Board, and the executive team, on a regular basis using the risk assessment approach.

5.3.5 A Briefings Booklet for executives

An important part of the Government Affairs work programme is to ensure that executives and their managers understand the prevailing policy and regulatory arena. It is also helpful that these important internal stakeholders share a common knowledge around which to have meaningful discussions and to aid their decision-making.

One way to achieve this is to create a Briefings Booklet that describes, at a high level, all the main issues that influence the market in which the organisation operates. This will begin with a description of the context for the policy development, an overview of the main underlying drivers that shape the market. For example, in the energy sector, the main drivers are decarbonisation, security of supply and cost to consumers; the first of these has dominated the agenda for a decade or so, but more recently the other two drivers have become more prominent with politicians. This highlights the fact that the context can change, and the policy focus with it, over a relatively short timescale, and the need for an organisation to stay alert and responsive to potential changes.

What is also important is that executives have a clear and simple summary for each policy issue that impacts the business to draw on, so that they are up to date and as well-informed as possible as they interact with their networks. One-page summaries have been shown to be effective, particularly if they are structured against a simple common template, for example, one that provides a background to the issue and explains what it is and how it works, what it means for the organisation, and finally, the key messages for decision-makers.

The Briefings Booklet should certainly address the issues covered by the Risk Register but it should also cover issues more widely of interest to other key external stakeholders, not least because they may become important for the organisation in time. For example, energy efficiency policy originally only affected retail companies, but unexpectedly the policy changed and other industry actors were brought into this area who then incurred unexpected additional costs to their operations. It is important to anticipate such potential outcomes, to raise their profile within the organisation, and whenever possible be active in forums where they are discussed.

Once the Briefings Booklet has been prepared for internal audiences, a second version with essentially the same information can be produced for external audiences. Experience with this approach suggests such briefing documents are simple and very effective in raising knowledge and awareness in the internal and wider stakeholder community.

5.3.6 *Regular highlights and briefings for the CEO and the executive team*

It is important that a protocol is established whereby there are regular meetings, perhaps monthly, when the CEO can be briefed on progress and recent developments on policy and regulatory issues. Such a commitment by the CEO demonstrates the importance placed on strategic stakeholder engagement and the CEO's role in it. Often issues of interest are discussed in the public space and questions are then asked internally; regular briefings ensure the CEO is not 'surprised' by developments, that they are sufficiently well-informed to brief the Chairman and the Board as needed, and they are able to respond to media queries with the high-level messages prepared. Regular briefings at executive team meetings are also appropriate, particularly in times when the policy and regulatory context for the business is changing.

As a minimum, the Government Affairs team should prepare monthly written highlights on developments in their area. This is important for several reasons:

- It provides a simple method of updating the executive team at regular intervals, and records developments over a period.
- It affords the executive team an opportunity to ask questions of those working on an issue.
- The highlights can be used in other documents and updates the organisation routinely produces.
- It provides an effective way of developing and maintaining the discipline of written communication that is fit for purpose.
- It provides a useful evidence base to review progress at end-of-year reviews.

It is not necessary to prepare highlights on every issue each month, but there are always new developments in the political, and policy and regulation arenas that should be shared with the CEO and their executive team.

5.4 Developing a 'story' and engagement strategy

The most important aspect of any stakeholder engagement programme is the 'story', and indeed there may well be more than one depending on the issues and stakeholders involved. The 'story' will bring something to the table for each stakeholder involved. If the stakeholder is the Government, it may be that what is presented by the organisation is consistent with its policy, such as bringing forward much-needed investment, employment and jobs; if it is Local Government, it may be related to economic benefit for the communities. If it is a key influencer such as the professional institutions, the organisation's 'story' may relate to maintaining existing skills or developing new ones.

> In the end, people follow stories, not policies, in politics. Governments and leaders who have a clear story that has a beginning, middle and end will generally be rewarded.
>
> *Nick Clegg, former MP and Deputy Prime Minister,*
> Politics Between the Extremes, *2016*

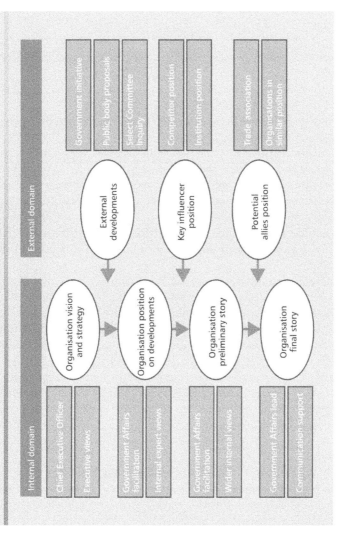

Illustration 5.11 Developing the organisation 'story'

An organisation's 'story' needs to be carefully developed, taking all the information available in the internal and external domains into account; it needs to be compelling and evidence-based when engaging with decision-makers.

The 'story' developed will consider the organisation's strategy and developments in the political, policy and public arenas; for example, a new initiative proposed by Government, one of the public bodies, or even a Select Committee inquiry will result in internal, expert analysis to develop the organisation's response. The 'story' will be more holistic and consider others in the external domain, for example, potential allies, and the position adopted by the institutions and even competitors.

Like all 'stories', it will have a beginning, a middle and an end, for example, the context for the issue, the concerns raised by the issue and potential solutions, and what action is being asked of decision-makers. The organisation will also improve its chances of success if it suggests credible solutions that will bring benefits beyond the organisation itself.

The engagement programme needs to satisfy several criteria if it is to be successful; the 5Cs are:

- A **coherent 'story'**, one that is credible, not overly partisan, evidence-based and timely.
- **Clarity of message**, one that can be easily understood and disseminated more widely.
- A **consistent approach**, with messages are well thought through and do not change, so that they remain credible.
- A **concerted effort**, sometimes over an extended period, if it is to reach all the relevant stakeholders and be successful.
- A **coordinated approach**, to ensure an effective engagement programme. This is important because there may be several elements to the engagement programme involving different issues, sometimes with the same external stakeholders and sometimes not; and different internal stakeholders will be involved and there needs to be good coordination for optimum effect.

Very few organisations address the 5Cs building blocks, but when they do, they can be very successful. One organisation that has done this well in the past is EDF Energy as they went about making the case for new nuclear build in the UK. They had a coherent 'story', one that was in tune with the Government's decarbonisation agenda and had the potential to bring significant economic benefit to the UK in terms of investment, jobs and high-valued skills, and economic benefit to hard-pressed communities. The high-level message was clear and consistent: *what we are proposing is good for the UK and the environment.* The company was unwavering in its efforts, presenting a credible 'story' over several years; and its engagement programme was opportunistic and very well coordinated across many diverse activities: consultations, conference roundtables and so on.

EDF Energy's 'story' went well beyond new nuclear build; for example, the company highlighted their efforts in renewable deployment, smart metres and their successful delivery of their social obligations. Crucially, each part of the 'story' reached a different set of stakeholders. They gained a Platinum award in the highly-regarded Business in the Community (BiTC) index and sponsored the 2012 Olympic Games, which gave them a platform to enhance their profile and credibility with the wider public. Public acceptability was important to EDF Energy because it had, and continues to have, a strong presence in the retail sector.

5.5 Building alliances and getting independent advice

There is only so much an individual organisation can achieve on its own, however significant in the sector, because decision-makers will want to be seen to act in a fair and impartial way, and to the benefit of the public. All organisations, then, will seek alliances, to be part of the sector trade association and to work closely with independent commentators in the policy space.

An organisation that is part of its sector Trade Association will benefit in several ways, because such a body can:

- Facilitate access to decision-makers and key influencers when it may be difficult for individual organisations.
- Develop a consensus on issues that would be helpful when Government is developing new initiatives for the sector.
- Provide specialist experts and forums for sharing knowledge among its members, something that is particularly helpful to smaller organisations that have limited resources.
- Provide an opportunity for an organisation to share its position, key messages and arguments on policy issues with others in the sector.

However, there are also some drawbacks, for example:

- There may not be consensus on some issues and this can make interactions with decision-makers difficult.
- Some organisations can devote more resources to the association than others; this allows them to be very active in the work of the association and therefore to take a position of influence.

An organisation may decide on an informal alliance with others in the sector, ones that share a common interest. There would need to be a clear rationale for the alliance and decision-makers must be receptive to this alliance. This could be a powerful grouping with many of the benefits of the formal trade association and, because of the shared interests, few of the drawbacks.

Forming alliances can be incredibly effective.
Expert Panel Member Tom Greatrex, former MP and
Shadow Energy Minister, UK Parliament

One alliance rarely mentioned is that between an organisation and the companies that contribute to its supply chain. This relationship is critical to both communities because one cannot work without the other; there is a clear link, then, between the well-being of an organisation and that of its supply chain. For example, any changes to the regulatory framework that may impact an organisation's existing operations in the market or policy developments that affect potential new developments will be important to both groups; an alliance to present a common position would be powerful and difficult for decision-makers to ignore.

Trade Unions remain an important stakeholder group for Government of whatever hue, despite the fact that their membership is falling – around seven million people out of a working population of around 31 million in the UK in 2016, compared to a peak of 13 million and 25 million, respectively, in 1979 – and they are partisan in their support of political parties. Unions are the stakeholder group most concerned with issues such as workers' rights, employment opportunities and the skills agenda; but their interests are broader, covering the economy, industrial policy, climate change, workplace environment, social and equality issues, and international developments. They represent employees in companies with a direct interest in policy-making, and those in the supply chain further away from the policy 'coal face'; and they represent employees in private companies and in the public sector.

Trade Unions develop positions on all the major policy issues and participate in the government's formal engagement processes. Alliances between unions and private organisations are unlikely because their membership is drawn from many organisations, but in energy, for example, they do support some sectors such as nuclear power and oppose others such as shale gas. They can work with business on apprenticeship schemes and with non-profit organisations on social issues such as poverty alleviation.

The investment community is also, potentially, a powerful lobby group because it can influence Government policy by providing fundamental information to help inform the decision-making process. In practice, this community may have a strong interest in government policy but tends to leave lobbying activity to the companies they invest in. Nevertheless, there are occasions when organisations can call on their investors to help them with their engagement programmes by providing, for example, data to support economic analyses and argument.

An organisation also enjoys a close relationship with the local communities in which it operates, because its activities often bring much-needed employment and other economic benefits. There may be a local liaison group the organisation uses to keep the community informed of its activities; and the local Member of Parliament will also want to be kept up to date with issues that concern their constituents. There will be opportunities for an organisation to use its relationships with the local Member of Parliament as it responds to policy and regulatory changes, and developments in the market, that affect its operations; it can, for example, raise issues with the local MP who then writes formally to Ministers on its behalf.

A wealth of knowledge and experience to draw on

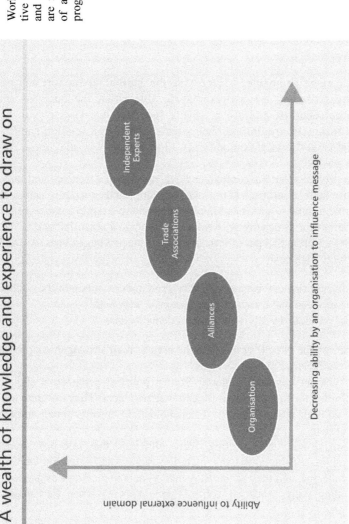

Illustration 5.12 A wealth of knowledge and experience to draw on

Working with others can be very effective when dealing with decision-makers and key influencers; such interactions are needed to complement the efforts of an organisation's own engagement programme.

5.5.1 The importance of independent advice

The importance of political advisors

Advisors are essential to the organisation's political engagement programme because they help to manage political and policy risk. They have an intimate understanding of the workings of Parliament, in both the Lower and the Upper Houses, and their respective influence on the legislative process. They also understand the importance of the institutions that support the politicians, and the crucial roles played by Special Advisors to the Ministers and the Clerks who serve the Select Committees.

There is a range of political advisors to call on, from small, excellent, specialist companies like Brevia Consulting to large public relations firms such as Hill and Knowlton. Both ends of the spectrum have their strengths and weaknesses:

- Small niche companies can provide the individual support and responsiveness needed, are very knowledgeable about the business and the political context, and are relatively low-cost; weaknesses can be that their resources are limited, their political networks smaller, and they are perhaps overly reliant on one or two individuals who may move on from their positions.
- Large public relations companies have significant resources and networks, can use their larger reach to transfer knowledge and experience across clients, are able to fund research and publish authoritative reports, and have a strong communications capability; weaknesses include a potential lack of focus on the organisation that pays for their services due to a large client base and their relatively high cost.

Crucially, political advisors have a very good understanding of the political and legislative process, and also how best to engage with both.

Services provided by advisors to their clients include:

- Advice on the overall strategy for the organisation's engagement programme with politicians and civil servants.
- Feedback on company material from a political perspective and help in developing the key messages for external audiences. They also provide feedback on draft letters to political stakeholders to ensure content and tone are appropriate.
- Organising individual meetings with politicians; they also provide detailed biographies of the politicians, including some intelligence on key interests and concerns, and they accompany their clients to meetings as needed.
- Providing daily briefs on political developments when Parliament is in session.
- Arranging for Parliamentary Questions (PQs) on issues important for the organisation.

- Providing briefings on topical issues, on an ad hoc basis or on specific issues required by the organisation; when appropriate they produce substantive reports on specific areas of interest.
- Providing analysis of recent political developments and their implications for the business at regular monthly meetings.
- Organising participation at party political conferences and ensuring an effective engagement programme during the events.
- Organising and supporting the overall process when preparing executives for oral evidence to Parliamentary Committees. This will involve developing a substantial Question and Answer brief around the questions suggested by the Clerk to the Committee, and organising a rehearsal session with an expert Chair who is very familiar with such proceedings; they will provide feedback on the rehearsal, not only on the content but also on the tone of the speaker, and suggest the best approach to adopt, considering the Committee interests.
- Helping to organise company events around, for example, selected themes such as 'think tanks' or key influencers, and by suggesting potential attendees drawn from their networks.
- Hosting roundtable discussion forums with a key speaker and range of other interested parties, often in informal settings.

Advisors are important facilitators, but the lead must always be taken by the organisation, from defining the agenda it wants to progress and the detailed narrative for external stakeholders, to the actual lobbying of decision-makers or briefing of key influencers.

Using Advisory Boards

In a rapidly changing marketplace with many stakeholders it is important that business tests its ideas, strategy and messaging in a positive and encouraging environment. One way of achieving this is to create a discussion forum for executives and external experts, in the knowledge that it is confidential, and that advice is provided by people who have the appropriate experience of the business environment but who are unencumbered by the day-to-day running of the business.

Research shows that Advisory Boards are used by companies right across the economy; for example, extraction companies in the primary sector, energy and construction in the secondary sector, and those in retail, tourism, banking, entertainment, and communications and IT services in the tertiary sector.

What is also interesting is that some companies have more than one Advisory Board. EDF Energy in the UK, for example, has in the recent past had three 'Boards' or 'Panels' at the same time, each having different functions and membership: A Stakeholder Panel, a Sustainable Business Panel and a time-limited Competition and Markets Authority (CMA) Stakeholder Panel.

The Carbon Trust, whose mission is to accelerate the move to a sustainable, low-carbon economy, has adopted a slightly different approach, creating a more broad-based Advisory Board to provide their ideas and views on the various

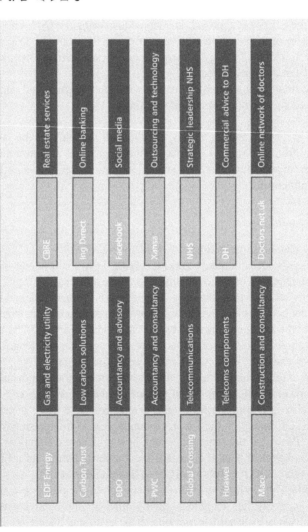

Advisory Boards across the economy

EDF Energy	Gas and electricity utility	Real estate services
Carbon Trust	Low carbon solutions	Online banking
BDO	Accountancy and advisory	Social media
PwC	Accountancy and consultancy	Outsourcing and technology
Global Crossing	Telecommunications	Strategic leadership NHS
Huawei	Telecoms components	Commercial advice to DH
Mace	Construction and consultancy	Online network of doctors

CBRE	
Ing Direct	
Facebook	
Xansa	
NHS	
DH	
Doctors.net.uk	

Illustration 5.13 Advisory Boards across the economy

Advisory Boards provide much-needed independent knowledge, advice and support for an organisation's Executive team.

Notes: BDO, Binder Dijker Otte; PWC, PricewaterhouseCoopers; CBRE, CB Richard Ellis; NHS full title is NHS Leadership Academy; DH, Department of Health.

activities of the organisation. The external advisors were chosen to provide advice on their specialist knowledge and expertise.

There are, then, several options when seeking external expert advice, from individual advisors to a small, high-level Advisory Board. Each option has its strengths, and it is important that they are assessed against a set of criteria that best describe the needs of the business. The ability to influence both the internal and external domain is important, and in simple qualitative terms a high-level Advisory Board may well provide a good option. Such Boards are popular, helping to position the business in a changing market place. They can support the executive by providing expert insight or contacts not readily available elsewhere, and they can augment the knowledge, understanding and strategic thinking of the executive team. Advisory Boards could be a resource to be used to aid the success of the business.

The detailed make-up of the Advisory Board is dependent on what is needed by the business. Ideally it should provide views on market developments and challenge the prevailing business direction; it should also provide knowledge of key decision-making arenas such as Government and its officials, and the regulators, and it should provide insights on public relations and reputation management. Board members may also be needed to make introductions and facilitate discussions with other companies and institutions; and they could act as ambassadors.

Successful Advisory Boards are clear about their collective purpose from the outset, and about the roles and expectations of the chair and the individual members. In terms of modus operandi, this can be light-touch, nimble, flexible and able to focus on a narrow set of issues. There is no need for elections, term limits, committee structures or extensive disclosure of the roles, remuneration or performance.

Ultimately, if the business is to benefit from a high-level Advisory Board, the CEO and his executive team must fully engage with the initiative, to make the best use of the time they have with the Board and to be active in seeking advice and support.

Using consultants

It is almost impossible to carry out a holistic stakeholder engagement programme without using consultants at one time or another. Political Advisors are essential, supporting the formal engagement programme with Parliament and their officials. Independent consultants provide a different essential service, usually on an ad hoc basis for a clearly defined outcome.

It is possible to get advice from a range of independent consultants on almost any issue related to an organisation's activities. At one end of the scale such consultants are 'singleton' experts who have gathered knowledge and experience in an area over a long period of time, perhaps within similar organisations. However, their knowledge can quickly become dated unless refreshed through regular projects from which new useful information and analysis can be added. Some can maintain their credibility with stakeholders by providing specialist forums for discussion that serve not only to maintain valuable networks but also to highlight prevailing interests and concerns. 'Singletons' may be academics, providing

Assessing options for external advice

Criterion [1]	Individual Advisors	'Ad hoc' Advisory Group [2]	'Broad based' Advisory Board	'High level' Advisory Board
Provision of specialist knowledge	YES	YES	YES	POSSIBLY
Able to consult at any time	YES	NO	POSSIBLY	POSSIBLY
Access at operational level	YES	YES	POSSIBLY	NO
Access to expert/board member networks	NO	NO	YES	POSSIBLY
Synergistic benefits	NO	POSSIBLY	YES	YES
Commitment to the organisation	NO	NO	YES	YES
Organisation 'commitment' to follow advice	NO	NO	POSSIBLY	YES
Experts/Board Members as ambassadors	NO	NO	YES	YES
Public relations benefits	NO	NO	POSSIBLY	YES
Ability to refresh at short notice	YES	YES	NO	NO

Illustration 5.14 Assessing options for external advice

There are several options for an organisation in terms of external advice which can be assessed against a set of proprietary criteria.

Note: (1) Cost may be an issue – with ad hoc expert advise the cheapest option and perhaps the Advisory Boards the most expensive, but the benefits are different; (2) Not necessarily the same group each time.

advice or carrying out consultancy services alongside their academic work; they have the advantage of being seeing seen as independent and this affords them a certain credibility with decision-makers and key influencers.

At the other end of the size scale are the large consultancy companies who have significant resources to draw on when carrying out projects. These organisations can conduct their own research and analysis that informs the market, and because of this they can be key influencers. They have their own discussion forums for clients and provide access to their networks. Large consultancy companies are also commissioned to carry out work on behalf of decision-makers and this means they are very well-informed when it comes to new policy developments.

There are many advantages to employing consultants:

- They can provide specialist knowledge not readily available in an organisation, and have strong analytical skills.
- They can devote appropriate resources and their whole attention to the issue or project.
- They have major knowledge networks to draw on for information and analysis.
- They can bring knowledge and experience from similar projects in other organisations and environments.
- They are not compromised by internal 'politics' or bias within organisations.
- Considerable learning by internal stakeholders can result from such interactions.
- They tend to have good communication skills, which makes it easier to deliver concepts and messages.
- They can act on the organisation's behalf with internal and external stakeholders.

There is, naturally, a cost associated with using consultants, and there is a danger that what is thought to be proprietary work ends up being used, perhaps in a different context, to the benefit of others. However, beyond the boundaries of the project, there are no other commitments the organisation needs to worry about.

The major advantage of using consultants is that they are considered to be independent, and therefore their ideas, analyses and proposals are likely to be received as such by decision-makers. It is important that consultants can carry out their brief without being compromised by the demands of the organisation beyond the agreed scope of the work; it is also important they are able to present the output of their work with commitment, making it more likely that it will be accepted in the external domain. In addition to meetings involving the organisation, the consultants and decision-makers, it is possible that the study commissioned can be shared in discussion forums, thus reaching other key influencers, or that a report of the findings can be released through a formal launch event, or selected media, to solicit wider coverage.

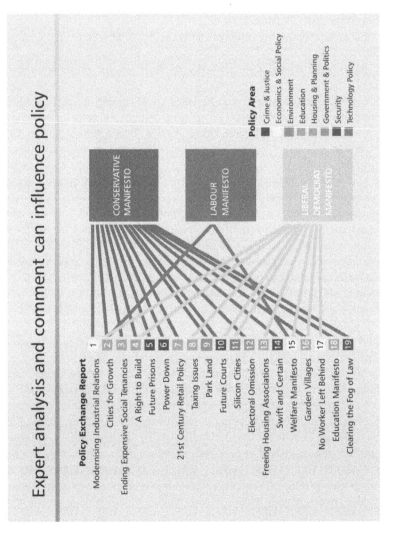

Expert analysis and comment can influence policy

Policy Exchange Report

1 Modernising Industrial Relations
2 Cities for Growth
3 Ending Expensive Social Tenancies
4 A Right to Build
5 Future Prisons
6 Power Down
7 21st Century Retail Policy
8 Taxing Issues
9 Park Land
10 Future Courts
11 Silicon Cities
12 Electoral Omission
13 Freeing Housing Associations
14 Swift and Certain
15 Welfare Manifesto
16 Garden Villages
17 No Worker Left Behind
18 Education Manifesto
19 Clearing the Fog of Law

CONSERVATIVE MANIFESTO

LABOUR MANIFESTO

LIBERAL DEMOCRAT MANIFESTO

Policy Area

Crime & Justice
Economics & Social Policy
Environment
Education
Housing & Planning
Government & Politics
Security
Technology Policy

Illustration 5.15 Expert analysis and comment can influence policy

Think tanks, and other groups and individuals, provide much useful analysis and comment that can inform policy development.

Source: Adapted from the infographic Policy Exchange in the 2015 Manifestos, Policy Exchange infographic, 16 April 2015. Reprinted by permission.

The work of 'think tanks' can provide much useful information for organisations. They can be influential, with their policy work often adopted by political parties to help inform their manifestos. Perhaps more strikingly, Special Advisors appointed by Ministers during their terms of office are often drawn from this group of experts. It is important that organisations create opportunities to interact with 'think tanks', to help inform themselves on new policy ideas that could impact their business.

Summary key points

- A qualitative assessment of political risk and a quantitative assessment of policy and regulatory risk are essential to inform the organisation and its stakeholder engagement programme.
- Executive leadership and commitment are essential in defining the ambition for an organisation in stakeholder engagement, and resources must be made available to match that ambition.
- A 'virtual' team representing different functions within an organisation will be needed to develop and deliver the organisation's story and engage with strategic stakeholders.
- An organisation can draw on a variety of sources for independent advice to complement its own capability.
- A holistic ethical policy supported by strong governance protocols is essential for organisations in their interactions with decision-makers and key influencers.

Case Study 5.1 On the rewards of ambition

One of the most important issues that the leadership of an organisation needs to address is the level of ambition in strategic stakeholder engagement. The rise of EDF Energy in the UK over the past 15 years shows what can be achieved in this area if that ambition is clearly stated, and the resources are deployed to achieve it.

Background

The UK liberalisation process in the 1990s saw considerable inward investment into the energy sector by foreign companies. The EDF Group, largely owned by the French Government, took a strategic decision to enter the market and by 2004 it emerged as a major UK utility with several power stations, a supply business and a networks business.

The rise and rise of EDF Energy

Recognising that the UK government was increasingly sympathetic to New Nuclear Build (NNB), EDF Energy took the highly ambitious step in 2009 of acquiring British Energy, the operator of the eight newest nuclear power stations in the UK. It believed that with its strong nuclear base in France, it could deliver a new fleet of power stations in the UK.

A key feature of EDF Energy's approach was to be very well-organised fully so that it could engage with Government right across the policy and regulation arena, with its CEO Vincent de Rivaz and his Executive team leading the effort and committing considerable resources to the activity. New nuclear stations at Hinkley Point and Sizewell were seen to be the future for the company, but the organisation was also keen to maintain its fossil assets, to develop a renewables portfolio and to bring new innovations to the market.

The company engaged in all the formal government processes, with emphasis on those that affected its nuclear generation. It also ensured it was represented in forums everywhere, from expert roundtables where policy was discussed, to sponsorship of the London Olympics in 2012.

Outcomes

Today EDF Energy is arguably the most prominent energy utility in the country. It has used its existing nuclear power stations to provide resources, both human and financial, for the NNB programme, and has won a contract from Government that guarantees an excellent price for the new stations' output for a significant part of their operating lifetime. The organisation's lobbying effort has been exemplary and a model for all; in addition to its efforts in NNB, its existing nuclear stations have also benefited from new policy initiatives that reward its existing nuclear and renewables generation.

From very humble beginnings, EDF Energy in the UK under the determined leadership of their CEO Vincent de Rivaz articulated an ambitious vision for the company, and then delivered it through an active stakeholder engagement programme.

Case Study 5.2 Stakeholder mapping is an essential activity

A stakeholder mapping process is an essential part of a stakeholder engagement programme. It helps identify the key stakeholders for an issue and establishes how an organisation goes about getting its voice heard by decision-makers and key influencers.

Background

The example in the mapping exercise below relates to carbon pricing, an issue that became part of the Coalition Government's programme in the UK in 2010. The top part of the table shows the entries for one of the key external stakeholders, the Government and its Treasury; the bottom part of the table focuses on the position and actions of an organisation with a mixed portfolio of power station assets including carbon-intensive fossil-powered generation. There are many other stakeholders that would be captured in a similar way in this mapping exercise. The stakeholder map is updated as new information becomes available and the outcomes from mitigation actions are known.

Example entries on carbon pricing in a stakeholder mapping exercise:

Specific issue or activity	Stakeholder group	Role of stakeholder group	Stakeholder sub-group	Role of stakeholder sub-group	Position on issue or activity	Stakeholder action on issue or activity
Carbon pricing	Government	To meet carbon targets	Treasury	Manage UK's finances	Increase environmental taxes	Bring forward appropriate policies

Organisation position on issue of or activity	Mitigation actions on issue or activity	Potential outcome of mitigation actions	Actual outcomes mitigation actions	Potential further mitigation actions	Actual outcomes of further mitigation actions	Review and lessons learned by the organisation
Against the introduction of the Carbon Price Floor arguing: a price for carbon already exists through the EU ETS; other regulation will force high carbon technologies off the electricity system; and the new initiative will create unwarranted windfalls for existing nuclear and renewables.	Respond to the formal consultations; hold bilateral meetings with key officials and provide a detailed analysis of the implications; and seek alliances with those who oppose the creation of the carbon price floor.	Optimal outcome would be for the carbon price floor initiative not to go ahead; alternatively, if it does go ahead that the price trajectory going forward should not be too far removed from the price in the EU ETS.	Price trajectory was set at a level considerably higher than prevailing cost of carbon in the EU ETS. Also, Climate Change Levy exemptions removed for Combined Heat and Power (CHP).	Continue to make the case for modifying the price trajectory at the HMT annual review; and work with others who have CHP assets to lobby for a return in value of the exemptions removed.	The carbon price floor trajectory was abandoned for the short term and the carbon price was kept at a constant value; the value of the original exemptions returned, albeit in a different way.	Lessons learned: pay close attention to the policies set out in political manifestos; agree on organisation position early in life of administration; use stakeholder mapping exercise to identify potential allies and competitors.

Case Study 5.3 Getting organised to meet specific challenges

An organisation must always be ready and able to respond to consultations, inquiries and investigations by various Government bodies. Any response to these requires an effective internal process that draws on knowledge that resides in the organisation, and a governance protocol to ensure that the submission is validated and signed-off by an Executive lead in the process. A Competition and Mergers Authority (CMA) investigation is particularly difficult for organisations because it tests all aspects of the internal process.

Background

On 26 June 2014, the independent regulator Ofgem (Office of Gas and Electricity Markets) formally asked the CMA to carry out an investigation into the electricity and gas markets in the UK. ENGIE (previously known as GDF SUEZ), along with all others in the electricity sector, were required to respond to consultations and to provide data and other information, over an expected 18-month investigation. It was important that the company was organised for what would be a long and resource-consuming interaction with the CMA.

The approach adopted by ENGIE

An internal briefing was carried out when the investigation was announced, which focused on the fundamentals: issues in scope, the legal requirements on the company, the timetable and CMA Panel Member profiles. The briefing identified:

- Areas of business likely to be involved and the ENGIE contact for these areas.
- The nature and scope of likely requests.
- Support that might be needed (analytical, legal and finance).
- Confirmation of the internal process to ensure expeditious, accurate, and thorough responses.

A 'virtual' team of experts was set up within the company, led by one of the executives. The team covered all the CMA's potential areas of interest, and was supported by an administrative assistant who created an electronic platform to facilitate interactions between the team, and to maintain a secure area for all confidential data and formal responses to the inquiry. A protocol was established for sign-off of any data, information or document that was sent to the CMA.

Outcomes

Over the course of the next two years, the company responded to a number of formal consultations and requests for data sets and information on the company's operations that went back several years; follow-up questions were common and there were several formal meetings between the CMA and ENGIE experts. The way the company was organised for this task was crucial to its successful interaction with the CMA. The inquiry outcomes did not impact ENGIE operations and were helpful to the industry.

Case Study 5.4 Focusing on risks to the business

Policy and regulatory risk is now high on executive and Board agendas. An organisation needs a methodology that provides this information in a clear and credible way, one that expresses the scope and scale of these risks, and the potential for mitigation actions. Below are two example entries to a *Policy and Regulatory Risk Register* that demonstrate how risks can be assessed and the implications for an organisation's stakeholder engagement programme.

Background

ENGIE (previously known as GDF SUEZ) owned and operated several power stations in the UK, traded electricity and gas in the wholesale markets, and had a retail business servicing the industrial and commercial sector in 2012. These activities were subject to several new policy and regulatory initiatives that would be brought forward over the next few years and impact the business, mostly negatively, but in a few cases positively. In total 19 individual risks and four opportunities were identified for the business.

Risk Register entries

The Government Affairs Policy and Regulatory team developed a Risk Register that contained all the key elements associated with each risk. Below are two examples of new policy initiatives aimed at limiting the impact of fossil plant operations on the environment, with all the relevant information captured in one place. The methodology is described in detail in the text.

Issue number	Owner	Risk opportunity	Description	Timeframe urgency (1)	Estimated value per year	Initiative lifetime	Total estimated value
1	LB	Risk	**IED Transposition** – IED emission limits may force some fossil power stations to close early or limit operation severely if abatement upgrade is not available or is prohibitively expensive	Short High	£8m	5 years	£40m
2	LB	Risk	**Water Abstraction Reform** – Existing plant may lose valuable abstraction rights. New plant may not be able to secure abstraction rights for whole planned lifetime of the plant	Short Medium	£1m	20 years	£20m

Issue Number	Start date	Initial Probability	Initial Impact	Mitigation	Forecast Probability	Forecast Impact	Rating
1	2016	5	5	Develop concept of mid-merit plant to be included in the BREF to allow continued operation	5	3	25
2	2016	4	3	Engage with DEFRA throughout the consultation process	4	1	12

Notes to table: LB, the internal expert lead; IED, Industrial Emissions Directive; (1), 'Timeframe' and 'Urgency' relate to how soon the initiative will impact the business and how soon action should be mobilised, respectively; mid-merit power stations are brought onto the system when the electricity demand lies between peak load and base load; BREF, Best Available Technology reference documents; DEFRA, Department of Environment, Food and Rural Affairs.

Illustration 5.16 Mitigating specific risks

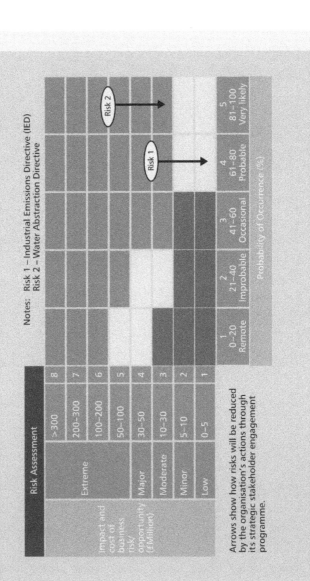

Mitigating specific risks

Notes: Risk 1 – Industrial Emissions Directive (IED)
Risk 2 – Water Abstraction Directive

Risk Assessment							
Extreme	>300	8					
	200–300	7					
	100–200	6					
	50–100	5					
Major	30–50	4					
Moderate	10–30	3					
Minor	5–10	2					
Low	0–5	1					

Impact and cost of business risk/opportunity (£Million)

	1	2	3	4	5
	0–20	21–40	41–60	61–80	81–100
	Remote	Improbable	Occasional	Probable	Very likely

Probability of Occurrence (%)

Arrows show how risks will be reduced by the organisation's actions through its strategic stakeholder engagement programme.

Outcomes

The Risk Register was a live document. The entries were of sufficient detail to give the executive team comfort that policy and regulatory risks associated with the business had been identified and quantified, and that mitigating actions were under way. Government interventions can also bring opportunities for the business, and these too were treated in the same way. The register also helped to focus resources on the issues that would result in the greatest benefit to the business.

Case Study 5.5 The importance of governance protocols

A governance protocol ensures that any material sent outside the organisation has been agreed, validated and signed off by an appropriate executive. This is particularly important in relation to data and information provided to Government departments and their public bodies who may use this information to make decisions. The lack of an adequate protocol can have potentially damaging outcomes, which was the case for ENGIE in its interactions with the Department of Environment Food and Rural Affairs (DEFRA).

Background

Companies were asked to provide DEFRA with nitrogen oxide emissions information from their fossil power stations so that they could be included in the UK's Transitional National Plan (TNP); this was needed for the implementation of a European Union Directive. Failure to enter the TNP would have severely restricted the running of ENGIE's fossil power stations and compromised their future.

The company response

The company made an error in the data that it provided to DEFRA in the preliminary call for information, omitting one of the two gas turbines at its Deeside Power station. The error came about because of an inadequate governance protocol, and this meant that if the data was not corrected, this turbine would not be allocated a nitrogen oxides emission 'bubble', and this would restrict its future operation. In the event, getting DEFRA to make the correction took a long time and required considerable effort on behalf of the company, with a very real risk of failure right up to the time the TNP was submitted to the European Commission.

Outcomes

A review of the TNP experience was carried out and a new protocol established, which was used when the company was asked to provide data and other information to the Competition and Mergers Authority (CMA) Investigation into the workings of the energy market:

- An executive was charged with leading the project and providing the requisite oversight and sign-off of any data and information sent to the CMA.
- A single point of contact was established between the CMA and the company.
- A project team was set up involving all parts of the business that would be called upon to contribute data and information.
- An electronic platform was set up where all the material was kept for review and filing, including requests for data, follow-up queries, meeting notes and email exchanges.

The company complied with all the CMA requests in the correct form and on time. The protocols established proved a very effective way to deliver complex requests from different parts of the company in an efficient and highly effective way.

Case Study 5.6 Briefings Booklet for executives and managers

It is crucially important that executives and their managers have a good understanding of policy and regulatory issues. One way of achieving this is to create a Briefings Booklet that contains one-page summaries for each policy and regulatory issue, using a simple template for all entries; below is the briefing on the UK's Carbon Price Support Mechanism used for Executives at ENGIE.

Background to the issue

The UK Government was concerned that the EU Emissions Trading Scheme (EU ETS) was not providing a sufficiently strong carbon price on its own to encourage investment in low-carbon technologies; the Government was also keen to see a higher contribution by environmental taxes to overall taxation. An important consideration is the extra revenue to the Treasury from this initiative. The Government has focused its attention on the electricity sector believing that this will feed through to all parts of the economy.

What is it? How does it work?

A Carbon Price Support (CPS) mechanism imposes a minimum price for carbon dioxide (CO_2) for fossil generation in the electricity sector; this cost is passed through to the wholesale price for electricity. The CPS came into force on 1 April 2013 and a price set at £16/tonne CO_2 for the financial year 2013/14, rising to £30/tonne CO_2 in 2020/21 (all in 2009 prices). The carbon price levied is made up of two components:

1. The EU ETS carbon price; the electricity sector will buy carbon permits in Phase 3 of the EU ETS scheme (2013–2020) from government via an auction.
2. The Climate Change Levy will be modified so that a tax on fossil fuels will be applied at rates that take their carbon content into account.

Treasury will take a view on the forward market price for carbon and then set the carbon tax on fossil fuel to bridge the gap to the minimum carbon price for that year. Treasury will set an actual price for carbon two years ahead in the budget and indicative values for the two subsequent years.

GDF SUEZ Energy UK-Europe (now ENGIE UK and Ireland) perspective

The Carbon Price Support Mechanism is arguably not needed to underpin investment in low-carbon technologies because the Contact for Difference mechanism has been designed to do this. It also places the UK economy at a competitive disadvantage when compared to other European countries and indeed countries further afield. Future Governments will have to consider whether the carbon price floor values to 2020, and beyond to 2030, are sustainable or even necessary.

Case Study 5.7 Building alliances

Trade associations provide forums for their members to meet with decision-makers and this is helpful to companies. But there are occasions, however, when an informal alliance amongst a group of companies may be a more effective way of engaging with decision-makers. This was the case when the Independent Generators Group was formed to give this group an important voice within the electricity industry.

Background

In 2010, the electricity sector was dominated by the six biggest utilities, who between them supplied nearly all domestic customers, a significant part of the Industrial and Commercial sector, and most of the electricity needed to meet demand. This group not only had individual power and access to decision-makers, but also created the UK Business Council for Sustainable Development to promote their interests; they also continued to play a prominent role within one of the main industry Trade Associations.

Market participants' response

The Independent Generators' Group (IGG) was created by a group of companies that decided to work together, informally, on issues of common interest. The group provided a focus and a more effective voice to represent the views of an important group within the UK electricity industry. Collectively, the IGG brought with them some attributes that were attractive to decision-makers; for example, they:

- Contributed more than 20% of the UK's capacity and generation, contributing to the UK's electricity security of supply.
- Had interests in a wide range of technologies including, gas, coal, oil, pump-storage, renewables and nuclear.
- Provided employment for several thousand highly-skilled people, directly and indirectly.
- Participated in all parts of the electricity demand profile, providing an additional source of electricity to the wholesale market and promoting competition in the markets.
- Wanted to invest heavily in improving their existing assets, and in a wide range of new generation projects, both small and large, thermal and renewable.

- Included several, financially strong international companies, with knowledge and experience across different markets.

Outcomes

Once formed, the IGG was of great interest to Government, regulators and other key stakeholders because it was a new 'voice' to go alongside the views being propagated by the six large utility companies. The CEOs of the IGG companies met regularly with the Secretary of State to discuss issues of common interest. At the working level, an IGG Steering Group met with officials and regulators, again on a regular basis, to provide comment on new policy developments. It was not necessary for all companies to agree on every issue, but rather to present views and potential solutions for policy development, and to note differences that existed.

Case Study 5.8 Importance of independent advice

In a rapidly changing political, technical and market environment it is important that an organisation can seek independent advice on its activities. In many cases this advice may come from non-executive directors (NEDs) on the Board, but there are cases where the independent advice needed to support a business may not be available to executives, so an alternative is needed. This was the case when ENGIE in the UK decided to create an Advisory Board to help inform their decision-making.

Background

ENGIE, a global company listed on the Paris Stock Exchange, and with headquarters in that city, was reorganised to form 24 largely geographical Business Units (BUs) and several support functions that cut across them. There is no formal direct link between the Board in Paris and the leadership of the BUs, and very little access to the NEDs of the main Board. Independent advice was not readily available.

Approach adopted

The creation of a high-level Advisory Board was chosen as the best option for ENGIE in the UK. A project team was set up that included the CEO and an ENGIE manager to oversee the process, supported by an external specialist provider who had a track record in this area.

A briefing paper for potential Advisory Board members was prepared and this was in three parts: a description of the wider ENGIE Group, a focus on the activities of ENGIE in the UK and a summary of expectations from the Board and its members. A critical part of the process was to establish what was needed in terms of the specialist knowledge to support the business. Briefly, this ranged from the workings of government at national and local levels, to the markets in which the company operates; knowledge of the many aspects of sustainable development, and of potential future developments, particularly in the digital revolution, was also important for the business. By necessity, then, each of the members of a small high-level Advisory Board had to be able to contribute to more than one area for effective coverage of the issues.

Outcomes

Following a thorough selection process driven by the external specialist provider, the Advisory Board was complete. An induction programme for the Board was developed and implemented. Each Board meeting had a theme, and an internal expert and a Board member were designated as leads for the discussion; this approach proved highly effective in eliciting a series of recommendations from the Board. An engagement programme was also developed for the Board that involved internal and external activities and events, so that all parts of the organisation could benefit from this initiative.

Case Study 5.9 Strategic stakeholder engagement programme review

An often-forgotten aspect of a strategic engagement programme is a formal, end-of-year review of activities. It is an important activity because it helps highlight what was achieved during that year, and informs the future stakeholder engagement programme; it also gives comfort to the executive team that resources are being used effectively. Below is an example review of the political strategy component of an engagement programme.

Context for the review

British Energy (BE, now part of EDF Energy) had a small team of Government Affairs professionals who developed and delivered the political engagement programme in the financial year 2007/08. Below is a summary of the formal review of the programme presented to BE's executive, which highlights the nature, scope and deliverables by the political engagement programme.

Elements of the review 2007/08

Political strategy: The political strategy focused on Ministers and their Advisors and MPs in Westminster; this was complemented by separate Government Affairs programmes with officials in Whitehall, and political audiences in Scotland. The programme had four aims:

- Repositioning British Energy as the key British nuclear actor, around a wider theme of 'competence, jobs, skills, communities'.
- Influencing the Conservatives (then in opposition) to encourage them to support Nuclear New Build (NNB) and BE.
- Reinforcing Parliamentary understanding of, and support for, NNB at all levels.
- Managing the process of relevant Bills – and their Committee stages – to ensure that BE's interests were heard.

Political audit: An annual audit of opinion among key political opinion formers was undertaken for BE by a Public Affairs consultancy. This included views on BE itself and on the Company's place within wider energy issues.

Lessons from 2007/08 programme: The year proved to be significant for BE in Westminster. The Government provided support for NNB as a central part of its energy and environmental policy, and set in motion a range of initiatives to encourage timely delivery. A consensus also emerged between the two major political parties on the principal of a balanced energy mix which included nuclear. Politicians increasingly saw British Energy as an important company in the future of energy policy.

Looking ahead to 2008/09: It is proposed that the Government Affairs team will refine the organisation's messages and the stakeholders it will engage with, in light of the lessons learned from the previous year. There would be a greater focus on explaining 'deliverables', for example on the reality of the waste management process, and economic and commercial elements of NNB. The priority would be on engaging the political community in greater depth of detail as well as continuing to widen the breadth of contacts.

6 Delivering the stakeholder engagement strategy

Chapter summary

This chapter draws together the different elements covered in the earlier chapters but focuses on 'how to engage' rather than 'why it is important to engage'. It is rich in examples and Case Studies that will help the reader to establish what they can do in their circumstances. For example, it addresses how an organisation might approach formal processes such as consultations and inquiries, and informal processes such as briefing Ministers and officials. It highlights how to engage with political and Civil Service decision-makers, and with influential independent third parties; and it demonstrates the importance of having a presence in influential forums organised by an array of interested stakeholders. It also shows how to raise the profile of an organisation so that in time it is invited to the top table of decision-making. Reviewing performance and measuring success or otherwise, however difficult, are essential activities; to help with these activities, a review process is suggested and several metrics are presented to measure success, both quantitative and qualitative, that will gain credibility with internal audiences.

6.1 The importance of formal and informal processes

The nature and scope of formal and informal processes available to organisations were discussed in detail in Chapter 4. An organisation can be reactive, by engaging with formal government processes, such as consultations, inquiries and investigations, and proactive through several informal processes including bilateral meetings with Ministers and officials. The formal processes provide a clear direction of travel in government policy and provide opportunities for organisations to present their views and comments; these views and comments can be disseminated to a wider community of interested stakeholders who may then relay the organisation's key messages within their networks. Informal processes, on the other hand, offer opportunities for organisations to set the agenda, to place key concerns and ideas in front of decision-makers and key influencers.

The nature of a company's engagement matters because organisations that take a more active approach are much likelier than others to connect directly

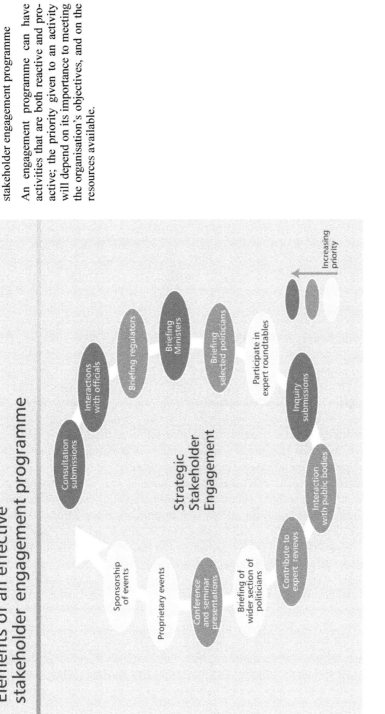

Elements of an effective stakeholder engagement programme

Illustration 6.1 Elements of an effective stakeholder engagement programme

An engagement programme can have activities that are both reactive and proactive; the priority given to an activity will depend on its importance to meeting the organisation's objectives, and on the resources available.

with stakeholders, instead of hiring lobbyists or relying on industry associations to engage on their behalf.

'How to reinvent the external-affairs function',
McKinsey, July 2016

Both formal and informal processes have their strengths and weaknesses when viewed from an organisation's perspective, and successful outcomes can be fleeting. But it is important that organisations engage in both processes or risk leaving the field open to their competitors. A mapping exercise will highlight the priority afforded each stakeholder and activity.

6.2 Submissions to Consultations, Inquiries and Reviews

There are several types of formal process that organisations can engage with to try and influence developments in the policy and regulatory arena, including consultations, inquiries and reviews. For example, the Department of Business, Energy and Industrial Strategy (BEIS) and its Parliamentary Committee address issues that affect the UK's economic activity, and they use these processes to engage with stakeholders:

- **Consultations:** These are the main vehicle by which Government and other public bodies such as the regulators seek views from interested stakeholders on new initiatives. A recent example is BEIS's *Building Our Industrial Policy*, a 'Green' Paper published in early 2017. This paper signalled the start of a process to establish the industrial needs of the country over the next generation and was aimed at organisations active across the UK economy. The paper not only provided much useful information on the economic and social well-being of the UK, but also posed a series of questions, 38 in total, to all who wanted to comment and express their views.
- **Inquiries:** These are carried out by Committees in both Houses of Parliament largely to scrutinise existing Government policy, and by doing so, to highlight areas of concern and present recommendations for improvement. A recent example is the BEIS Committee inquiry titled: *The Future World of Work and Rights of Workers*, launched in late 2016. As with all inquiries, it will involve both written and oral evidence, focused, on this occasion, on eight key questions; written evidence is voluntary but there is an expectation that an invitation by the Committee to provide oral evidence will be accepted.
- **Reviews:** These tend to be ad hoc in nature, carried out, for example, by prominent expert individuals such as Lord Stern or by a Royal Commission. In late 2016, BEIS announced it had commissioned a review of the Small Business Research Initiative (SBRI) to identify barriers facing small businesses in the innovation area. The review was led by an industry expert who is free to consult stakeholders, gather information and data, and to provide recommendations to Government.

There is an art to responding to consultations to make it more likely that an organisation's messages are heard, from the template it uses to the way the response is written. It is important that the organisation is consistent in the way it deals with consultations, and to develop a reputation for delivering high-quality, well-argued submissions. It is often helpful to the reader if the submission contains a brief description of the organisation and its operations, and a statement as to why the issue(s) is important. It is also helpful if it contains an executive summary with the main points highlighted, ensuring the officials do not miss what is considered essential.

Consultation responses often require considerable effort, with contributions from several internal and – on the odd occasion when appropriate – external experts; there is a clearly stated deadline to consultations. The organisation should have an established process of producing such responses, with a lead author who is charged with gathering views and preparing the organisation's position, and a stringent validation process and executive sign-off, before it is sent to external audiences. There may be added value if the organisation's response can be shared with other stakeholders, either directly or indirectly, by publishing it on the organisation's website; clearly this affords the opportunity that others will incorporate the key messages and supporting arguments in their formal submissions to the consultation.

Often the consultation exercises consist of a series of questions set around several specific themes associated with a policy initiative. It is important to answer the questions in as much detail and with as much supporting evidence as possible. The government sets out what it wants to achieve through these questions, but organisations are also able to provide additional information or raise other issues they believe have not been covered by the consultation document. It is not always clear whether these additional issues will be picked up by the Government's process, particularly in a consultation that is covering considerable ground, and when different officials or their consultants are assigned set questions and asked to analyse and to produce a summary of responses; it is possible that additional issues raised by the organisation, which are outside the scope of the questions, are missed.

The submission can be confidential, particularly if the evidence contains proprietary information. In the event of a Freedom of Information (FOI) request, officials will seek permission from the organisation before releasing the details requested and the organisation can deny permission.

Inquiries by Parliamentary Committees are slightly different from consultations. The questions are more general in nature, and if it is an issue that will solicit a large response, there is a limit placed on the number of words in an organisation's submission. Nonetheless, as with consultations, a rigorous approach is required when preparing an inquiry response, with relevant information and clear arguments underpinned by evidence. Once again, a description of the organisation and an executive summary are helpful to officials and their advisor(s), as they prepare a summary of views expressed by consultees, to help the Committee prepare for oral examination of witnesses.

An organisation can offer to provide oral evidence to a Committee, if the issue is sufficiently important, by approaching the Clerk who will then discuss it with the Chair; alternatively, the Committee may formally invite the organisation to put forward an executive, normally the CEO, to act as a witness and provide additional oral evidence. Such an invitation is not normally declined, and it is important that the CEO, or whoever is asked to represent the organisation, is well briefed on the organisation's submission and has a thorough Question and Answer brief. The 'witness' should also undergo a rehearsal with an Expert Panel, the members of which have experience in the way oral sessions are run. A rehearsal is crucial, however accomplished the witness may be in other forums, not least because the oral evidence is normally relayed live through the Parliamentary Channel and is recorded and formally published along with the Committee's findings and recommendations.

As with consultations there will be a deadline for written evidence but with a much shorter timescale, and little opportunity for an extension; oral evidence will be on set days and advertised to allow other interested stakeholders to attend.

Inquiries are an excellent way of putting views on the record because they are more transparent than consultations and the Government must respond to the Committee findings. Inquiries do tend to be backward-looking at existing policy, but do nonetheless offer an opportunity for change if that policy is not working.

Government-commissioned reviews tend to be highly influential. For example, the Committee on Climate Change (CCC), which advises the Government on how it could meet its decarbonisation targets, was set up following the Stern Review, and the recent creation of the National Infrastructure Commission (NIC) came about because of the Armitt Review. In both cases, it was possible for organisations to contribute to the Review in their formative stage by providing written submissions, or through working groups, roundtables and even bilateral discussions with the team supporting the lead author. These reviews are usually broader in scope to consultations and inquiries but can set the policy direction for the Government.

As indicated in Chapter 4, if organisations are unhappy with the way that Government has reached its policy conclusions, they can challenge the conclusions through a Judicial Review (JR) in a Court of Law. It is fair to say that the Government and its public bodies rarely lose a case that goes to JR. Nonetheless it is an important part of the checks and balances in the democratic system that organisations can, and occasionally do, take the government to task on its decisions. NGOs such as Greenpeace have proved very successful in raising awareness on issues such as new nuclear build through this high-profile legal process.

Organisations can engage with JR in one of two ways: they can initiate a JR through a formal legal process if they believe the Government decision-making is flawed and that it is harmful to their business; alternatively, they can be named as 'Interested Parties' and can contribute their views in written or oral form to the process. In both cases, they will need legal counsel to support their efforts.

6.3 Briefing key audiences

6.3.1 *Political decision-makers*

The most important decision-makers are Government Ministers in the form of Secretaries of State of Civil Service departments who sit in the Cabinet, and Ministers and Under-Secretaries who are responsible for portfolios within the departments. Unfortunately, there tends to be a high turnover in these roles; for example, the Department of Energy and Climate Change (DECC) was set up in 2008 and in the period to 2016, at which point it merged with the Department of Business, Innovation and Skills (BIS), it had four Secretaries of State and eight Ministers of State for Energy. This means the organisation must be willing to brief new Ministers, and their Special Advisors, often having to go over the same material and issues.

Gaining access to Ministers for bilateral meetings can be difficult for an organisation, but not impossible. It may be necessary, and sensible, to meet with the Minister's Special Advisor in the first instance to brief them on the nature of the issue and explore whether it is appropriate to escalate it to the Minister or if the issue can be dealt with elsewhere.

> Much depends on who Government think they should listen to – either by virtue of being important national players, or being seen to having something in the way of knowledge or information which policy-makers believe would be useful to them.
>
> *Expert Panel Member Joan MacNaughton, CB Hon FEI,*
> *Chair of the Climate Group and the Energy Academy of Europe*

It is often easier to meet with these decision-makers when more than one organisation is present; for example, as part of a group from industry, perhaps facilitated by the sector trade association. The organisation's messages, however, will likely be diluted by the number of comments around the table. Ministers prefer such group interactions because they can gather views on key issues from across the sector at the same time.

Somewhere between individual organisations and trade associations lie small groups of organisations that share common objectives on selected issues. A strategic alliance between these organisations often makes it more likely that a meeting with Ministers can be organised, particularly if the informal group has distinctive attributes they can bring to the table that are valued by Government. An example of such a sector sub-set is the Independent Generators Group, which was formed to provide an alternative voice of the electricity industry to the major utilities and proved very successful in having regular meetings with the Ministers on a range of issues.

All meetings by Ministers are attended by officials who may provide expert opinion if needed and who keep a record of what is said; Special Advisors may also be present. It is important that the briefings tabled at the meetings are documents that are self-explanatory in nature so that they can be shared by decision-makers outside of the formal meetings. However, there is also the chance that documents 'leak', so considerable care needs to be taken in their preparation, the assumption must be that even if the document is marked 'confidential', the content may be discussed more widely.

Another tranche of Parliamentarians that are influential in policy and regulatory issues are the Committees in both Houses of Parliament. Normally, each Committee has a Chair and around ten Members drawn from across the political landscape and they scrutinise Government policy, assess performance against objectives and make recommendations; it is normal practice for the Government to respond to inquiry reports. Committee Members are receptive to bilateral meetings because they can improve their knowledge of the sectors they have an interest in, and they can consider inquiry topics put forward by sector representatives.

Members of Parliament (MPs) in constituencies where an organisation has operations are very important because of the shared interest in the welfare of the employees and local communities. It is important that they are briefed on a regular basis, in Parliament or at the operational site so that they are kept right up to date. In the event of a problem at the site, or in the organisation, these MPs are high on the contact list for briefings on the issue. They can be valuable allies when a concern needs to be raised with Ministers, or the organisation wishes to table a Parliamentary Question. Occasionally, sites may need to be closed and the site MP is arguably the most important stakeholder; they will want to be briefed so that they can respond to local media enquiries and help seek solutions for the site, its employees and the local communities.

There will be MPs from the opposition parties who need to be briefed, particularly those whose remit covers the organisation's sector. These MPs are particularly grateful for such briefings because they do not have the resources or research capability to remain sufficiently informed as they go about their business of asking questions of the Minister. These briefings offer another avenue to get key organisational messages into decision-making circles.

There are highly knowledgeable and influential Members in the House of Lords. A holistic engagement programme will include those Members who retain an interest in the organisation's sector, perhaps because they have been Government Ministers in the past, responsible for the activities of the sector, or on rare occasions have worked in the sector before being awarded a peerage. Building a relationship with these Lords is important for three reasons: they tend to play the same role for a long period of time and are known for their knowledge and expertise in both Houses; they can be approached to consider amendments to new legislation as it passes through the House of Lords; and they can ask questions of the Minister in relation to issues of importance to the organisation.

There are many Parliamentary Groups, most of which continue across elections. Such groups hold seminars, events and occasionally roundtables; an example in the energy area is the Parliamentary Group on Energy Studies (PGES). The various PGES forums offer an opportunity for the organisation's experts to interact with interested stakeholders from both Houses of Parliament, and the wider community, to raise issues in a simple and non-judgemental way; it also offers an

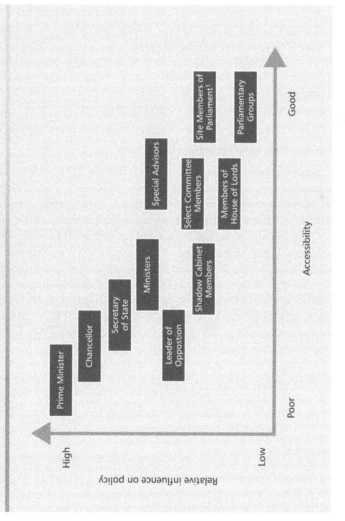

Engaging with political decision-makers

Relative influence on policy (vertical axis: High → Low)

Accessibility (horizontal axis: Poor → Good)

- Prime Minister
- Chancellor
- Secretary of State
- Ministers
- Leader of Opposition
- Special Advisors
- Select Committee Members
- Shadow Cabinet Members
- Members of House of Lords
- Site Members of Parliament1
- Parliamentary Groups

Illustration 6.2 Engaging with political decision-makers

Some decision-makers are more important than others and some are easier to engage with; nonetheless, an organisation should strive to engage with the full cross-section of politicians, increasing its chances of getting its views heard in decision-making circles.

Note: 1 Site Members of Parliament are those Members whose constituencies include an organisation's operations.

opportunity for the organisation to raise its profile by offering a presentation by the CEO on a topical issue, or by sponsoring the PGES annual dinner, which may be attended by the appropriate Minister and interested MPs and Lords.

It is also important to develop relationships with Special Advisors, since they are experts in their own right in the areas covered by the Department in which they serve, they have access to Ministers and Committee Chairs, and they can set the agenda of both offices. Their lifetime may only be as that of their Minister, a hazard of the role. Nonetheless, if the organisation has an urgent issue that needs addressing at high levels of Government, Special Advisors offer the first port of call, and it would be helpful if they were already briefed on the company and its operations.

There are also Advisors for Committee inquiries, although these are appointed once the issue being scrutinised is agreed upon. These Advisors tend to be academics and help the Clerk to the Committee in defining the scope of the inquiry, help to frame the required written evidence through questions, and brief the Committee Members ahead of the oral sessions. They will normally attend these sessions and help in the preparation of the final inquiry report.

It is often helpful to meet with those Clerks of Committees that have an interest in the organisation's sector for two reasons: to get an idea of the issues the Committees are looking at in the future, and to put forward ideas for issues they may want to consider as they consider their forward programmes.

6.3.2 Engaging with officials in the Civil Service

Officials are charged with implementing policy decisions, and this is often a difficult task because their work will likely affect organisations, with some 'winners' and some 'losers'. They must be seen to be fair and transparent even though in practice the policy direction and the broad outline of the potential outcomes of what needs to be achieved would have been set by their Ministers. Of course, when under pressure from stakeholders they can simply say they are carrying out the wishes of their political masters; for this reason, it is important that the engagement programme involves both politicians and officials because both play a role in the decision-making process: politicians have the final say as to what is implemented, while officials have a clearer appreciation of implications for the sector involved and its stakeholders, and can use this information to influence the detailed implementation of the policy initiative.

> Policy-makers can quickly be turned off, for example, by naked special pleading.
>
> *Expert Panel Member Joan MacNaughton, CB Hon FEI,*
> *Chair of the Climate Group and the Energy Academy of Europe*

As with politicians, it is easier to meet some officials and difficult to meet others; for example, it is perhaps unnecessary to meet with the Head of the Civil Service on policy-related issues unless there are initiatives in which Whitehall needs business as a whole to be involved. However, regular high-level discussions

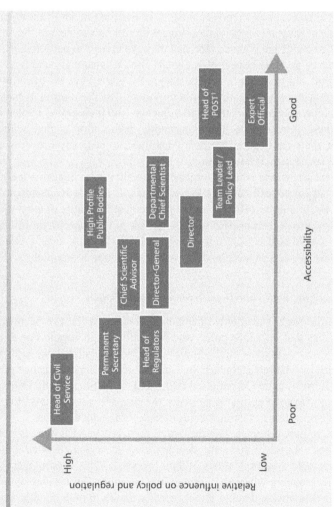

Engaging with policy and regulation key influencers

Illustration 6.3 Engaging with policy and regulation key influencers

An organisation should seek to engage with officials and other key influencers, although it may not always be possible to gain access in some cases. Bilateral meetings with key influencers will be appropriate on some issues, and sector meetings more useful on other issues.

Note: 1, POST, Parliamentary Office of Science and Technology.

between the organisation and Permanent Secretaries of departments are appropriate, particularly on policy direction. Permanent Secretaries are extremely able individuals who must look after the interests of their Ministers and manage resources that often involve several thousand expert civil servants and a budget to match. This level of responsibility is equivalent to that of a CEO of a major commercial organisation, and suggests that meetings with Permanent Secretaries should ideally be the same level.

The most common interaction with the Civil Service happens at the operational level between an organisation's experts and officials charged with the detailed implementation of policy. If there is a major shift in policy or a new initiative entirely, the Department will organise regular roundtables to keep interested stakeholders briefed and to gather views. It is important that the organisation is one of the stakeholders invited to such roundtables, either in its own right, or as part of an alliance, or as a representative of its trade association; an organisation's experts, then, must develop relationships with officials to ensure they are aware that such meetings are planned, and that they are invited to participate.

It is fair to say that expert officials are open to meetings, and have increasingly sought the opinions of organisations by embarking on their own stakeholder engagement programmes. It is important that these officials have a good understanding of the sectors they will influence with their policy implementation; organisations, then, can use the opportunities afforded to engage with officials to provide their views about the policy involved, to raise any concerns they may have, and suggest potential solutions.

There are occasions when an organisation believes its concerns are not being heard by an expert official, and in such cases, it will be necessary to escalate the issue beyond those officials, to the programme Directors or even the Special Advisors who will then bring it to the attention of the appropriate Minister. This approach should be used sparingly by organisations because it can erode goodwill between the two sets of stakeholders, even if the action is justified.

6.3.3 Engaging with Non-Departmental Public Bodies

The organisation's stakeholder mapping exercises will have identified those public bodies that influence policy and regulation for its sector. For example, in the energy sector, notable public bodies include the regulator, the Office for Gas and Electricity Markets (Ofgem), the Committee on Climate Change (CCC), the National Infrastructure Commission (NIC) and the National Audit Office (NAO). All of these have the ability to influence the success of an organisation, from its day-to-day operations to its future business development activities.

Experts in public bodies, like the rest of the Civil Service, are very bright but they do not necessarily have the detailed level of sector knowledge needed to fully understand the implications of their proposals. This is particularly the case on technical matters where they rely on the literature, discussions with academics and consultants, and some sector representatives to help develop their ideas.

There is a clear need and opportunity for organisations to help with this process to ensure the best possible outcomes for the public, the sector and themselves.

A holistic engagement programme should include regular meetings with public bodies. This is because they have a measure of independence from their sponsoring Government departments, which gives them credibility across the stakeholder spectrum, from politicians to the public, and because of this independence, they can be highly influential. Also, the work of some public bodies, like the CCC and NIC, receives considerable publicity, and rightly so, considering the potential implications of their recommendations. An organisation needs to engage with such influential bodies, to put forward its ideas with the underpinning evidence, and it is possible they will be adopted and disseminated widely.

6.3.4 Participation in sector working groups, roundtables and other forums

There is ample opportunity to engage with sector stakeholders through the work of trade associations at the regional, national and international level. These representative bodies rely on committees, working groups and task forces to establish common positions for the sector that can then be shared with Government and public bodies, and with the wider public. An organisation must engage with its trade association programme, not least because it normally pays a significant annual subscription and it wants to get value for that investment. It will also want to ensure that its views and ideas are heard alongside other, competitor organisations that are also members of the association. Government is very fond of consulting trade associations because it believes that it has a better chance of getting a consensus view on any potential policy proposals; and if that consensus is not there, it will get an idea of the degree of disagreement within the sector.

Some organisations with operations in one country can develop and deliver bespoke messages for its decision-making arena; it may have the option of bilateral meetings or small group meetings facilitated by its national trade association. Other organisations may have operations in different countries and they have two challenges: consistent messaging across national borders, and meeting with decision-makers and key influencers in international bodies. For example, an organisation would want to understand, and to influence, new policy development emanating from the work of the European Council of Ministers, the European Parliament and the European Commission, but it may only be able to do this through its sector representatives.

An organisation will also want to participate in roundtables, seminars and conferences that involve a range of stakeholders interested in the sector, including investors, supply chain organisations, non-governmental organisations and academics. These are useful activities providing valuable intelligence and information that can be used to test the organisation's ideas and modify them if necessary to make them more acceptable to a wider constituency.

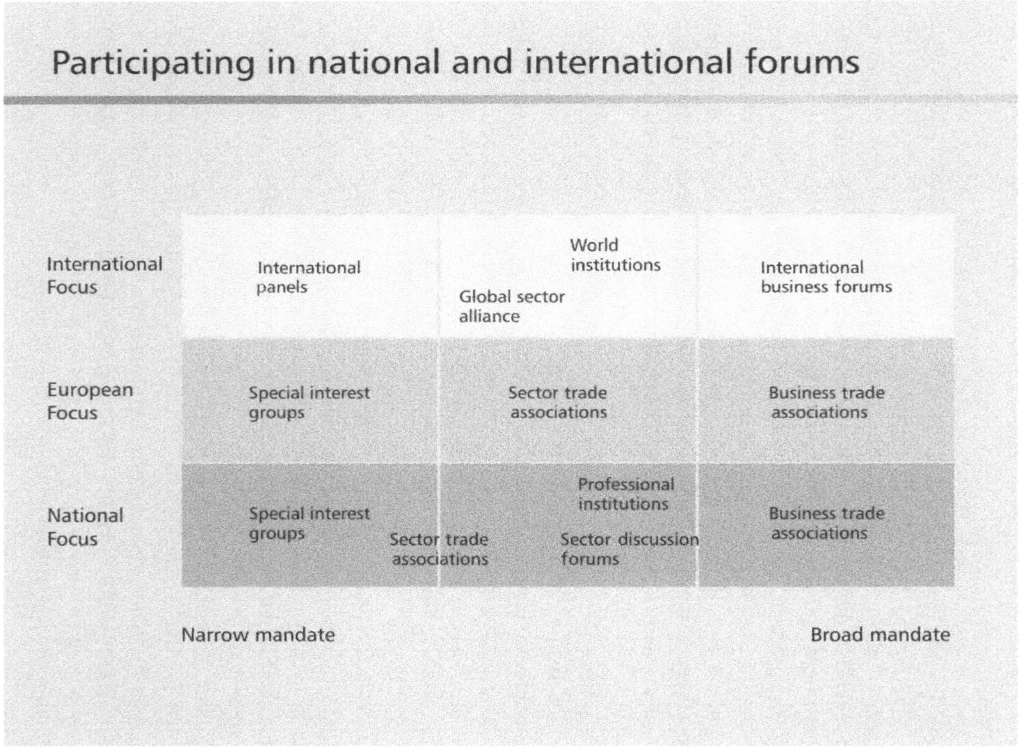

Participating in national and international forums

	Narrow mandate		Broad mandate
International Focus	International panels	World institutions / Global sector alliance	International business forums
European Focus	Special interest groups	Sector trade associations	Business trade associations
National Focus	Special interest groups / Sector trade associations	Professional institutions / Sector discussion forums	Business trade associations

Illustration 6.4 Participating in national and international forums

Early sight of new developments is very important for an organisation, and this can be achieved by participating in various national and, where appropriate, international forums, when potential developments may be discussed and the views of different stakeholders presented.

6.4 Responding to Brexit

The UK Government will negotiate the principles of the relationship it has with Europe post-Brexit, and it will also carry out a case-by-case examination of policy, consulting with its stakeholders as it does so. For example, the referendum debate and subsequent discussion suggests that the rules for immigration from the European Union (EU), and elsewhere, will likely be changed, and this will have implications for employment and the associated skills and training agenda. Climate change targets and other environmental legislation, on the other hand, are less likely to change significantly. The business community is anxious to have access to the European Market, with the financial services sector particularly keen to retain its pre-eminent position in Europe and the world. Stakeholders from sectors across the economy engage with the UK Government, putting forward their needs for the future.

Both formal and informal processes are available to organisations to influence the outcomes of the policy reviews planned by Government. From an individual organisation's perspective, there are three levels of issues to consider:

- **Primary:** Those policy/regulatory issues that impact the business directly.
- **Secondary:** Those policy/regulatory issues that address the markets in which the business operates.
- **Tertiary:** Those that affect the economy and consumer demand, and may compromise the ability for its business to operate effectively, for example, through a lack of skilled labour.

With this in mind, an organisation could begin to establish its position by addressing a set of questions:

- What are the processes, formal and informal, timing and milestones associated with Brexit?
- What are the high-level positions for the UK and the EU on key issues, and how might these influence the outcomes?
- What detailed policy/regulation that affects our business comes from the EU?
- What policy/regulation that affects our business is most likely to be transferred unchanged to the UK?
- What policy/regulation that affects our business is most likely to be changed following Brexit and how will this be integrated into UK policy/regulation?
- What are the threats and opportunities associated with potential changes in policy and regulation?
- What is our position on potential changes to policy and regulation?
- What forums exist, both formal and informal, to influence the debate?
- Who from the organisation is best placed to engage with decision-makers?
- What should an engagement programme focus on?

It may be that this exercise requires a small expert group drawn from around the organisation to establish what is needed and to implement an appropriate engagement programme.

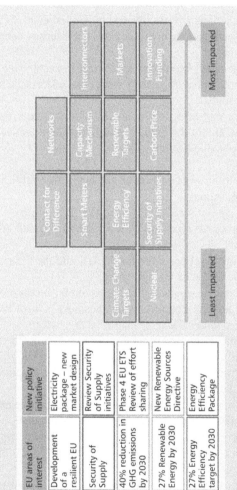

Illustration 6.5 Potential energy sector implications of Brexit

The UK leaving the EU (Brexit) is, arguably, the defining issue for this generation. An assessment of the policy and regulatory implications of Brexit is necessary at the sector and organisation levels.

Notes: EU, European Union; GHG, greenhouse gases; EU ETS, European Union Emissions Trading Scheme; Energy Efficiency targets are energy savings compared with the business-as-usual scenario.

6.5 Raising the organisation's profile

Credibility for the organisation and its leadership with decision-makers and key influencers comes from it being seen to present its position on issues with robust arguments underpinned with evidence, in a fair, transparent and consistent way. Every interaction is important in its own right but must also be considered as part of an overall strategy, gradually building an overall picture of the organisation in the minds of those who influence the debate. It is important that an organisation is innovative in the way it goes about enhancing its credibility, and that of its leadership, with stakeholders.

6.5.1 Reporting performance

Fundamental to any organisation is the need to demonstrate that it is being run effectively for the benefit of its shareholders, its consumers, its employees and the communities in which it operates. The traditional Annual Report, then, is fundamental for this purpose, providing as it does a transparent and audited review of the basic operational and financial performance; this confirms an organisation's licence to operate. The report is usually available to stakeholders, and the metrics used to measure performance can be compared with past years to provide an accurate reflection of the path of travel of the organisation. It also provides an opportunity for the Chairman and the CEO to articulate their vision for the future for the organisation and the markets in which it operates.

An organisation's Corporate Social Responsibility (CSR) activities address elements of both the licence to operate and the social licence to operate discussed in Chapter 5. The content of the CSR review signals the intent by the organisation to be an ethical and responsible organisation in the way it behaves towards its customers in the marketplace, its employees and supply chain organisations in the workplace, its local community and the environment. The more holistic approach to reporting performance in the review is a powerful vehicle to establish an organisation's credentials. Like the Annual Report, the metrics for each area demonstrate the progress being made; unlike the Annual Report, the content of the review is largely driven by the organisation and better reflects an organisation's culture. This annual document is crucially important to an array of external stakeholders.

6.5.2 Speeches, presentations and discussion forums

One of the most effective ways of raising the profile and credibility of an organisation is for its executives to make speeches, give presentations at conferences and seminars, and participate in Expert Panels. There are advantages to these activities:

- Such events usually have an opening address by decision-makers – for example, a Minister or even a Secretary of State – and this affords an opportunity for informal discussions around issues of mutual interest.

Building credibility and trust by reporting performance

Illustration 6.6 Building credibility and trust by reporting performance

The organisation's story will draw on all its activities: in the workplace, the marketplace, the environment and the communities in which it operates. Its performance in these areas will be very important in gaining the trust of decision-makers and key influencers.

- An opportunity to position the company as a leader in the field of interest, by considering the wider interests of the UK alongside those of the organisation.
- An opportunity to disseminate key messages and positions on policy to stakeholders from the sector, officials and regulators, supply chain organisations and so on.
- Media are often at such events, and it may be possible to offer a brief interview with the CEO to relay views on what has been discussed by stakeholders participating in the event.
- The opportunity to network with stakeholders from across the spectrum who have an interest in the same issues as the company.

It is important that the CEO makes speeches regularly at such events, although it is also helpful if other members of the executive team contribute to the programme, thus enhancing the reputation of the company. It is possible that the CEO and his executive team are expert speakers, but it is more likely they will need media training. A good speech-writer is needed, someone who can work closely with the executives to ensure an interesting 'story', one with consistent messaging and delivered with clarity and energy; it may also be supported by a visual presentation that can be 'free-standing', that is, one that when seen by stakeholders not at the event, is clear in the messages being conveyed in the presentation.

Most important is that speeches should not be seen in isolation; rather, they should be part of a series in which nuanced messaging and ideas are conveyed over a reasonable period. In this way, it is possible to reinforce messages that were communicated in the past, and new messages can be introduced to 'freshen up' the story and keep stakeholders interested.

Organisations tend to have many talented people who are expert in their areas. They should be encouraged to participate in conferences and seminars at the expert level where much of policy development occurs. It is surprising how little this occurs and it is a missed opportunity by many organisations. Participating in such events not only brings the company considerable credit and opportunity to influence at the detailed level; it is may also provide a development opportunity for the individuals involved.

An organisation may choose to enter the public debate on issues that impact its business in different ways. It may choose to circulate its own analysis and views to decision-makers and key influencers although this may be seen as a self-serving exercise; alternatively, it can commission work by consultants or academics with the advantage that this is seen as more independent and therefore more credible. An organisation can enhance its credibility by supporting independent studies, particularly if it they make a decisive contribution.

6.5.3 Supporting Government initiatives

What has been encouraging over recent years is the willingness of officials to take the time to understand the workings of commercial enterprises and this has allowed organisations an opportunity to build relationships that are helpful to both parties. There are several avenues to exploit when engaging with officials depending on the sector involved; for example, organisations have provided brief-ings on key criteria for investment decisions, or real-time trading activities, or the ways assets operate and so on. The briefings can be in bilateral meetings or through visits to the organisation's operational sites, and it may even be possible for some international companies to arrange discussions with experts in other regions who perhaps have adopted solutions that officials would find helpful.

Officials may also seek proprietary data and information to give them a bet-ter understanding of where the industry is heading. The conditions for providing what may be confidential information have to be carefully established to protect the company from disclosure under the Freedom of Information (FOI) Act. But so long as the correct safeguards are in place, providing such information makes for better policy.

Those organisations that are open to such discussions would not only be pro-viding a valuable service to their sectors, but will also get a much better under-standing on how officials go about their business, the stresses and constraints they operate under, and the issues that concern them most.

Officials tend to be moved to new roles within the Civil Service on a regular basis, which means that not only has a potentially effective relationship gone, but there may be a need to repeat the process at intervals with their replacements. This can be frustrating, but it is the way the Government operates and organisations must be patient and flexible in their approach.

Providing support for officials need not be resource-intensive but it does nor-mally involve internal experts from across the business, so it is important that these experts understand what is needed from them and to ensure that they are able to devote the time needed. It is also vital that an organisation understands that if it wishes to help officials in this way, there is an internal education process needed for the experts involved, their managers and the executives.

One of the most important questions companies have of officials who develop policy is whether they are sufficiently expert in the markets they are affecting. There are a few reasons for these concerns:

- Civil servants tend to join Whitehall and the other executive offices in the Devolved Administrations straight from university without any wider experience.
- Career development is almost entirely within the service, usually by moving from one post to another on a regular basis and often without seeing a particu-lar policy development through to completion.
- The graduate intake is lean with respect to science and engineering and it is also lacking in people with experience in the technical and commercial sector.
- There is a strong concern within the Civil Service that any one interest group should not be too influential in policy initiative, so there is a reluctance to rely on a single organisation for information or ideas.
- The Civil Service relies heavily on consultants and academics to provide analytical support for policy development. Although they may be considered

independent, the information these experts have access to is more limited than that held by commercial organisations, and so their advice may be based on data and information that may not be up-to-date or complete.

Civil servants tend to be bright and energetic and they can become very good at their roles relatively quickly. Their understanding of commercial operations can be augmented through regular meetings with organisations and through site visits. But in some cases, this is insufficient, and it is helpful if officials could spend extended periods working in external organisations, to deepen their knowledge and experience working in a very different environment. What is also clear is that if there is a lack of understanding of the commercial environment by officials, the reverse is also true, with those working in the private sector having a poor understanding of the environment in the public sector.

A better understanding, then, of how the private and public sectors work is beneficial for all stakeholders involved. A Civil Service initiative – the Civil Service High Potential Secondment programme – has proved very helpful in this regard. The idea was to encourage young, talented professionals from the public sector to be seconded into private sector companies, and vice versa. Those organisations that supported such initiatives learnt much about their Civil Service counterparts, gaining considerable credibility within the public sector and improving their stakeholder engagement with an important group.

6.5.4 Sponsorship of selected events

A company's profile can be raised in decision-making circles in a number of ways. At one end of the spectrum is sponsorship of events that reach a relatively large number of people in an appropriate networking setting. For example, the Parliamentary Group on Energy Studies (PGES) provides its members with a series of seminars on topical issues throughout the year. Once a year it has its annual dinner in the House of Lords where a wide cross-section of stakeholders can network and interact, the event punctuated with a small number of speeches, often with the Secretary of State or a Minister providing the keynote address.

It is possible to sponsor or co-sponsor such a high-profile event, and this offers an opportunity to showcase some of the organisation's activities and to be mentioned in the speeches; it may even be possible for the CEO to make a short address.

Party political conferences also offer an opportunity to engage with the debate through sponsorship of 'side-bar' events. Clearly it is not only the party's MPs and their advisors that attend these annual events but the 'grassroots' supporters and activists, who help in the development of policy. Although these events tend to be somewhat chaotic, it is possible to have a Minster or influential MP to chair a roundtable discussion or a lunch or dinner event, and these offer opportunities for the CEO or members of his executive team to frame the discussion and express their views, and also to build relationships.

At the other end of the scale are small group hospitality events that cannot be used to engage with MPs but can include advisors, members of 'think tanks', other key influencers, commercial allies and media. A variety of sporting, musical, charity and trade association events are popular with stakeholders and provide an informal setting for networking, discussion and relationship-building.

The offer of a periodic award where topical issues can be aired in public can be a highly effective, if unusual, stakeholder engagement activity by an organisation. For example, British Energy sponsored the John Collier Medal and the accompanying Memorial Lecture; the medal was awarded to outstanding individuals in the general area of sustainable energy. British Energy worked closely with several professional institutions, most notably the Institute of Mechanical Engineers, and over time, the medal became a prestigious award with some outstanding individuals recognised for their contributions to the area. The Memorial Lecture was published and widely disseminated. The fact that the organisation was associated with this event gave it credibility with an important and influential group of stakeholders.

6.5.5 *Gaining recognition for individuals in an organisation*

There are many ways an organisation can gain recognition for its activities, and raise its profile with stakeholders; for example, it can be ranked best performer in its sector as judged by certain stakeholder groups, or it can perform well when assessed against certain criteria in exercises run by credible organisations such as Business in the Community (BiTC) or FTSE4Good. Such recognition is important for an organisation because of the credibility it affords and the positive publicity in the media, and because its performance distinguishes it from its competitors. It is also important for employees because they have contributed to, and take pride in the achievements of their organisation, and are motivated to continue improving their own performance.

The recognition of individuals is also helpful for an organisation since this is reported in the media, and, as with other forms of public recognition, employees take pride in the fact that one of their colleagues has been successful. The most important recognition for an individual in the UK is the award of an Honour by the Queen for a significant contribution in their sphere of influence. For example, the most popular group of Honours is the Order of the British Empire. In this group, the award of Commander of the Order of the British Empire (CBE) recognises those who have held a prominent role at national level, or a leading role at regional level; the award of Officer of the Order of the British Empire (OBE) recognises those who have played a major local role in any activity, including being a national illustration in their chosen area, while the award of a Member of the Order of the British Empire (MBE) is for those who have made an outstanding achievement or service to the community.

These are highly prestigious honours, awarded to a very few in civil society. The number of awards in business, for example, is very low, with perhaps one or two individuals recognised in each sector, each year. Such recognition often goes to people who are at the end of a successful period and are moving on to new ventures or into retirement.

Engagement through informal processes

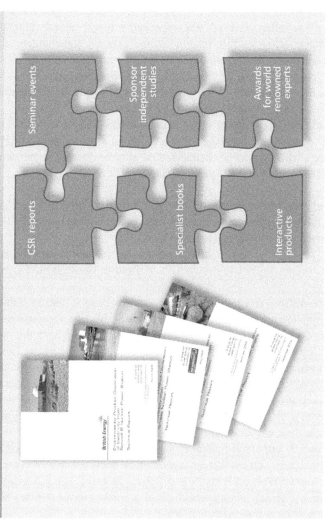

Illustration 6.7 Engagement through informal processes

Adopting a proactive approach to engagement allows an organisation to help set the agenda in the external arena, and to be seen in a positive light by stakeholders.

Note: CSR, Corporate Social Responsibility.

6.5.6 Using all forms of media

It is possible to use media either passively or actively when engaging with stakeholders. A passive approach focuses on, for example, the use of a website that provides a portal to the outside world. This is the simplest and most effective way of providing information about developments affecting the organisation to interested stakeholders; it is important, then, that it is accurate, up to date and engaging.

There is, rightly, considerable emphasis placed on the 'look' of the website, and in particular the ease with which those who access it can move around the website to get the information they seek; this is important because the time spent on a website by stakeholders will depend on these features as much as on the quality of information provided. There is also a need for some homogeneity in the way in which information is conveyed, no easy task when activities across an organisation differ markedly.

The website offers a wonderful opportunity to get added value from other organisational activities that may influence external stakeholders: interviews, speeches and presentations, submissions to Government consultations and inquiries, and Corporate Social Responsibility (CSR) programmes. Organisations will also want their employees to use the website as a source of information, so that they too can convey its messages through their networks.

The rapid rise in the use of social media requires a more active and immediate approach to conveying messages. It is a powerful medium, particularly for those stakeholders who want to be 'connected' at all times; for an organisation, it provides another source of intelligence on developments in its markets.

> Social media has also transformed the way in which politicians, commentators, advisers, spinners, journalists, activists and other members of the political and media elite speak to each other.
>
> *Nick Clegg, former MP and Deputy Prime Minister,*
> Politics Between the Extremes, *2016*

It can be difficult to engage stakeholders through social media if the organisational culture has not evolved to make best use of this new approach to delivering messages. One way to improve the use of social media within the organisation is to develop an internal version of the tool and encourage its use in the normal course of business. This approach can provide a new platform for exchanging views and encouraging employees to interact. These tools require a 'cultural shift' in the organisation but evidence suggests that as employees become familiar with social media tools, they become more confident in sharing their knowledge and ideas with colleagues across the business.

It is crucially important that an organisation remains proactive and innovative in its approach to stakeholder engagement, to seek out new ways in which to deliver its core messages. With the appropriate protocols and governance on messaging, the wide reach of social media is clearly one avenue that can be exploited to good effect by organisations. This is a rapidly evolving form of media, so it's also important to learn how stakeholders respond to this form of engagement, and to look beyond to the next generation of communication tools.

6.6 Reviewing progress

The best organisations tend to schedule regular meetings, usually monthly, to review progress. There are generally two types of meetings: one for the CEO and his executives, and one for all those involved in the engagement programme. The meetings with the executive team offer an opportunity to confirm that the engagement programme is on track, with all the main risks and opportunities being addressed. Such a meeting also provides an opportunity to get ongoing reaction and substantive comment on the programme; it encourages shared ownership and responsibility for the programme activities and reinforces the organisation's high-level messages with an important internal stakeholder group.

Regular review meetings are also important at the operational level, involving all members of the internal 'virtual team'; that is, all those being asked to contribute to the engagement programme or who provide valuable expert knowledge and analysis underpinning the organisation's narrative on policy issues. A monthly roundtable provides an excellent forum for an update on any new developments and for providing feedback from the executive meetings; it also offers an opportunity for each individual member to report on progress on their contributions, and seek clarity and help on specific issues as needed.

Such review meetings are also valuable in international companies where similar groups are carrying out engagement programmes in different countries. Although the policy initiatives and the political and market context will differ, experience suggests that important learning can be transferred from one jurisdiction to another.

6.6.1 The importance of an annual review

An annual review is an important activity for those leading the strategic stakeholder engagement programme. It offers an opportunity to:

- Deliver an overview of progress, annotated with the associated success factors.
- Identify strengths and weaknesses in the programme.
- Highlight successes and recognise those involved.
- Make the case for additional resources in the forward programme if needed.
- Highlight lessons learned.
- Summarise the key elements of the forward programme.

Once again, the annual review can give comfort to the executive team that the programme has achieved what it set out to do, and if it is found lacking in some areas, that there are measures in place to improve the situation. The review

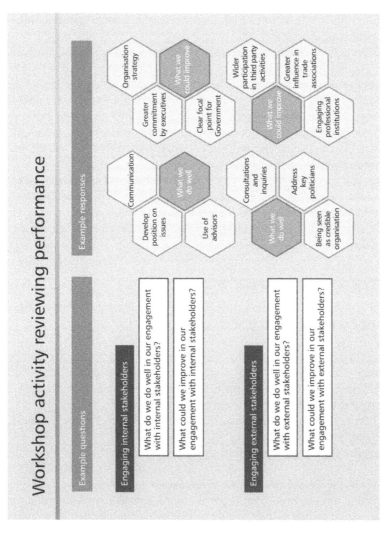

Illustration 6.8 Workshop activity reviewing performance

A strategic stakeholder engagement programme can always be improved. It is often helpful, then, to facilitate a workshop that reviews the programme and elicits observations from the internal stakeholders involved.

can also be shared with Board Members, and an abridged version reported in the Annual Report for investors and other interested stakeholders. The appropriate information in the review can also be shared with the wider community in the Corporate Social Responsibility report, demonstrating openness, honesty and ethical practice in an important area.

6.6.2 Measuring success

There are several ways of measuring the success or otherwise of a stakeholder engagement programme using both quantitative and qualitative metrics. From a strictly business point of view, the number of risks mitigated or opportunities realised, and the total cost avoided or money value gained, are probably the most important measures and the ones that most interest the CEO and his Executive team.

> Measure success on output not input.
>
> *Expert Panel Member Bernie Bulkin OBE,*
> *former Chief Scientist of BP and Chair for the UK's Office of*
> *Renewable Energy Deployment*

An annual update of the risk register, then, will highlight:

- Those risks mitigated and the total avoided cost to the business.
- Those opportunities realised, and the value to the business.
- Those risks that have not been mitigated, a review of which should provide valuable learning for the organisation.
- Those risks that remain active, with a clear mitigation strategy identified.
- Those risks on the horizon that may, or may not, arise in the near future.

Another measure is the number of decision-makers or key influencers met who had been identified in the stakeholder mapping exercise and stakeholder engagement programme. In the political arena this will include Ministers, Committee Members, Members of Parliament whose constituencies include the organisation's operations, members of the Shadow Cabinet, and where appropriate, their Special Advisors; it will also include Members of the House of Lords and politicians in the Devolved Administrations. In some cases, there will be more than one meeting, and the forums may differ with some bilateral meetings and some meetings that will involve others in the sector. What is important is to assess what has been achieved following these meetings.

> Always need to be mindful to never confuse access with influence.
>
> *Expert Panel Member Dr Doug Parr,*
> *Chief Scientist, Greenpeace UK*

A similar exercise can be undertaken for officials in departments and public bodies and will involve meetings right across the board, from department Permanent

Secretaries to their policy leads at the other end of the hierarchy, and from CEOs to experts responsible for a stream of work in the public bodies. There will be other key influencers identified in the stakeholder mapping exercise outside of political and Government departments, and these will also need to be assessed.

An end-of-year review of the stakeholder engagement programme, then, should assess the value of these meetings against a simple, proprietary set of criteria. For example, a helpful measure is how often the organisation is asked to contribute to expert roundtables or working groups; and in how many bilateral meetings:

- Did the organisation get what it asked for?
- Did the organisation get some of what it asked for?
- Did the organisation not get what it asked for?
- Was the organisation asked to provide further information?

A further useful measure would be the number of 'platforms' accessed for the organisation's key messages. For example, the number of:

- Written responses to Government consultations.
- Submissions to inquiries by Committees in the House of Commons.
- Submissions to inquiries by Committees in the House of Lords.
- Written responses to consultations by Public Bodies.
- Committee oral sessions in which the organisation participated.
- Presentations by the CEO and his/her executive team members at sector conferences and seminars.
- Times the CEO and executive team members were quoted in the media.
- Decision-makers and influencers engaged through proprietary events.
- Influential third-party events participated in.

Once again, this information will be captured in the 'live' stakeholder mapping document, which is available to and updated by all members of the 'virtual' team. This will make it easier to ensure that the 5Cs necessary for an effective stakeholder engagement programme – a *coherent* story, *clarity* of message, a *consistent* approach, *concerted* effort and *coordinated* action – are adhered to.

> The true measure of success is if you make a call [to a decision-maker] and that call is returned; a greater measure of success is if the decision-maker contacts you.
> *Expert Panel Member Bill Coley CBE, former President of Duke Power and CEO of British Energy Group*

There will be intangible, hard-to-measure benefits that will arise from the engagement programme. For example, some activities will enhance reputation, increase credibility and engender goodwill for the company that could lead to more tangible benefits at a later time. However, it is also possible for an organisation to lose these intangible benefits if it does not take sufficient care with its programme.

It is important that those representing the organisation in the external world are well briefed. It is also crucially important that they conduct themselves according the organisation's ethical policy when interacting with decision-makers, key influencers and other stakeholders.

Summary key points

- The stakeholder mapping document provides a valuable tool to ensure that all internal stakeholders understand the organisation's activities in the engagement programme and their contributions.
- An effective engagement programme will place emphasis on working with politicians and their officials and advisors, and putting the organisation's views on the record through the formal processes available.
- Engaging with a wider cross-section of stakeholders is also important, requiring a more proactive approach by the organisation's executive team and experts.
- The organisation can engage in a number of formal and informal activities aimed at raising the profile and credibility of the organisation and engendering goodwill and trust among key stakeholder groups
- It is important to hold regular review meetings on the engagement programme with the executive team and with the internal 'virtual' team, and to assess progress against agreed success factors.

Case Study 6.1 Positioning the organisation for external stakeholders

An organisation needs a 'story' to tell the external world. The narrative must have the capacity to engage external audiences and present a positive vision for the future. That 'story' must be credible and, crucially, it must discuss issues that are important to decision-makers and of interest to a range of stakeholders. Such a 'story' was a very important first step in raising awareness of the role that nuclear power could make to the UK's electricity mix.

Background

In the late 1990s, nuclear power was rarely discussed in public arenas and when it was, the focus was normally on the negative aspects of the technology: costs, waste and proliferation. What was needed was a 'story' that told the positive side of this much-maligned technology, one that demonstrated its importance in mitigating climate change, in improving air quality and its contribution to security of supply.

The approach adopted

Scenarios, particularly with a strong narrative, have proven to be excellent vehicles to engage stakeholders; British Energy, the nuclear operator, adopted this approach in the early 2000s. It created a few credible scenarios of the electricity sector to 2020 using the best available information at that time. This analysis yielded several important insights that were used by the organisation to engage stakeholders; for example:

- The industry in general, and British Energy in particular, were crucial to the UK economy; it had delivered large quantities of electricity in the past and would continue to do so for several decades into the future. It was contributing to the country's security of supply.
- It was making a major contribution to the UK's decarbonisation targets by avoiding the emission of tens of millions of tonnes of carbon dioxide that would otherwise have been emitted through fossil generation. It would continue to do so for the foreseeable future and if it did not, then electricity sector emissions would rise. The same was true for other air pollutants from fossil generation.

Outcomes

These insights were shared with stakeholders in presentations, briefings and interviews, they were placed on the company website, and on leaflets at the company's visitor centres and operational locations and offices. The narrative also opened up the opportunity to discuss nuclear using the three 'pillars' of sustainable development – protection of the environment, benefits to the economy and societal well-being – alongside other energy technologies such as coal, gas and the renewables. This approach and the messages it delivered gradually brought the industry into the mainstream for many stakeholders and was an important first step towards the new nuclear build programme now under way.

Case Study 6.2 Dealing with risk through active stakeholder engagement

In many cases, an organisation will respond to new government policy initiatives through the formal processes available, such as consultations and inquiries. However, there are occasions when the organisation will need to be proactive in engaging decision-makers, and in a timely manner, if it is to protect its interests. The UK Government's Energy Company Obligation (ECO) policy initiative was such a policy.

Background

Successive UK Governments had adopted the practice of placing 'obligations' on utility companies to carry out and pay for energy efficiency measures for their domestic customers. In 2010, the Government was considering the next stage of these 'obligations', ECO, to run from January 2013 to December 2017.

The approach adopted

The financial implications for International Power, an independent generator (now part of ENGIE in the UK) would have been severe if it were included in the initiative. The company responded to the formal consultations, and raised this issue in bilateral discussion with politicians and officials in a concerted effort to be exempted from ECO. The company also worked closely with other major independent companies through the Independent Generators Group (IGG). The arguments were simple and based on experiences under an earlier initiative, the Community Energy Savings Programme (CESP), which had surprisingly, and unfairly, included independent generators (IGs) as well as the utility companies:

- IGs obligated under CESP had no ability to pass through the costs of the scheme onto domestic customers since they had none, or through the wholesale market.
- IGs had no experience or capability in energy efficiency and were forced to pay a premium to a third party, sometimes a competitor, for delivery of the 'obligation'.
- Including IGs in ECO would jeopardise their position in the UK market, erode competition and threaten their planned investments in low-carbon, flexible generation.

These arguments were presented to the Secretary of State by IGG CEOs, and the underpinning evidence was presented to his advisors and officials. IGs also shared these arguments with their network of decision-makers and key influencers. In this way, the issue had a high profile and the inequities of the scheme were made plain. Cornwall Energy, a respected independent organisation providing intelligence and analysis, helpfully picked up the issue and supported the IG's position.

Outcomes

International Power and the other IGs were exempted from the ECO scheme, saving considerable time and resources that would be better spent elsewhere. A successful stakeholder engagement exercise was based on a strong 'story' supported by credible evidence, a concerted engagement programme in alliance with others in the sector, and a proactive approach.

Case Study 6.3 Escalating issues in decision-making institutions

There are occasions when an organisation can do everything right when engaging with the Government's formal consultation processes but the organisation fails to elicit the response it needs. In this case, it may be necessary and appropriate to escalate the issue to the next level of decision-making. ENGIE was forced to do this during a government process to implement new European legislation.

Background

The Industrial Emissions Directive (IED) sought to limit nitrogen emissions from fossil-powered plants and each European member was required to present a National Transitional Plan (TNP) as part of the implementation process. The Department of Environment, Food and Rural Affairs (DEFRA) asked operators who would participate in the TNP to provide specific information for its draft submission in December 2012. Unfortunately, due to an administrative error by ENGIE, data for one of the two gas turbines (GT1) at its Deeside power station was omitted from its submission. The error was identified by the company shortly after submission of the draft UK plan to the European Commission, and DEFRA were informed immediately in mid-January 2013.

The approach adopted

Early indications from DEFRA suggested that there were no legal or process barriers preventing correction of the draft TNP data. Further assurances were given to operators during the DEFRA-led stakeholder meetings throughout 2012.

Two years of meetings and communications followed. Initially ENGIE received positive feedback on the inclusion of GT1, but following a change of lead official, there emerged a new reluctance to address this error. ENGIE made it clear to DEFRA that if the error was not corrected, the plant would not be able to operate in an effective manner going forward, placing it in a difficult financial position; it would likely close.

With the deadline for the final TNP submission approaching and with officials unresponsive, ENGIE decided to escalate the issue and briefed several interested stakeholders: the Member of Parliament whose constituency included the power station, and several Special Advisors in departments with an interest in this issue. The ENGIE CEO wrote directly to the Secretary of State for DEFRA, by-passing officials, explaining the basic facts of the case and seeking a positive resolution.

Outcomes

Escalation of the issue proved successful, with the Secretary of State instructing officials to include ENGIE's Deeside GT1 in the UK's final Transitional National Plan. There was important learning for the company from this exercise: it needed to improve its internal governance process to eradicate errors in material sent externally; and the escalation process should have been activated much earlier by the organisation.

Case Study 6.4 On the vagaries of Government policy

It is sometimes difficult for organisations to understand decisions made by Ministers. Logic would suggest that developments that deliver the Government's aims, have wide stakeholder support and are backed up by sound analysis would be encouraged. Wind farm development on the Isle of Lewis showed that this is sometimes not the case.

Background

There has been interest in developing renewables, and wind projects in particular, on the Isle of Lewis for around 15 years. Such developments were not only consistent with Scotland's aspirations for the sector but potentially very beneficial for the local community, which had seen a gradual depopulation of the island.

By 2012, there was sufficient confidence that with careful siting, about 450MW of wind projects could be developed, and the cost of a new grid connection could be borne by these projects. On revisiting the project, the local grid operator indicated that the estimated cost of connection had doubled, although no detailed explanation was given; this led to a major review by the UK Government of wind deployment on all the Scottish Islands of Lewis, Shetland and Orkney.

Developer response

Organisations developing the projects participated in all the formal UK Government consultative processes, and held discussions with the Scottish Energy Minister and his advisors, and the Member of Parliament for Lewis; there were also discussions with the local grid developer and the UK regulator.

The companies, individually, came forward with several proposals to address the increasing cost of the grid connection. One company also made the point that the islands were not unlike offshore wind developments, in terms of scale and distance from the mainland, and that they enjoyed a much higher subsidy than those onshore; it also highlighted the wider economic benefits to the islands that it felt should be factored into the final decision.

Outcomes

In the event, the UK Government's decision on the level of incentive it would apply to the island projects was disappointing; the level set might encourage development on Shetland and Orkney but was insufficient for the projects on Lewis. Furthermore, the Government offered a much higher price for riskier offshore projects at that time, projects that would provide little in the way of economic benefit to local communities.

The decision had a profound impact on Lewis, and at least one major company decided not to go ahead with its project. The Government's decision disappointed the local communities who were hoping these developments would regenerate the island economy, and alienated the Devolved Administration. An important lesson here is that organisations need to have a good understanding of the political context as it applies to their areas of interest if they are to avoid the cost of developing projects.

Case Study 6.5 When politics trumps argument

If Government wishes something to happen then it will happen. Politics does trump argument even when there is strong opposition from stakeholders who present credible evidence. The question is: what should organisations focus on in this situation? The creation of the Carbon Price Support (CPS) mechanism in the UK provides an opportunity to explore this issue.

Background

In 2010, the UK Coalition Government expressed concern that the European Union Emissions Trading Scheme (EU ETS) was not providing a sufficiently high carbon price to encourage investment in new low-carbon technologies such as nuclear, renewables and carbon capture and storage. The Government was also keen to see a higher contribution by environmental taxes to overall taxation. It adopted the Conservative Party Manifesto commitment to reform the existing Climate Change Levy to deliver a floor price for carbon.

Response by market participants

A significant number of stakeholders argued against the creation of the CPS mechanism and the arguments were compelling:

- The Government's *Energy Market Assessment* had as one of its aims the need to provide a new incentive scheme to encourage new low-carbon investment; a carbon price floor was not needed.
- The EU ETS set the price for carbon, and if this was thought less effective than it needed to be, it would be better if Government supported efforts to improve the performance of the EU ETS by working with its European partners.
- A higher carbon price would place the UK economy at a competitive disadvantage when compared to other European countries, and indeed countries further afield.
- A higher cost of carbon brought about by the CPS mechanism would deliver unwarranted 'windfall' profits to existing nuclear and renewables generation.

Outcomes

Despite the arguments against the creation of the CPS mechanism, it came into force on 1 April 2013 with a minimum price for carbon dioxide for carbon dioxide (CO_2) set at £16/tonne CO_2 for the financial year 2013/14, rising to £30/tonne CO_2 in 2020/21 (all in 2009 prices). However, organisations continued to make the case against the CPS, even after it was brought into force. In March 2014, the Government, under pressure from business, decided that the CPS support would be capped at £18/tonne CO_2 for the period 2016 to 2020; and in the summer of 2014, compensation was provided to energy-intensive industries and an exemption provided to good quality Combined Heat and Power (CHP) generation from 2015/16.

The political context has also changed with the decision by the UK to leave the European Union. The UK's economy would have to be competitive, and this may provide an opportunity for stakeholders to seek further changes to the CPS mechanism.

Case Study 6.6 Dealing with Government policy uncertainty

Policies change, and they can change rapidly, and this can create considerable uncertainty in the environments affected. For example, the sudden removal of incentives for some renewable technologies in the UK could and should have been foreseen. This example shows that it is important to continually assess existing policies and the context in which they operate.

Background

In 2007, the UK Government, in concert with its European partners, agreed to an ambitious renewable target that would require new policies to incentivise action in the electricity, heat and transport sectors. The electricity sector was expected to be the major contributor to meeting the target with more than 30% of generation coming, in the main, from onshore and offshore wind, solar and biomass. A high target and the provision of a generous incentive scheme encouraged many companies and considerable investment into the sector in the years that followed.

Government action

Shortly after its election win in May 2015, the new Conservative Government ended subsidies for new onshore wind farms. This was the first of several announcements in the immediate aftermath of the election that would essentially discourage new onshore wind and solar projects, and large biomass projects.

There were three main reasons given for the sudden change in policy: subsidies were only provided to encourage a decline in the cost of new technologies, that sufficient wind and solar technology was being deployed, and that the Government's budget for renewables would likely be breached if no action was taken.

Impact on market participants

The impact was profound. Hundreds of megawatts of capacity across the three renewable technologies would now not go ahead and the development costs were lost. In the onshore wind sector, companies would focus on the relatively few sites that would still be profitable due to high load factors.

Companies could and should not have been surprised. For example, a precedent had been set for reducing subsidies for solar in Spain, albeit because of the Government's dire finances following the 2008 economic crisis. Also, the Conservative Government had indicated it would cut subsidies to onshore wind in its Election Manifesto, largely to appease those Members of Parliament with rural constituencies where opposition to this technology was fierce. Nonetheless, these signals were not heeded by companies who continued to spend valuable resources in developing potential projects that would not proceed.

Those companies who carry out regular and thorough policy risk analysis as part of best practice are likely to be rewarded with early warning of Governments changing direction and mitigate the risk accordingly.

Case Study 6.7 Working with local Members of Parliament

It is essential to have a good working relationship with politicians, both national and local, who have an interest in an organisation's operational sites in their constituencies. There will be occasions when it will be necessary to consult with these politicians, particularly when the organisation has to address difficult decisions that affect these sites. The closure of Teesside gas-fired and Rugeley coal-fired power stations by ENGIE demonstrates the importance of these relationships.

Background

The period 2012 to 2016 was a difficult one for fossil-powered generation in the UK wholesale market as electricity prices fell due to low demand for electricity, and an oversupply in capacity as subsidised renewable technologies were deployed. Worse, the prospects to 2020 were poor with new policy initiatives putting further pressure on the sector.

Teesside power station was one of the first new gas power stations to be built in the UK in the 1990s. The power station ceased operation in 2011 and notice was given for its decommissioning in 2014, a process completed in 2015. Rugeley power station was an old but relatively efficient 1,000MW coal plant; it was commissioned in 1970 and closed in 2016.

The approach adopted by the owners

In both cases, it was crucially important to have an active engagement programme with a range of stakeholders: employees, the local community, energy specialists in Whitehall, the system operator, the regulator and the local Members of Parliament (MPs).

The Teesside process was protracted as the company explored options for keeping the plant open. The local MP was fully briefed because they would be expected to protect the interests of the employees and local community. The briefings were carried out by the CEO of the company, and it was helpful that the MP understood the difficult market conditions leading to closure.

A similar but much shorter process was followed for Rugeley. Once again, a key stakeholder was the local MP who was fully briefed. The MP was very active and visible in seeking options for the employees and the site, and helpful in supporting the company's discussion with officials as the company made every effort to keep the plant open.

Outcomes

The company came out of both processes with considerable credit for the way it had dealt with two very difficult situations. It had put the employees at the heart of the process, and with the help of the MPs had explored every avenue to keep the plants open. The MPs involved were sufficiently briefed and in a timely manner to be able to field questions from their local communities and media.

Case Study 6.8 Dealing with Brexit

There are events that have the potential to fundamentally change the environment in which organisations operate. Those events that are driven by Government action will involve a formal process, and this will offer opportunities for organisations to engage in discussions that will determine the nature of the new environment. It is important, then, that organisations first establish their position on the key issues that affect them in such cases, and the Brexit process helps demonstrate a potential approach to achieve this.

Background

The decision by the UK to leave the European Union (EU) has far-reaching implications for the economy, for business and for consumers and the wider civil society. The process involved is complex and it is likely that implications will take many years to fully unravel. However, there is ample opportunity for organisations to engage in the decision-making process, particularly as the Government develops its negotiating positions on issues and in establishing what will be in place once the UK has left the EU in 2019.

Establishing an organisation's position and strategy

An organisation must first establish a series of questions it will need to address if it is to develop its position and strategy for external engagement. Below is a potential response to a series of questions by an organisation that has generation assets trading in the electricity wholesale market. It establishes the Brexit process involved, identifies the threats and opportunities for the business, and highlights elements of a potential engagement programme for the organisation. Clearly a company offering different products and services and with different attributes will produce a different response to these questions.

Question	Example response
What are the processes, timing and milestones associated with Brexit?	• Article 50 was triggered by UK Government on 29 March 2017. • Up to two years of negotiation will follow to reach an agreement, which is expected to be bespoke to the UK; the UK will leave the EU, with or without an agreement, on 29 March 2019. • If no agreement is forthcoming, the EU will treat the UK like any other country within the World Trade Organization.
What are the high-level positions for the UK and the EU on energy and how might these influence the outcomes?	• The UK has taken a lead role in many areas and will continue to have common aims in this area going forward. • The UK will transpose all EU laws into UK legislation and then assess what changes, if any, it wants as each Government department carries out policy reviews with its stakeholders. • The EU's first Energy Action Plan of 2007 focused on three main challenges – sustainability, security of supply and competitiveness – and these have remained largely intact. • The UK adopted its share of the 20:20:20 climate change targets for 2020 in relation to carbon reduction, renewable contrition to energy and energy efficiency, respectively. • The EU proposed measures to complete the internal market for gas and electricity.

Question	Example response
What policy/regulation that affects our business comes from the EU?	• Regulation of markets. • Those that address physical connection across markets. • Government support schemes need to satisfy the EU's State Aid rules on competition. • Environmental and security of supply targets. • Access to skills and labour.
What policy/regulation that affects our business is most likely to be transferred unchanged to the UK?	• Those that promote/encourage competition. • Medium-term climate change and other environmental targets. • Efficient trading of power and gas over interconnectors to enhance security of supply. • Financial Services Regulation as applied to the electricity sector. • Those that affect the EU Emissions Scheme (for greenhouse gases).
What policy/regulation that affects our business is most likely to be changed following Brexit?	• The level of interconnection from the Continent to the UK, and the treatment of electricity and gas flows into the UK market. • Innovation capacity. • The Carbon Price Floor trajectory. • Access to skills and labour from the EU (and from elsewhere).
What are the threats and opportunities associated with potential changes in policy and regulation?	• Investment flows into the UK. • Treatment of interconnectors. • Overall cost of carbon. • Market access for new technology. • New measures related to access to skills and labour from the EU (and elsewhere).
What is our position on potential changes to policy and regulation?	• Support a level playing field for interconnectors. • Support a strong and predictable overall cost of carbon. • Support measures to ensure continued access to skills and labour.
What forums exist, both formal and informal, to influence the debate?	• Bilateral meetings with officials and, if necessary, Ministers. • Government stakeholder engagement forums. • Trade association working groups that deliver industry positions. • Participation in third-party seminars and roundtables.

Question	Example response
Who from the organisation is best placed to engage with decision-makers?	• CEO and executive team at Ministerial-level meetings. • CEO and executive team members at high-level industry discussion forums. • Company experts in meetings with officials. • Company experts in industry working groups and other discussion forums.
What should an engagement programme focus on?	• Being present at all the key forums; and this will require a small core team drawing on the expertise that resides with the organisation. • Bilateral meetings with officials to present company views and proposals on the key issues for the business.

Outcomes

What is important is that organisations need to go through this exercise or something similar, to help inform their activities; they will then be in a position to support and to influence the Government's efforts as needed during the negotiating period and the transition period that follows.

Case Study 6.9 Challenging erroneous messages

There are many issues that divide stakeholders. There are occasions when one group of stakeholders will try to influence Government policy by presenting unsubstantiated claims. It is necessary to counter such claims through well-argued and credible arguments. An initiative by British Energy that established the carbon credentials of nuclear power proved very effective in this regard.

Background

Prominent non-governmental organisations (NGOs) have been consistent in their opposition to nuclear power in the UK. They have argued that it is no longer needed in a world where new renewable technologies can be deployed. They have also claimed that carbon emissions associated with nuclear generation are at the same level as gas generation. This last claim was left unchallenged for some time.

The approach adopted

British Energy, the operator of the UK's eight newest nuclear plants, wanted to address the claim on life-cycle carbon emission and decided to commission an independent study. The study used an established methodology which allowed the life-cycle carbon dioxide emissions in grams (g) associated with the production of a unit of power, a kilowatt-hour (kWh), by an existing nuclear power station – Torness in Scotland – to be established.

The methodology considered all aspects of the station in estimating carbon emissions: the extraction, conversion and fabrication of the fuel, the construction and decommissioning of the plant, its operations, reprocessing and dealing with the waste streams during its construction and lifetime operations. The total carbon emissions from electricity generated were estimated to be just 5g/kWh, subsequently revised to around 7g/kWh when more accurate data became available. This compares to carbon emissions from typical UK coal and gas plants of around 900g/kWh and 350–400g/kWh, respectively, based upon the operational stage of the plant alone.

Outcomes

It was clear from this detailed analysis that the NGO claims were false, and it was important that this message was relayed to key stakeholders. The results were shared with the Government's Chief Scientific Adviser and the Head of the Parliamentary Office of Science and Technology (POST), whose main role is to brief Parliamentarians on issues of interest in the technical arena. In fact, prompted by this work, POST carried out its own life-cycle study of all the major energy technologies, including nuclear.

The most important outcome was the acceptance that carbon emissions from nuclear operations were very low, even on a life-cycle basis, a fact accepted by Parliament's Environmental Audit Committee who cited the Torness study in one of their reports. The British Energy initiative confirmed the importance of challenging erroneous messages in the public domain, using credible analysis and active stakeholder engagement.

Case Study 6.10 Raising an organisation's credibility with officials

The Civil Service in all countries plays an important role in helping Government develop and implement policy, and this means they are highly influential. Organisations must be prepared to support Government initiatives that improve the capability and the policy-making ability of civil servants. ENGIE and many other organisations did this by participating in the Civil Service High Potential Secondment programme, and by doing so raised their credibility with officials.

Background

The UK's Civil Service is filled with many bright and very able professionals, but they often lack knowledge and experience of the environment in which commercial organisations operate. This means they are not always aware of the full implications of their initiatives on the organisations affected. It is also fair to say that there is a similar lack of knowledge in private organisations of the environment in which Civil Service professionals operate. This makes the interaction between these two sets of stakeholders less effective than it could be, to the detriment of the policy-making process.

The approach adopted

Secondments from the private sector into Civil Service Departments are not uncommon, primarily to provide specific knowledge and expertise; but relatively few officials spend significant periods in private organisations. It was encouraging, then, that the Civil Service themselves came forward with a scheme for their aspiring managers to spend time in the commercial sector, with private sector experts spending time in Civil Service Departments; it was called the High Potential Secondment Programme. The main objective of this initiative was to improve capability and increase understanding across the public and private sectors; scheme participants would have an opportunity to learn from, and develop in, environments which are important to the UK's long-term economic and environmental performance.

Outcomes

ENGIE, a private sector energy and services company had, independently, arranged a successful secondment from one of the non-department public bodies into the corporate area of its business. ENGIE was then approached with a request that it participate in the High Potential Secondment Programme, and following a formal selection process, two young and talented Civil Service professionals were seconded into the company, and a similarly talented ENGIE expert joined a Government department.

The scheme was respected, with secondees given interesting and challenging projects, and treated as employees of the organisations they joined. All secondees gained enormously from the experience, delivering excellent work and gaining a respect and understanding of each other's working environment. There is little doubt that ENGIE's profile and credibility was raised within policy-making circles.

Case Study 6.11 Public speeches a powerful engagement vehicle

An organisation must use all the forums at its disposal to present its messages. Conferences, seminars and other public stakeholder events offer opportunities for an organisation to present its views on key issues to a wide-cross section of stakeholders. A well-constructed programme of speeches that develops a theme over time, and in a concerted and coordinated approach, can be a powerful engagement vehicle.

Background

Fifteen years ago, nuclear energy in the UK was in the doldrums. The two main companies involved in this sector were not particularly successful, and one of them, British Energy, which operated eight nuclear power stations, had to go to the Government for financial support in 2002. This was the nadir for the company and the industry, their credibility with politicians and the public at a very low level. The British Energy executive team worked hard on the financial rehabilitation of the company over the next few years, and succeeded. But it was also recognised that it was important to engage with a wider group of stakeholders beyond politicians, officials and investors, and this would require the company to be represented on public platforms.

The organisation response

The company believed it had a good story to tell and embarked on a successful speech programme by Bill Coley, the charismatic CEO of British Energy; the company was proactive in developing the programme by, for example, working closely with conference and seminar organisers. It was very helpful that this CEO had an excellent knowledge of the electricity sector and nuclear power, having spent his career with and been President of Duke Power, a major utility in the USA. He was committed to the rehabilitation of the company, and a strong supporter of the nuclear industry in the UK. It was also helpful that he was a consummate communicator, making it easy for the audience to understand what was being conveyed.

Outcomes

In total Bill Coley made 32 major speeches, presentations or addresses over a three-and-a-half-year period from late 2005 to early 2009. Consideration of the speeches over this extended period shows that there is a clear thread running through them, and they address all the major issues associated with the technology.

What is also evident is that the speeches reached a broad section of the stakeholder spectrum: Government Ministers, officials and regulators, professional institutions and interest groups, market participants, and of course the media; it was also important for the organisation's employees who took pride in the fact their efforts were being recognised in the public domain. The speech programme would have been much less successful, and the 'story' less credible if it had been limited to opportunistic ad hoc events.

Case Study 6.12 Novel approaches to delivering messages

The communications revolution has allowed organisations to use different forms of media to engage with its stakeholders. However, sometimes it helps to look beyond what is currently available, and to be innovative in the way an organisation can deliver its messages. The *Power Game* was a simple tool that was developed to help stakeholders understand their electricity sector.

Background

Around 15 ago years, there was an emerging consensus on the need to address rising greenhouse gas emissions, and politicians and their officials were looking at new policy initiatives to do this. Most people focused on the need to deploy renewables and encourage people to adopt energy efficiency measures, but nuclear remained very much in the background, even though it was arguably making the largest contribution to greenhouse gas mitigation in the UK.

The approach adopted

The question, then, was how best to raise awareness of the benefits of nuclear power with stakeholders across the spectrum. British Energy, the company that operated nuclear power stations in the UK, decided to do this by developing a groundbreaking interactive game that encouraged players to design the country's energy mix to 2030. Its aim was to encourage people to explore the attributes of all the energy carriers: fossil fuels in its various guises, renewables and nuclear.

The company commissioned an independent consultancy to develop the game using the best available information. The objective of the game was to deliver the optimal generation mix to 2030: one that had the lowest carbon emissions, had the greatest security of supply and involved the lowest cost to consumers.

The game was made available on a disc and placed on the company website, making it accessible to a wide cross-section of stakeholders in the UK and elsewhere.

Outcomes

The evidence suggested that the game had a broad reach, and that it educated stakeholders on the benefits of nuclear power. It was also popular with the communications world as shown by Corporate Eye which came across the game while carrying out a review of websites on sustainable development and wrote (31 October 2008):

> This [Power Game] is a small little flash application which can be downloaded and played at your leisure. Your aim is to use available forms of energy to meet energy demands in the UK up until 2030. Simple, easy, and inspired. Any company can provide pages upon pages of content to educate its audience about the specific challenges it faces in a sustainable economy. It's quite another thing to give that audience experience of confronting those challenges and having to decide the choices you face.

Practitioners in stakeholder engagement need to be innovative in the way they communicate key messages. The social media revolution offers many opportunities to engage different constituency groups.

Case Study 6.13 Gaining recognition for employees

There are several ways in which an organisation can be recognised for its achievements in the public arena. Employees can also be recognised for their achievements, and in the UK, the most prestigious award is an honour that is given by the Queen. Such an honour is given to relatively few people but it is well worth going through the process of applying because a successful outcome also brings credit and respect to the organisation.

Background

International Power (IP) had grown to become a global independent power producer in the space of about a decade, with a listing on the London Stock Exchange. The company was much admired for its highly successful growth model and formerly combined with GDF SUEZ (now known as ENGIE) in 2011.

The CEO, who oversaw the growth of IP, and the success of the company, brought major credit to British business. There was a strong case for recognising his achievements by seeking an appropriate honour. A small project team within the business developed the case, and produced the *Citation* for consideration by the Cabinet Office Honours Committee; the *Citation* was supported by letters from five eminent people familiar with his work.

The *Citation*

The *Citation* made the case for awarding an honour; briefly, the main points were:

- The CEO was an internationally respected illustration in the energy industry with a wealth of knowledge and experience gained in a long and highly successful career.
- On becoming CEO of IP, he moved the company forward impressively through his vision, leadership, and financial and organisational skills; he encouraged a talented group of executives to seek and develop opportunities in power markets across the world.
- Under the CEO's astute management, IP was arguably the UK's most successful power utility overseas in 2010. In that year, the

CEO steered IP successfully through a major combination with GDF SUEZ, the French multinational utility, and at £16 billion, this was the largest transaction in the world in 2011.

- The CEO's influence extended well beyond the financial performance of the company. He has been a strong leader of the company's voluntary and charitable programmes and inspired strong commitment to these activities by employees.

Outcomes

International Power's CEO was awarded the CBE for services to business in the Queen's New Year's Honours list of 2012. This award was recognition not only for him but also for the employees of IP who had helped build a successful international group. It placed on record in a very public way the achievements of an exceptional group of people that contributed to the prestige of UK business.

7 Reflection

Chapter summary

This chapter begins by highlighting the fact that Governments around the world will always have an extensive slate of potential policy initiatives that will affect sectors right across the economy, and an organisation's ability to engage with the decision-makers will depend on the way in which the political institutions in a country function. With this in mind, it is important that an exercise is carried out to establish executive team ambition in strategic stakeholder engagement, and confirms their commitment to delivering this ambition. This chapter outlines an approach to the exercise; it presents a series of questions to the key internal stakeholders, the answers to which will yield much valuable information and, crucially, provide a clear mandate to those charged with delivering the engagement programme.

7.1 Policy arena is rich with opportunities for stakeholder engagement

A little research into Government policy activities at any one time will reveal surprising breadth and depth. The UK Government's website, for example, lists policy areas in which it is active, and the Civil Service departments and Ministries involved: at the beginning of 2017 there were a staggering 224 policy areas listed, involving 67 departments. There were policy areas in Economics and Social Policy, Environment and Energy, Housing and Planning, Education and Health, Crime and Justice, Security and many more. Each policy area has many activities, from Ministerial speeches that present a vision and path of travel for their policy interests, to formal papers that sketch out potential policy options being considered and formal consultations. All stakeholders in business, non-governmental organisations, institutions and others in civil society will find their area of interest is impacted by new policy developments.

> A change in Government policy is potentially as destructive as new technology is disruptive.
>
> *Expert Panel Member Tom Greatrex, former MP and*
> *Shadow Energy Minster, UK Parliament*

Example policy areas across the economy

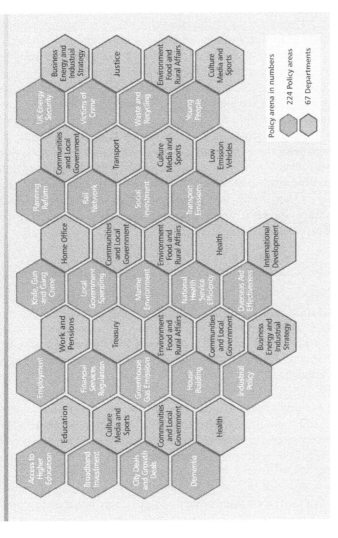

Illustration 7.1 Example policy areas across the economy

The policy arena is rich in new initiatives that address all parts of the economy. An organisation must be aware of as many as possible of the policies that can affect the environment in which it operates.

Source: UK Government website, February 2017.

7.1.1 Stakeholder engagement by officials

Stakeholder engagement is also increasingly recognised as an important part of government practice. In the past, this activity would have been carried out in an ad hoc manner most likely to help inform a question or market development. Each department would engage in its own way and would not coordinate its efforts with other departments. There was also a danger that the same external stakeholder would be approached by different departments, and often with short response times; this meant that only those stakeholders with sufficient resources could engage effectively, with the result that a desired cross-section of views was only rarely achieved.

The quality of the government engagement, then, was 'sketchy', often with a focus on the major actors in any sector. There was also a tendency to rely on networks developed by individual officials through their normal work programmes rather than a systematic stakeholder mapping exercise. The regular movement of individuals to new work areas or departments meant that the relationships developed over time were very rapidly lost, with new incumbents having to develop their own network organically.

The decision by the UK to leave the European Union (Brexit) gave fresh impetus to the nature and scope of the Government's stakeholder engagement programme because there is a need to gather information and opinions from those impacted across the economy. The programme is more systematic, with every Government department encouraged to have a dedicated Stakeholder Engagement team and a Cabinet Office group, made up of high-level departmental representatives, to coordinate action across Government. The fact that Government has stepped up its efforts in this area means that organisations must also make greater efforts to be on the Government's radar and be ready to contribute their views, ideas and supporting evidence.

7.2 Strategic stakeholder engagement in different countries

Organisations need to focus on decision-makers and key influencers in relation to policy and regulation across the world. Is it possible to identify those countries where organisations are more likely to be heard? Can the ideas and approaches presented in this book be applied in different jurisdictions? And what basic information is needed for an organisation to be able to engage with stakeholders in these environments?

The ability of those in Public Affairs to have their views heard and perhaps to influence developments is affected by a number of important factors: the nature of the political institutions, the formal and informal processes available to organisations for engagement, the level of consultation sought by government and its executive, the level of scrutiny and transparency involved in the decision-making process, the ability to use the law to protect interests and so on.

The Economist Intelligence Unit (EIU) publishes an annual *Democracy Index* based on five factors: electoral process and pluralism, functioning of government, political participation, political culture and civil liberties. It ranks each of these out

Engagement with political institutions

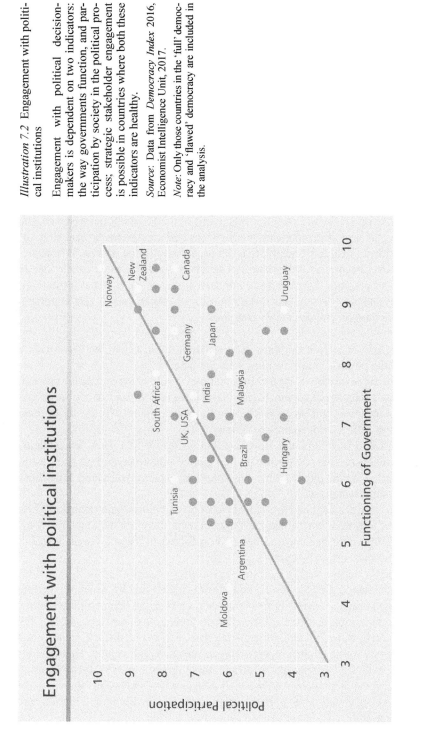

Illustration 7.2 Engagement with political institutions

Engagement with political decision-makers is dependent on two indicators: the way governments function, and participation by society in the political process; strategic stakeholder engagement is possible in countries where both these indicators are healthy.

Source: Data from *Democracy Index* 2016, Economist Intelligence Unit, 2017.

Note: Only those countries in the 'full' democracy and 'flawed' democracy are included in the analysis.

of ten and then, giving each an equal weight, produces an overall ranking, again out of ten; one way of interpreting these results is that the higher the country's *Democracy Index* the greater the opportunity to engage with decision-makers and to be heard, and the more useful the ideas and approaches presented in this book. In reality, it may be that one or two of these factors may be more important than the others; for example, for the purposes of engagement with decision-makers, it may be more appropriate to consider the ratings given to two of the components: *Functioning of Government* and *Political Participation*; once again, higher values for these may signify a greater opportunity for engagement.

The EIU has four main categories: *Full Democracies* (for example, Sweden and Canada), *Flawed Democracies* (for example, the USA and Poland), *Hybrid Democracies* (for example, Turkey and Thailand) and *Authoritarian* (for example, China and Russia). According to the Index, *Full Democracies* and *Flawed Democracies* make up 11.4% and 34.1%, respectively, of the 167 countries assessed, and represent half the world's population. The ideas and approaches presented in this book are most likely to be helpful to those organisations that operate in countries in these two categories. Further layers of detail are needed to establish the kind of engagement possible; for example, an understanding of the political institutions, their roles and membership, and the relationships between them is also important. There are common features across countries:

- The Head of State is normally separate from the leader of the Government, with the political power residing with the latter.
- There are invariably two chambers that play a role in the legislative process: a 'Lower House' where much decision-making resides, and an 'Upper House' that scrutinises and proposes changes; however, the relative power of these Houses differs from country to country.
- With odd exceptions, the election cycle is four or five years, encouraging politicians to come forward with new policy initiatives in their manifestos, and allowing the public ample opportunity to express their views and refresh their representatives.
- There is significant and growing devolution of political and financial power today – in addition to national governments there are regional and local assemblies, but once again, the power afforded to these different levels of governance differs by country.

An understanding of the formal and informal processes by which the institutions go about their business is also important. Once again there will be common elements; for example, there will be consultations by Government and its Civil Service, and by the regulators, although the precise form will differ by country and perhaps by sector depending on the nature of the markets involved. Transparency of action will also be important allowing ample opportunity for organisations to react to new developments. And the legal system will also play an important role in allowing organisations an opportunity to challenge decisions, and to safeguard their operations.

Decision-makers in representative countries

Country	Political System	Head of State	Government Leader	Election Cycle	Legislative Institutions Lower House	Upper House	Levels of Government
Sweden	Constitutional Monarchy	Monarch	Prime Minister	4 years	Rikstag	None	EU; national; regional; local
Canada	Parliamentary Democracy/ Federation	Monarch	Prime Minister	4 years	House of Commons	Senate	Federal; provincial; local/minicipal
Australia	Federal Parliamentary Democracy	Monarch	Prime Minister	3 years	House of Representatives	Senate	National; state/territory; local
UK	Constitutional Monarchy	Monarch	Prime Minister	5 years	House of Commons	House of Lords	EU; national; regional; local
USA	Federal Republic	President	President	4 years	Congress	Senate	Federal; state; local
India	Federal Republic	President	Prime Minister	5 years	Lok Sabha	Rajya Sabha	National; district; local
South Africa	Republic	President	President	5 years	National Assembly	National Council of Provinces	National; province; local
Brazil	Federal Republic	President	President	4 years	Chamber of Deputies	Federal Senate	National; state; local

Illustration 7.3 Decision-makers in representative countries

There are similarities in the way political decision-making is organised in democracies around the world. There is considerable devolution of power, with many countries having three levels of decision-making: national, regional and local.

7.3 The importance of reflection

There are four layers of management in an organisation that need to consider the strategic stakeholder engagement programme: the CEO and the Board, the Executive Team, the Executive responsible for the organisation's stakeholder engagement activities, and the Head of the Government Affairs function. Others across the business will also need to reflect on their contribution to the programme: those in external communications, business development, investor relations, and marketing and trading; and those in operations that are in close contact with their local communities will also have an important contribution. Employees are important ambassadors for the organisation and as such are also important to the engagement programme; internal communications, then, will need to be active in the programme to help disseminate the organisation's high-level messages.

> An organisation needs to want to engage.
>
> *Expert Panel Member Robert Armour OBE,*
> *Former Deputy Chairman, NuGeneration*

There are a number of activities that are needed to ensure a stakeholder engagement programme is effective, and these have been discussed in detail in earlier chapters. Reflection is particularly important for the higher echelons of an organisation since the ambition, commitment and tone are set by the CEO and the Board.

7.3.1 On the context for stakeholder engagement

Reflection can begin with each internal decision-maker addressing a series of questions that touch on their areas of responsibility; this challenges their perceptions and encourages them to think creatively and holistically. The answers to these questions are important: they will establish the organisation's ambition for its strategic stakeholder engagement programme; they will recognise the resources needed to meet that ambition; and they will establish whether the right governance structure for the programme is in place.

There are three potential outcomes to this exercise, each resulting in a different profile for the organisation in the external domain. The lowest profile is when the executive team decide to ensure the organisation simply maintains its 'licence to operate' and complies with the laws that govern its operations. It may choose to engage with the Government's formal processes but only insofar as they have an immediate bearing on the business.

A medium-level profile will involve an organisation taking a more active role in the decision-making arena. It may do this on its own or in concert with others, depending on the issue involved. It will take a longer-term view, perhaps one to three years, when addressing new policy and regulation. It will have a presence in decision-making forums and ensure its voice is heard alongside its competitors.

A decision to adopt a more proactive, higher-profile approach would suggest an ambition to be opinion-formers in the sector and as such have the organisation's

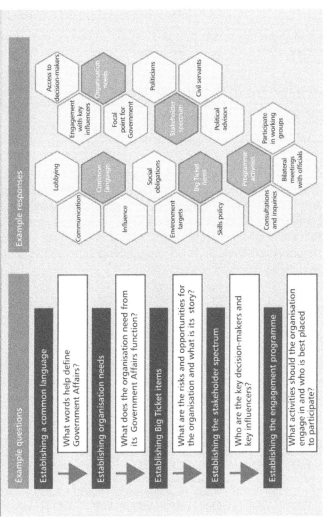

Workshop activity to aid organisation positioning

Example questions

Example responses

Establishing a common language

What words help define Government Affairs?

Establishing organisation needs

What does the organisation need from its Government Affairs function?

Establishing Big Ticket items

What are the risks and opportunities for the organisation and what is its story?

Establishing the stakeholder spectrum

Who are the key decision-makers and key influencers?

Establishing the engagement programme

What activities should the organisation engage in and who is best placed to participate?

Lobbying · Communication · Common language · Influence · Social obligations · Environment targets · Big Ticket items · Skills policy · Programme Activities · Consultations and inquiries · Bilateral meetings with officials · Participate in working groups · Political advisors · Civil servants · Politicians · Stakeholder spectrum · Focal point for Government · Engagement with key influencers · Organisation needs · Access to decision-makers

Illustration 7.4 Workshop activity to aid organisation positioning

As part of an annual 'reflection' process by an executive team, it is often helpful to facilitate a workshop that refreshes its views on where the organisation wants to position itself in the external world.

Internal stakeholder	Some questions
CEO, Chairman and Board Members	• Has sufficient thought been given to engaging decision-makers? • Are we showing sufficient ambition in this area? • Do we want to focus on our licence to operate, or should we commit to activities covered by a social licence to operate? • Is the Board briefed on a regular basis on the organisation's strategic stakeholder engagement programme? • Has a Board Director been appointed responsible for the programme? • Am I willing to devote time to this activity?
Executives	• Am I willing to commit experts to support the organisation's strategic stakeholder engagement programme? • Am I getting regular briefings? • Am I willing to devote time to this programme?
Executive responsible for Government Affairs	• Has a benchmarking exercise been carried out on the organisation's capability in the Government Affairs area against its competitors? • Am I willing to devote time to this activity?
Head of Government Affairs	• Do I have a good appreciation of what the organisation needs/wants from its strategic stakeholder engagement programme? • Have I made the case for the programme?

views and ideas solicited by decision-makers. The organisation will take a longer-term view of policy and regulation, perhaps up to five years, or a period consistent with its planning cycle. Its engagement programme will be more holistic in approach, going beyond its obligations under its licence to operate. There is recognition that all members of the executive team and Board have a role to play as part of an overall positioning of the organisation and those leading the programme will be given the resources to be successful.

7.3.2 On key stakeholders

Understanding the key stakeholders is fundamental for an organisation, irrespective of the level of engagement. There are two main questions when dealing with stakeholders: does the organisation have a full appreciation of all the stakeholders it needs to engage with? And is it clear who in the organisation will own the individual relationship involved? Questions that will help this exercise are as follows.

Internal stakeholder	Some questions
CEO, Chairman and Board Members	• Has there been a formal stakeholder mapping exercise carried out? • Which stakeholders can Board Members engage with? • Could Board Members be the main contact in the organisation for key stakeholders?

Internal stakeholder	Some questions
Executives	• Which stakeholders should executives and their direct reports engage with? • Could executives be the main contact in the organisation for key stakeholders?
Executive responsible for Government Affairs	• Which stakeholders can the Government Affairs team engage with? • How comprehensive does the stakeholder mapping need to be, and how are the priority stakeholders being identified?
Head of Government Affairs	• Have I canvassed all the key internal functions in relation to their stakeholders? • Do I have appropriate relationships with the decision-makers and key influencers? • Am I confident that our stakeholder mapping is complete?

What is clear is that a stakeholder mapping exercise needs to involve people from across the organisation if it is to be meaningful. The first step will be to have as wide coverage as possible capturing stakeholders at the national, regional and local levels; the second step will prioritise stakeholders, making it easier to match the engagement programme with resources, and the final step will be to identify relationship holders.

The stakeholder list will be a 'live' document, and it will be incumbent on its custodian to establish a protocol whereby the content is refreshed over time.

7.3.3 On stakeholder processes

Which formal and informal processes the organisation will engage with will largely depend on its ambition and strategy. Nonetheless it is worth addressing a set of questions that not only helps inform that ambition but also addresses the governance needed to ensure that a consistent approach is adopted when dealing with the external stakeholders.

Internal stakeholder	Some questions
CEO, Chairman and Board Members	• Which formal processes should the company engage in? • Are we prepared to give oral evidence to Select Committees? • Do we want to devote time to informal processes?
Executives	• Are we prepared to give oral evidence to Parliamentary Select Committees? • Do we want to devote time to informal processes?
Executive responsible for Government Affairs	• What governance process is in place for engaging with formal and informal processes? • What is the optimal balance of effort between formal and informal processes?

Internal stakeholder	Some questions
Head of Government Affairs	• Have I sufficiently briefed Board Members and executive on the formal processes, and on their potential contribution to the organisation's participation in these processes? • Have I made the case for external resources needed to help with stakeholder engagement processes?

It is probably easier to indicate which of the formal processes the organisation could engage with because Government takes the lead role on an issue and an organisation simply decides to participate in the process or not. More difficult is to decide which informal processes the organisation should participate in, and what resources to devote to them; an informal programme that targets some key influencers will benefit the organisation as it goes about trying to influence the policy debate.

7.3.4 On organisational issues

McKinsey in their excellent review titled 'How to reinvent the external-affairs function', published in July 2016, highlighted the importance of organisational capability, and in particular, that all organisations could enhance their performance through better organisation of the external affairs function. The questions below address this important aspect of stakeholder engagement.

Internal stakeholder	Some questions
CEO, Chairman and Board Members	• Have I given those leading the stakeholder engagement programme my vision for the organisation? • Have I indicated my ambition for the stakeholder engagement programme?
Executives	• Have I identified those activities under my direct reports that will contribute to the stakeholder engagement programme? • Have I given those who are needed to support the programme the time and resources to do so? • Do we recognise these efforts, for example, in the end of year appraisals of my direct reports contributing to the programme?
Executive responsible for Government Affairs	• Have I provided sufficient resources to match the organisation's ambitions in this area? • Have we established the forums for regular, formal internal stakeholder meetings? • Do we have the right external advice needed to run an effective programme? • Do we have the right success factors and programme reviews?

Internal stakeholder	Some questions
Head of Government Affairs	• Do I have sufficient internal and external resources to deliver a successful engagement programme that matches the organisation's ambition? • Do we have the tools needed to deliver the engagement programme? • Have I established the right internal briefing programme to all contributors to the engagement programme?

An effective engagement programme needs a strong organisation where all internal stakeholders understand their contribution to the overall programme. Clear leadership by the executive team and their active involvement in the programme are important; also crucial is that the individuals involved embrace a collegiate approach, all working together towards a common end.

7.3.5 On stakeholder engagement

Once the level of ambition for the organisation has been established, it is important that all internal actors understand their role in the engagement programme. They must be supported with the agreed 'story' and key messages, and provide feedback and intelligence to those charged with implementing the programme. The following questions will help ensure that all participants are working towards the same overall objectives.

Internal stakeholder	Some questions
CEO, Chairman and Board Members	• What role do individual members of the Board play in the programme? • What are the three high-level messages we would want to voice? • What process is in place to capture outcomes and learning?
Executives	• How can I and my direct reports in my area of responsibility contribute to the engagement programme? • What do I need to ensure my effective contribution to the organisation's engagement programme?
Executive responsible for Government Affairs	• What would it take to be a leader in this area? • Is the team fit for purpose? Does it have the tools available to deliver a successful programme? Is there a role for external providers to support the programme? • Are all the key decision-makers and key influencers identified by the Stakeholder Mapping Tool being engaged by the internal 'team'? • Is a record being kept of key stakeholders, their interests, the engagement options available and the organisation's key messages for each stakeholder? • What review process is in place? How would you measure success? • Is the Governance structure fit for purpose?

Internal stakeholder	Some questions
Head of Government Affairs	• Is the organisation's story up to date? • Does the team have the resources available to carry out its programme? • Are all the tools available being used? Are there sufficient innovative practices?

The engagement programme needs to be flexible enough to allow the organisation to respond to emerging developments; for example, there may be new stakeholders to brief, unforeseen potential changes to emerging policy or existing regulation, favourable treatment of competitors by government that is harmful to the business, or ad hoc issues arising at the devolved and local levels that affect existing and potential new assets. Of prime importance is that the programme, and those involved in delivering it, adhere to the 5 Cs discussed elsewhere: a *coherent* 'story', *clarity* of message, a *consistent* approach, *concerted* effort and *coordinated* action.

Summary key points

- Governments all over the world have an active policy programme that touches all aspects of economic, environmental and societal activity. It is important that organisations are actively reviewing these policies and assessing the implications to their interests.
- There are democratic processes around the world, and this means there are opportunities for organisations to engage with decision-makers in Government and key influencers in the Civil Service and other institutions.
- The organisation's leadership team need to think strategically about the way it engages with key external stakeholders.
- The leadership in an organisation needs to establish its ambitions in strategic stakeholder engagement and empower those who are charged with delivering it.
- A strategic engagement programme will be successful if there is a shared belief in what the organisation is trying to achieve and a commitment to deliver it.

Index

academics, role of 59, 80, 156, 166–7
advice, independent sources of 121, 145–6
advisory boards for companies 125–7, 145–6
alliances 15, 121–2, 144, 153, 158
Annual Reports 163, 171–3
annual reviews of progress 171–4
Apprenticeship Levy scheme 68–9
Armitt, Sir John (and Armitt Review, 2013) 53, 62–3, 152
Armour, Robert 105, 201
Attenborough, Sir David 61, 64–5
audiences for briefing 153–60
awards 168; *see also* Honours list

Beamer, David 108
Better Regulation Task Force 77
bilateral meetings 79, 153–4, 166, 174
Brevia Consulting 124
Brexit 13, 29, 41, 50, 75–6, 78–9, 161–2, 182, 185–8, 198; questions for the electricity generation industry and possible responses 186–8
briefings booklets 117
British Energy 1–9, 65, 89–90, 97, 146–7, 168, 176, 188–9, 191, 193
British Management Data Foundation (BMDF) 83
British Nuclear Fuels Ltd (BNFL) 2–3
Bulkin, Bernie 99, 173
Business, Energy and Industrial Strategy (BEIS) Committee 150
Business in the Community (BiTC) 89–90, 168

the Cabinet 26–7
Cabinet Office 50, 52, 194
Cabinet Secretary and Head of the Civil Service 49

Calder Hall 2
capabilities, organisational 101–4
Carbon Price Support (CPS) mechanism 143, 181–2
carbon tax and carbon trading 5–6, 143
Carbon Trust 125
chief executive officers (CEOs), role of 11, 15, 82–3, 99–100, 118, 152–6, 163, 165, 167, 171–4, 178, 185, 191, 194–5
Chief Scientific Advisor to the Government 189
China General Nuclear (CGN) 2
Civil Service 49–50, 61, 166–7, 189–90; engagement with 156–8; Head of 49, 156; for Wales and Northern Ireland 52
Civil Service High Potential Second-ment programme 167, 190–1
civil society 95
Clegg, Nick 22, 49, 74–6, 95–6, 118, 170
Climate Change Levy (CCL) 5–8, 76–7, 143, 182
climate change targets 43–6, 161
Coley, Bill 1, 11, 96, 174, 191–2
Combined Heat and Power (CHP) generation 5–6, 182
Committee on Climate Change (CCC) 52–4, 62–4, 71, 80, 152, 158–9
Committee of the Regions 56
'communication' function in a firm 101, 103
Competition and Markets Authority (CMA) 53–4, 136–7, 142
Confederation of British Industry (CBI) 80
conferences 159, 163; *see also* party political conferences
confidentiality 153–4, 166
consultants, use of 80, 127–30, 166–7

consultations 67–70, 150–1
consumer groups 14
Cornwall Energy 178
corporate social responsibility
    (CSR) 89, 95, 163, 173
cost of a stakeholder
    engagement programme 106–8
Court of Appeal, UK 76
credibility of an organisation 163, 180–91
Cromwell, Oliver 25
culture, organisational 18, 170

decision-makers, access to 16, 19, 153–6
Democracy Index (EIU) 198–200
Department for Business, Energy
    and Industrial Strategy (BEIS) 50,
    52, 150
Department of Energy and Climate
    Change (DECC) 50, 153
Department of Environment, Food
    and Rural Affairs (DEFRA) 179
Department for Exiting the European
    Union (DExEU) 50
Department of International Trade
    (DIT) 50
Department of Trade and Industry (DTI) 8
Department for Transport 50
devolved administrations 28–36,
    41, 88, 200
Digital Infrastructure and Inclusion
    Task Force 78
Dinorwig power station 86–7
Drax Group 76
Duke Power 191

Economist Intelligence Unit 198–200
EDF Energy 1–2, 9, 93, 120–1,
    125, 132–3, 146
Eggborough power station 2
Electoral Commission 49
Electricity Market Reform (EMR) 42–3
Emission Performance Standard 84–5
end-of-year reviews of progress
    in stakeholder engagement 174
Energy and Climate Change (ECC)
    Select Committee 70–1, 84–5
Energy Company Obligation (ECO) 177–8
ENGIE (company) 136–7, 142–3,
    145–6, 177–80, 184, 190–1, 194
Environmental Audit Committee 189
erroneous messages, challenging of 188–9
'escalating' an issue 178–80
ethical considerations 95–7, 131, 175
European Commission (EC) 54–6
European Council 38

European Court of Auditors 56
European Data Protection Supervisor 56
European Economic and Social
    Committee (EESC) 56
European External Action Service
    (EEAS) 56
European Investment Bank (EIB) 56
European Ombudsman 56
European Parliament 38–9, 56
European Union 33; Council of 38;
    Court of Justice of (CJEU) 56;
    Emissions Trading Scheme (ETS)
    143, 181–2; influence of national
    policy 45–6; institutions of 38–41,
    54–7; legislation of 95
Eurozone 41
executive summaries in reports 151
expert groups and expert panels
    11–15, 161, 163
expert reviews 62–4
experts: external 130, 151; from
    the Civil Service 158; internal
    105, 165–6; *see also* consultants;
    'singleton' experts
external affairs function in a
    company 9–11, 18, 97, 206–7

Festiniog power station 87–8
Fish Legal 77
fitness for purpose 105
five Cs of stakeholder engagement
    91, 120, 174, 208
Freedom of Information (FOI) requests
    72–4, 96, 151, 166
Fukushima power station disaster 86

governance protocols 141–2
the Government 13, 25–7
'government affairs' function in a
    company 91, 105, 110, 117–18, 147
government policy: new initiatives
    in 165–8, 196–7; transformational
    nature of 42; uncertainty about
    183–4; vagaries of 180–1
Greatrex, Tom 121, 196
greenhouse gases 8
Greenpeace 74, 85–6, 152

Helm, Dieter 61
Hendry, Charles 87
Hewitt, Patricia 6
Hill and Knowlton (PR firm) 124
Hinkley Point C power station 2
Honours list 168, 194–5
hospitality events 80, 167–8

House of Commons 23–5, 27, 34
House of Lords 23–5, 27, 34, 54, 167

immigrants from the EU 161
Independent Generators Group
  (IGG) 82, 144–5, 153, 177–8
individuals' influence on policy 61
industrial policy 150
Infinis (company) 76
influences on Government 47–52
inquiries 70–1, 150–2; Advisors to 156
Institute of Mechanical Engineers 168
internal infrastructure of a company
  105–18
internal organisation of a company
  18, 97, 206–7
international companies 171
international contacts 159–60
International Power (IP) (company) 194–5
Internet of Things (IoT) 13
investment community 122

John Collier Medal and Memorial
  Lecture 168
Jones, Carwyn 88
Judicial Review (JR) 76–7, 85–6, 152

leadership, importance of 99–100, 131
'leaks' 153–4
legislation 71–3, 78
Levy Exemption Certificates 5
Lewis, Isle of 180–1
licence to operate 93–5, 163;
  social 95, 163
Lisbon Treaty (Article 50) 76
lobbying 95–8
local government 35–8;
  responsibilities of 37
London Electricity 2
Lovelock, James 61, 64–5

McKinsey (consultants) 9, 16,
  93, 97, 150, 206
MacNaughton, Joan 153, 156
Marshall Report (1998) 5, 62
media training 165
media usage 170
Members of the European
  Parliament (MEPs) 39, 57
Members of Parliament (MPs)
  23, 72–4, 103, 122, 154, 184–5
Miliband, Ed 53
Miller, Gina 76
Missions 78
Montague, Sir Adrian 1

National Audit Office (NAO) 49, 158
National Infrastructure Commission
  (NIC) 53–4, 62–3, 152, 158–9
national insurance contributions 5
Natural Resources Wales (NRW) 77
networking 165, 168, 198
New Electricity Trading Arrange-
  ments (NETA) 2–3, 8
Non-Departmental Public Bodies
  (NDPBs) 52, 63–4; engagement
  with 158–9
Non-Governmental Organisations
  (NGOs) 14, 59, 67–8, 74, 85,
  95–6, 152, 188–9
Northern Ireland 28–9, 33, 52;
  Assembly and Executive 31
Nuclear Electric (company) 99

Office of Gas and Electricity
  Markets (Ofgem) 136, 158
Ombudsman services *see*
  European Ombudsman;
  Parliamentary and Health Ombudsman
opposition parties 27, 154

'pariah' technology 97
Parliament 23–5, 41
Parliamentary Committees 33–6,
  70–1, 125, 150–4; Advisors to 156;
  Clerks to 34, 70, 124–5, 153, 156;
  see also Select Committees
Parliamentary Group on Energy
  Studies (PGES) 154–6, 167
Parliamentary Groups 155
Parliamentary and Health Ombudsman 49
Parliamentary Office of Science
  and Technology (POST) 49, 189
Parliamentary Questions (PQs) 72–4, 96,
  154
Parr, Doug 173
party political conferences 167
performance of companies,
  reporting of 163
Permanent Secretaries 157–8
personal networks 112
'platforms' for engagement 174
policy initiatives 165–8, 196–7
political advisors for companies 124–7
political context 181–2
political institutions: British 22–33;
  of the EU 38–41
political risk analysis 112–14
politicians' role in decision-making 156

'positioning' of an organisation 176–7
The Power Game 192–3
presentations 163, 165
pressure groups 95–6
Prime Minister 25–7
privatisation 2, 39
professional institutions 14, 57
profile of an organisation 163, 167
public relations 93, 101, 124

The Queen 23, 168, 194

recognition for organisations
    and individuals 168, 192, 194–5
reflection 18, 201–8
regulators 54, 150
renewable energy 5, 8, 183–4
reviews of programmes 146–7, 150;
    commissioned by the Government
    152; in the form of regular progress
    meetings 171–5
Riley, Steve 84–5
risk registers 114–17, 137–41
de Rivaz, Vincent 132–3
roundtables 83, 158–9, 174
Royal Assent 72
Royal Commission on Environmental
    Pollution 77
Royal Commissions 77
The Royal Society 57
Rugeley power station 184–5

scenario development 112, 176
Scotland 28–33, 36, 43–4, 50, 52
Scottish Nuclear 99
Scottish Parliament 29–33, 43–4, 52
secondments from the private
    sector into the Civil Service
    and *vice versa* 190
Select Committees 84–5, 100
seminars 83, 159, 163
shale gas 65
Shell (company) 112
'singleton' experts 105–6, 127
Sizewell C power station 2
Small Business Research Initiative
    (SBRI) 150
small businesses 14
social media 13, 170–1, 192–3
Special Advisors to Ministers 27,
    47, 79–80, 124, 131, 153, 156, 158, 179
specialist forums 82–3
specialists in stakeholder engage-
    ment, qualities and skills needed by 100–1
speeches 163, 165, 191–2

sponsorship of events 167–8
stakeholder engagement 1, 18–19, 38,
    41; *active* and *passive* approaches to
    22, 92–3; context for 91–6, 201–4;
    developing a programme of 97–105;
    importance of 9–16; formal processes
    of 66–78, 83, 148–50, 175–7; informal
    processes of 66–7, 79–83, 148–50,
    175; intangible benefits from 174; by
    officials 158, 198; opportunities for
    196–8; in other countries 198–200;
    proactive and innovative approaches
    to 170, 175, 177, 193; questions to
    be asked about 204–8
stakeholder mapping 108–12, 133–5,
    150, 158, 173–5
stakeholder processes 205–6
stakeholder spectrum 20–1
stakeholders: categories of 20–2;
    strategic 22, 41, 208
Stern, Lord (and Stern Review, 2006)
    62–3, 150, 152
'story' for stakeholder engagement
    118–21, 176, 178
success, measurement of 173–5
success factors 16, 120, 175
supply chain relationships 14, 121–2
supply chains 14
Supreme Court, UK 76

task forces 77, 159
tax-raising powers 33
Teesside power station 184–5
'think tanks' 14, 131
Thompson, Dorothy 77
'tool' for stakeholder engagement
    108–12
Torness power station 189
trade associations 13, 57–9,
    80–2, 121, 144, 153, 158–9
trade unions 59, 95, 122
Trump, Donald 13

United Kingdom, emergence of 28–9

virtual teams 105–6, 110, 131, 171, 175
vision 15, 163

Wales 28–31; Civil Service 52;
    National Assembly 31
websites, corporate 170
Westminster Energy Forum (WEF) 83
working groups 159

Yeo, Tim 6

For Product Safety Concerns and Information please contact our EU
representative GPSR@taylorandfrancis.com
Taylor & Francis Verlag GmbH, Kaufingerstraße 24, 80331 München, Germany